Here's what others are saying about *The Power of REAL* **and Dr. Joseph W. Daniels, Jr.**

At a time when most churches are stuck in the way it "used to be," Pastor Daniels reminds us of what churches are called to be – dynamic and authentic catalysts for transformation in the lives of individuals and communities. *The Power of REAL* is a primer for those seeking to create ecclesia, called out communities of love, militant and triumphant, as Jesus intended His churches to be.

Kaya Henderson
Chancellor, District of Columbia Public Schools

Filled with wisdom, spiritual insight and practical application *The Power of REAL* is a timely parable that unfolds with spiritual power and hope. If you are being called by God to transform your local church and only have the time and resources to invest in one book—this is it!

Rev. Gary A. Shockley
Executive Director of Path 1 New Church Starts and author of
The Meandering Way *and* Imagining Church

"Dr. Joseph Daniels is a transformational leader in the life of the Church and humankind. His wisdom and forethought, as shared in *The Power of REAL*, provides the reader a realistic view of Church through Dr. Daniels' eyes; and, it helps each reader connect to the God within them. As with *Begging for REAL Church*, focused on the desire for Church relevancy, *The Power of REAL* is a must read for denominational leaders, pastors and laity who want to better understand making the Church relevant today and in the future. This book is a powerful resource, which needs to be read by leaders across our nation.

ob Brown
iates, Inc.

For Pastor Joe Daniels, "REAL" is "Relevant, Enthusiastic, Authentic and Loving." Joe is all of these things and he has built a vital congregation. In research, we call this a "primary source" because it is the honest account of the struggles and wisdom of a real pastor. It is a resource in practical divinity, where what we know about how humans work and how God works can come together for Christian disciples trying to make church real.   It is written in a very accessible style that will make a good "coaches manual" for both clergy and lay.

David McAllister-Wilson
President, Wesley Theological Seminary

Joe Daniels is one of the most creative and effective United Methodist pastors whom I have had the privilege to know. This new book demonstrates, both in its form and its content, his extraordinary creativity for ministry. From planning and leading worship, to articulating an understanding of leadership, to casting a vision for a "real" church, Joe Daniels is a man called to serve with a capacity to inspire. His book will inform and transform its readers with a bold mission for the church.

William B. Lawrence, Dean
Professor of American Church History
Perkins School of Theology at Southern Methodist University

"*The Power of REAL* is the logical following to *Begging for REAL Church*. In this sequel, Joe Daniels dares the intricacies of how assemblies of the spiritually needy become baptized ministers of the Gospel. Safe religious routines are challenged to become responses to life's wrestlings. Through *The Power of REAL*, Joe Daniels, along with Christie Latona, invite us to what church can be! Don't delay. Read it!

Rev. Vance P. Ross
Senior Pastor, Gordon Memorial United Methodist Church

Rev. Joe Daniels, prophet, organizer, teacher and preacher, has spoken truth to power and shared powerful truth with those he serves. He is one of the few pastors in the United States that has transformed an urban congregation and an urban community. *The Power of REAL* provides key insights for all congregations and pastors on how to connect with people and how to connect people to God. It is a real telling of how to make the Gospel plain and transformative.

John R. Schol, Bishop
The Baltimore-Washington Conference of the The United Methodist Church

Words cannot adequately describe TRUTH. However, Truth leaps from the pages of this remarkable book. We either accept it or reject it at our peril. Under the power of the Holy Spirit, Laity and Clergy will be set free to serve God and humankind, with Holy Boldness, by living THE REAL CHURCH, thereby taking on the Body of Christ as their flesh and blood.

Dr. Felton Edwin May, DD
United Methodist Bishop (Retired)
Pastor, Turning Point United Methodist Church, Trenton, New Jersey

"After reading *The Power of REAL*, I was moved by its relevant content and timeliness. It infused additional and fresh hope for seeing transformation and revitalization of churches, especially Black and Multicultural congregations modeling the life and ministry of Jesus as the approach for offering men, women, children and youth, authentic receptivity and "radical hospitality" into the kingdom of God here on earth as it is in heaven. Hence, *The Power of REAL* is a must read. It is liberally illustrated by real life stories and punctuated by challenging life-application tools.

Dr. Fred A. Allen
National Director, Strengthening the Black Church
for the 21st Century of The United Methodist Church

Joe Daniels, as the pastor of Emory United Methodist, Church, and as co-chair of Washington Interfaith Network in Washington, D.C., has exhibited a unique talent to not only build a congregation, but also to build a community and city that cares for all. Rev. Daniels is a powerful voice for church, justice, love and community. He is a prophetic voice that is too often missing in our country today. I count Rev. Daniels as one of the most important voices that I have worked with in the over 40 years of my experience in community organizing working with pastors of many different faiths.

Arnie Graf, Co-Director,
Industrial Areas Foundation

Pastor Daniels is a dynamic and wonderful individual committed to the growth of the local church. He represents a wonderful group of church leaders with the wisdom to teach and demonstrate the power of church growth and systems. He is a mentor and guide and his leadership example is a blessing.

Olu Brown, Lead Pastor,
Impact Church in Atlanta and author of
Zero to 80: Innovative Ideas for Planting
and Accelerating Church Growth

If ever there was a book best needed to strengthen the black church, this is it! Every aspiring young pastor and every weary urban minister toiling in a dying inner city church ought to read this lively, well-written narrative of a vision for re-energizing the urban church. What makes it so compelling is that it is based upon the real church experience of the author.

Cornish R. Rogers
Professor Emeritus,
Claremont School of Theology

If your church is more like the Church of the Last Chance than the Church of Living Hope, then you want to read this story of changed lives and communities through the power of Christ. Joe Daniels knows what it means to help dry bones come alive in vital ministry. There are lessons here for all.

Lovett H. Weems, Jr.
Distinguished Professor of Church Leadership and Director,
Lewis Center for Church Leadership,
Wesley Theological Seminary

~

As Joe, a novice preacher being mentored by the older, wiser Pastor D in *The Power of REAL* realizes early in this highly readable parable, this is some really powerful stuff! In his sequel to *Begging for REAL Church,* Reverend Joseph Daniels presents a clear call, with concrete ideas, to help urban church leaders merge with and transform their city surrounds through worship that is Relevant, Enthusiastic, Authentic, and Loving (REAL). In practical, "non-churchy" language, he offers practical advice for urban ministers, disciples, rank-and-file worshippers, and lay people who seek resurrection through dependence on the Divine. The Power of REAL is the story of a man, his mentor, his church, and his church community, who begin not only to rise above their desperate circumstances but also to speak a united vision of hope and lay out a strategic plan for bringing their collective dreams and aspirations to pass. Daniels shares practical tips for urban congregations, worship cultures, and communities to grow together in and through the Word. Most importantly, he provides something readers of all, little, or no faiths can use: some Holy Spirit CPR. Through fellowship, service, and healing, Daniels reveals, churches can manifest REAL-ness, serve as change agents in their underserved communities, and make worship work. And that's some really powerful stuff!

D. Kamili Anderson,
Writer/Editor/Community Activist,
Washington, DC

The Power of REAL

Changing Lives. Changing Churches. Changing Communities.

Dr. Joseph W. Daniels, Jr.
with Christine Shinn Latona

NOT JUST A CURTAIN PULLER
WASHINGTON, DC

Dedication

This book is dedicated to my treasured family members who have gone on to Glory since the publication of ***Begging for REAL Church***. Each of them has had a profound impact on my life, and on *The Power of REAL* for countless others. I love you Uncle Pete, Aunt Mabel, Cousin Ray, Cousin Patrice, Cousin J.J., Aunt Sadie and Uncle Johnny. My family and I would be incomplete had you not touched us with your love. God bless you and continue to rest in peace.

Acknowledgements

When you truly think about it, every day is a day to give thanks to God and thanks to those who make your life possible. I've discovered that life is only possible with the love of God, and the love and support of others. With that, I could say thank you to a multitude of people who would fill up many pages of this book, and I do say thank you —thank you from the depths of my soul!

But specifically, I want to say thank you first to the queen of my life, my wife of 25 years, Madelyn. You continue to define and redefine the love a spouse is to have for her companion. I am not, unless you are, and I have no words that can say thank you for the deep and abiding love you have for me. The marriage makes it, the family survives and thrives, the ministry expands because God has graciously given me the special helpmate that is you. Thanks to my daughter, Joia and my son, Joey. Thanks for the fantastic love you have for your father. I am proud to have the best children in the world. Thanks to my mom, Jeanne, who loves me more than a son deserves, and my sister, Jeannie, whose refusal to quit in the face of obstacles is always an inspiration to me.

Thanks to all of the people who make up the Emory United Methodist Church, affectionately known as The Emory Fellowship. And thank you to Emory's Lead Team led by Philipia Hillman and lay leader Philbert Benjamin. Truly, Emory, you are the greatest congregation on the face of the earth, making church REAL for so many seeking healing and hope in the name of Jesus, in the midst of a hurting world. This book happens because of you, and I am humbled and honored to serve as your pastor.

Thanks to the Emory Beacon of Light, Inc. and board president Hazel Broadnax for your phenomenal sacrifices to make our community better.

Thanks to my prayer partners Vance Ross, Gary Henderson, Dred Scott, Rudy Rasmus, Tim Warner, Kevin Smalls, Tyrone Gordon, Buster Samuel and Donald Jenkins. You have no idea how your prayers, along with those of my family and church, daily sustain me.

Thanks to Ewurama Ewusi-Mensah, our chief editor, and Gary Shockley, Vance Ross, Nancy Shinn, Carolyn Anderson and Bob Kallen for your comments and contributions just the same.

And last but not least, thanks to my book partner, Christie Latona. Because of your amazing God-given gifts, wisdom, creativity, and tenacity, this book is a reality! Your sacrifice has been nothing short of a labor of love. Your passion to see God's Church transformed is unparalleled. And the sacrifice of time made by your husband Peter, and your children, Melina, Andrew and Christopher, will always be remembered and appreciated.

For all of this, I am grateful to God, who makes all things possible.

Contents

Foreword

n his first book, *Begging for REAL Church*, Dr. Daniels took a look at
the hunger our world has for a relevant experience. His latest work,
*The Power of REAL: Changing Lives. Changing Churches. Changing
Communities.*, moves us from dialogue to practice. Joseph Daniels and
Christie Latona do amazing work by bringing you face to face with the
necessities of real ministry. Fasten your seatbelts and witness the tension
within the Church of the Last Chance as it struggles for relevance and as
the dynamic fellowship at Hopeville takes a community by storm.

In a world filled with superficiality, phoniness, and inauthentic expressions, occasionally a clear, resolute voice pierces through the chatter with a
prophetic statement and prolific direction. Joseph Daniels is a person quali-
fied to define REAL like few others. The principles of his ministry are indeed
relevant, enthusiastic, authentic, and loving and have been for many years. A
time as cynical as this current age requires not only a strong grasp of theory
and theology but also an understanding of what's missing and what needs
to change in the church in order for the institution to fulfill the tenets of its
founder, Jesus.

The prophetic presence of the church is often represented as something
inherent to the institution, and people often point to by-gone days and
past deeds for evidence of this fact. Dr. Daniels unpacks this notion right
at the beginning of the book in the Fellowship of the Used-Tos. In each
instance, a backward glance defines the content of the church's stance in the
present—justifying its continued relevance and authorizing its voice. The
church's task, because it has become estranged from the present moment in
which it exists, is to make us idolize and conform to it. Such a church has
lost its power. This book reminds us of "a deep hunger, thirst and desire to
experience REAL church—church that makes a difference in the lives of
the people it touches and the communities in which they live."

The Power of REAL addresses what I have discovered are the
essentials required for a ministry to do more than just survive—
to thrive. This includes an honest deciphering of the mysteries

surrounding the call experience, taking on an in-depth look at the qualities of a leader poised to tackle the demands of the real world, and incorporating a meticulous perspective on the essential elements of ministry vitality: worship and community development.

When I am seeking guidance in my work and life, I look for individuals who have experience, courage, and wisdom to offer from their own life. Joseph Daniels has been my friend and prayer partner for over ten years, and I have sought his insight on many occasions during that time primarily because I have witnessed an actual manifestation of his talk in his daily walk. Doing REAL begins with being REAL, and this man is a fusion of authenticity and reality.

Will we exhaust our prophetic voices by battling issues that have very little to do with the well-being of the people God cares about or will we offer our voices to the voiceless, hurting masses who have historically been helped by the church Jesus founded? Maybe it is time to bury aspects of the church that are no longer relevant and raise up an *ecclesia*, a community, a church where people share a perspective of the twenty-first century that prioritizes God's radically inclusive ideas around being relevant, enthusiastic, authentic, and loving—in a word, REAL.

Rudy Rasmus
Co-Pastor, St John's United Methodist Church, Houston, Texas
Author of *Touch: Pressing Against the Wounds of a Broken World*

Chapter 1
The Fellowship of the Used-To's

Worship. Destiny. Possibility.

The Fellowship of the Used-Tos was a different kind of church. It was perched on a hill at the odd intersection of Leadership Lane, Culture Crossing, and Systems Street—but the physical location wasn't what people talked about. People talked about the church being a place to go if you needed help. A place that felt safe and warm no matter what was going on in your life. A place that was full of people who tried their best to love you. A place where you could get connected or reconnected to Jesus. The Fellowship was a beacon of light and hope.

When you walked through the door of the church, you couldn't help but notice the unique, ornate wallpaper. On closer inspection, you'd see that the pattern was created from written testimonies etched on the walls. This was how people in the fellowship shared their liberation stories— their release from behaviors, habits, and attitudes that had separated them from God.

In naming their "used tos," the people gave credit where credit was due.

I used to get drunk all the time...I used to be anxious...I used to steal a...I used to try to be in control...I used to cheat on my wife...I used to be impatient with people...I used to avoid people who weren't like me...I used to shake my booty on the stage for money...I used to feel left out and alone...but since I started learning about Jesus and following him, I don't do that anymore. Thanks be to God! I used to get drunk all the time...I used to be anxious...I used to steal a...I used to try to be in control...I used to cheat on my wife...I used to be impatient with people... I used to avoid people who weren't like me...I used to shake my booty on the stage for money...I used to feel left out and alone ...but since I started learning about Jesus and following him, I don't do that anymore. Thanks be to God! I used to get drunk all the time...I used to be anxious...I used to steal a...I used to try to be in control...I used to cheat on my wife...I used to be impatient with people...I used to avoid people who weren't like me...I used to shake my booty on the stage for money... I used to feel left out and alone...but since I started learning about Jesus and following him, I don't do that anymore. Thanks be to God! I used to get drunk all the time...I used to be anxious ..I used to steal a...I used to try to be in control...I used to cheat on my wife...I used to be impatient with people...I used to avoid people who weren't like me...I used to shake my booty on the stage for money...I used to feel left out and alone...but since I started learning about Jesus and following him, I don't do that anymore. Thanks be to God! I used to get drunk all the time ..I used to be anxious...I used to steal a...I used to try to be in control...I used to cheat on my wife...I used to be impatient with people...I used to avoid people who weren't like me. ..I used to shake my booty on the stage for money...I used to feel left out and alone...but since I started learning about Jesus and following him, I don't do that anymore. Thanks be to God!

But it hadn't always been like that. The Fellowship of the Used-Tos was formerly known as the Church of the Trying-to-Stay-Open. The name change had followed major renovation; the members had torn down the shrines and altars of traditionalism and started building up REAL church. Before the renovation, no one but the members had even known the church existed. But now, seven years later, people came from near and far to try to figure out how the Fellowship did what it did.

The people who made up the fellowship were surprised by the response. It seemed that those visiting from other churches saw the Fellowship as something exceptional. Some visitors thought it was outstanding that the Fellowship included people from all walks of life: executives, community leaders, the homeless, recent immigrants, and everything in between. Others thought it was extraordinary that the Fellowship was made up of people from more than twenty-five different nations. Some thought the turnaround story itself was special, and others couldn't believe that there was one new decision to follow Christ for every six people who regularly attended worship.

The Fellowship of the Used-Tos celebrated all that the Lord was doing in their midst even as they saw all the brokenness within themselves and their community—but they didn't see that as exceptional. Surely all churches celebrated what God was doing in their midst. Surely all churches sought to live out the realization that they were blessed to be a blessing to others. The fellowship aimed to be like Christ, feel the Holy Spirit, and do what mattered to God. They weren't perfect—far from it! They continually wrestled with how to be bolder and more effective in their ministry. What could others learn from them? They were about to find out . . .

At the altar one Sunday night after a powerful worship experience, a bewildered-looking young man, Joe Stephens, paced back and forth as Pastor D uttered the final blessing.

"Is there anything I can do for you?"

Joe felt a hand on his shoulder. As he turned to face the woman who had spoken to him, the first thing he noticed was her smile, and then the sparkle in her eyes, and the energy that seemed to rush forth from her touch. Before Joe had a chance to collect his thoughts, the woman asked another question: "Is this your first time here with us?"

Joe could answer the easier question. "Yes, it is. I've heard many great things about Pastor D and the Fellowship of the Used-Tos, but none of the stories speak to the uniqueness of what God is doing here."

"Yes, God is up to something! We are so happy to have you with us. My name is Paula, and I've been a part of the fellowship for about four years. What's your name, and what brings you here today?"

Joe's face took on a thoughtful expression as he tried to determine how much detail to subject Paula to. What was the simplest way to describe the series of unusual events that had literally driven him to the Fellowship of the Used-Tos and left him restless at the altar?

It had all begun with a call from his supervisor, who had asked if Joe would be interested in serving as the pastor for the Church of the Last Chance. A flood of uncertainty had ensued: *Is this the right place? The right time? Is this where God is calling me? Will this be a good experience to add to my resume? What will my wife say? Will we have to move?*

Before he said yes, he wanted to be sure he could make a difference in that congregation. He read everything he could about how to turn around a church. There were lots of great ideas, tips, and frameworks. But nothing felt quite right. Some authors offered too specific a perspective ("Here's what I did—you can do it, too") or a perspective that was depersonalized and too general ("Of all the churches surveyed . . . "). In other cases, Joe recognized that the advice wouldn't be helpful until the church was more stable and larger. Each approach seemed to be missing something that he couldn't quite put his finger on. Joe knew that, before he did anything, he had to get people who felt defeated and defensive to open themselves up to the influence of the Holy Spirit. While he personally had experienced such a transformation, he had never seen a church go from being "Last Chance" to "the Used-Tos." So, on this evening, he had come to see if the Fellowship of the Used-Tos held any clues for him.

The words of the sermon that night had left him shaking.

There is a deep hunger, thirst, and desire to experience REAL church— church that makes a difference in the lives of the people it touches and in their communities.

Rev. Joe Whalen, pastor of Marsden First United Methodist Church in Bermuda, says, "Traditionalism is the dead faith of the living; while tradi- tion is the living faith of the dead." You and I are called to make disciples for Jesus Christ because that is the tradition passed down to us. But arguing and wrestling over ecclesiastical, institutional matters that have nothing to do with saving lives from sin is where we get caught in traditionalism. And traditionalism causes the church to become stagnant. Traditionalism has no positive response to an already stagnant world needing to be transformed.

But when the tradition is alive in you, you are filled with the Holy Ghost. When you are filled with the Holy Ghost, you are never stagnant. You are always on the move—always doing something to reach somebody for Jesus Christ.

In the first ten verses of Acts 3, Peter and John are fresh off revival and doing something to reach people for Jesus Christ. Their revival was Pentecost, a street revival that led masses of people to experience the transforming power of God through the Holy Spirit. Peter and John and about 120 others had been in prayer, seeking the kingdom of God—"in the same place, at the same time, with the same frame of mind," as Rev. David Jackson, former pastor of A.P. Shaw United Methodist Church in Washington, DC once said. And God's power showed up.

As the Holy Ghost descended, Peter and John joined with others in speaking the Word of God boldly. We get a picture of the disciples and crowd speaking the language and talking the talk of the street with all of its diversity—communicating with strangers in their community. We see them lifting those who are down. Healing those who are hurting. We see them unifying what has been divided. Meeting the needs of those who don't have.

Everyone gathered was filled with the Holy Ghost, filled with God's power. And we find in Acts 2:42 that they strengthened their relationship with Jesus and with one another by devoting themselves to the apostles' teaching and to Bible study, fellowship, breaking bread with each other, and prayer.

That was the original Pentecost moment. Depression, betrayal, fear, and failure were replaced by power, peace, harmony, and joy. They were filled with world-changing power. They'd been transformed. On that day, in that moment, more than three thousand souls were added to the community of believers.

In fact, Acts 2 and beyond tells us that, day by day, folks were getting saved because revival was happening. Day by day, they were telling their stories of what the Lord had done for them. Day by day, they were sharing what they had so that nobody was in need.

Day by day, they spent time visiting one another, eating together, praying together. Day by day, they went into the community and began changing the world. Can you imagine what might happen if the Holy Spirit initiated this kind of revival in congregations all over the world?

The world would not be the same.

The Holy Spirit can create another revival like what we see in Acts 2 . . . when you and I dedicate ourselves to being REAL church. Living out a relevant, enthusiastic, authentic, and loving movement that transforms lives, communities, and the world—in the name of Jesus.

That's what Peter and John did. They came out of a street revival and started a REAL church movement. Acts 3:1–10 is the first recording of their movements after Pentecost. And in Peter and John's first movements outside of their fellowship, we find the Holy Spirit moving them to the temple—to the institutional church—to bring revival and transformation to it.

That afternoon, as described in the Acts 3 account, when Peter and John got to the front of the church, they ran into a man who was being carried in. As the story goes, the man had been lame since birth, and every day, people would lay him at the gate of the church—called the Beautiful gate—so that he could beg for alms from those who were entering.

There's a lot in this one passage. The lame man's situation is reflective of the condition of many people, communities, and churches today.

1. The man is lame.

Being lame means that you are stuck and unable to move. There are a lot of people in the church and in the world who can walk, but who are still stuck and unable to move—they find themselves unable to carry out God's plans and purposes for their lives. There are a lot of churches that are stuck—unable to move into the destinies, plans, and purposes that God has for them because somebody's fighting the pastor or the pastor is fighting the congregation. There are wars in the music ministry. Battles in the church council. Skirmishes in the pews. The church is bogged down in chaos and confusion, instead of being focused on the main thing: developing people. Helping them to learn about Jesus Christ and follow him. Meanwhile the community suffers.

2. The man has been lame from birth.

If you read more into his situation, you see that he's forty years old. So, he's been lame for a long time. A lot of folks with big dreams and big aspirations have been stuck and unable to move for a long time, and they are frustrated, mad, hurt, and hopeless. Or maybe they're just tired. A lot of churches with big dreams and big aspirations are stuck and unable to move because the infighting is keeping them from getting out into the world to do the work the Lord needs done.

3. The lame man's community lacks the power to help him.

The text doesn't tell us where the man lives. We don't know who his family is. We don't know who's bringing him to the temple, where they are carrying him from, or where he goes in the evening. But what we do know is that the people around him, the ones tending to him, do not seem to have the power to help this man be whole. Every day they leave him in front of the church to beg. Today we see the same dynamic. The helpless and hopeless are dumped—sometimes at the steps of the church—because communities don't have what is needed to turn around the fate of the marginalized. As a result, many people are suffering needlessly.

4. The lame man's church lacks the power to heal or help him.

The church is supposed to be the catalyst for community change in the name of Jesus. And here we see a community bringing a lame man to the place where healing is supposed to take place. The man has been there in the same condition for forty years because the folk who go to that church keep walking by him every day and giving him a handout when what he really needs is a hand up. Every day they walk by him, unable to heal him because they lack revival in themselves. They are powerless because of their own need—to be filled with Holy Ghost power.

Not only do we find the lame man begging, but we also find the community and church begging silently in the background. Begging for transformation. For relevancy. Begging for enthusiasm. Begging to be possessed by God. Begging for authenticity. Begging for love. Indeed they are all begging for REAL church.

That's what Peter and John found when they went to church that afternoon. But they were determined not to leave the man begging for REAL church. They were intent on being REAL church with the man, expecting that Jesus would heal him. And when Jesus did heal him, it opened the door for everybody to be healed—even those in the church.

Peter and John went to the temple to heal the institution through a profound interaction with a man the temple viewed as unclean—unworthy to be a part of the temple. But it wasn't complicated. They did it through a simple process. They were relevant: they paused where the beggar was so they could lift him to a better life. They were enthusiastic: because they were possessed by God, they had the power to heal the lame man. They were authentic: they were honest and open, telling the man, "Silver and gold we don't have." And they were loving: love compelled them to stop in the first place and to offer him Christ.

As the sermon continued to play in the back of his mind, Joe blurted out to Paula, "I think God wants me to discover how the church I'm supposed to pastor might become REAL. I came here looking for clues, and now I realize how much I want to ask and to learn. I feel like the books I've read and the conferences I've attended haven't given me what I need to start transforming a congregation into another Fellowship of the Used-Tos."

"That's wonderful! Let me introduce you to Pastor D," Paula said as she started walking Joe toward the thinning crowd surrounding the pastor, "and let's see where God leads."

Chapter 2
Understanding REAL

Relevant. Enthusiastic. Authentic. Loving.

I feel like I'm a long-lost family member. It's like I'm the only person in this room, Joe thought as Pastor D greeted and embraced him. Paula introduced the two men, and Joe felt a level of joy he hadn't experienced for quite a while.

"Why don't we sit for a minute and talk?" Pastor D offered. The two men got settled around a small table in the pastor's office that had been prepared with care. It was laden with fruit, juice, tea, and muffins, and decked out with a colorful tablecloth.

"You have a very special place here," said Joe, a little misty-eyed. "Not only was your preaching inspirational to me, but the people are so genuinely warm. You had me by the seventh hug during the passing of the peace. The lesson on Acts 3 really got me thinking, and God started speaking to me in that." He paused for a moment, lost in thought. "Do you mind if I ask you some questions?"

"I'm humbled by your enthusiasm. I'd be honored to answer your questions," replied Pastor D warmly.

Joe seized the moment. "I want to know how my church can be filled with people like this? How can we turn our temple into a REAL church? Sometimes I even wonder if it's even possible for all churches—especially one like the Church of the Last Chance—to be relevant, enthusiastic, authentic, and loving!"

With a broad smile and infectious laugh, Pastor D simply asked, "Last Chance? Is that really the name of your church?"

"Well, it's the name of the church I've been asked to pastor," Joe said a little sheepishly.

"Yes, you can turn around your church—even one called Last Chance! All it requires at the outset is an expectation that REAL church is possible. And that expectation has to be born out of your own Pentecost experience. A part of turning around a church like Last Chance is allowing your experience to reenergize exhausted souls in the pews."

Joe nodded, listening closely as Pastor D continued.

"It seems to me," Pastor D said "that people in the church are getting tired and worn out by the tension between what they long for in church and what they experience in church."

"Why do you think that tension exists? What causes it?" Joe wondered aloud.

"In my experience, there is a wide variety of causes for this. And we need to address as many of them as possible if we are going to have a chance at making a REAL church movement happen."

Pastor D held up his hand and began listing nine reasons for the tension between what many churches have become and what people are begging for the church to be.

"For starters, not everybody in the church has a personal relationship with Jesus Christ. Second, not everybody in the church is operating in God's plan and purpose for their lives; and third, not everybody has embraced the divine vision that God put in their house of worship for the transformation of the larger community outside the walls of the church.

"Life has been difficult for many; but too often the church doesn't speak or act to address the challenges along life's journey—and on top of that," said Pastor D, holding up a fifth finger, "many of us haven't experienced a church that connects us to the One who can build us back up. The sixth reason is that you can't bring transformation to others, unless you've been transformed yourself. And, seven, if the church is going to bring transformation to a hurting world, then the church must experience healing itself. Oftentimes churches ignore the pain within their own body. Until this pain is dealt with positively, the congregation can't move forward as a transforming agent in its community.

"A lot of us and a lot of churches are stagnant because we've stopped working to make new disciples of Jesus Christ for the transformation of the world. And the last reason is that we are tied up in arguments that distract us from our mission or we have simply lost the urgency to 'go and make disciples'—or both."

"Wow, no wonder so many churches are in trouble!" said Joe. "I must admit I was a bit surprised to find you talking about REAL church in your sermon since that is one of the things you are known for. That's how you describe yourself, right? REAL church for real people? How often do you preach about that?"

"I preach on REAL church every now and then to keep us grounded in who God wants us to be and who we say we are. Preaching on the culture and vision of a place helps everyone stay on the same page, and it keeps those things more meaningful than any slogan ever could."

Joe nodded enthusiastically and asked for a piece of paper on which to continue the notes he had begun scribbling furiously on his crumpled church bulletin. Pastor D handed Joe a notebook and then grabbed a blueberry muffin from the spread in front of him.

"Can you explain in a little more detail what you mean when you say REAL?" Joe asked once his note-writing hand had managed to catch up with his brain. "From your sermon, I understand it is an acronym for relevant, enthusiastic, authentic, and loving. And I get that these are sort of foundational to everything you do here . . . so I want to be sure I understand what they represent for you."

"No problem," Pastor D said, as he bit into a muffin. "REAL church has to do with four elements that work in tandem. When these four are visible and evident within the life of a congregation, that congregation is transforming lives and *being* transformed on a regular basis. People in the congregation and community are being saved from their sins, finding their basic needs met, identifying with their dreams, and achieving God's purposes for them. People are sacrificing for the well-being of others and discovering they are being blessed so that they might better bless others.

When one or more of these elements is absent, transformation becomes much more difficult.

We must be RELEVANT.

"Now, the word *relevant* has two components to it. First, it means either getting closely connected or being appropriate to the matter at hand. It is sitting where people sit so that we experience their daily realities. If the church is going to be relevant, it has to be closely connected and appropriate to the daily struggles of people's lives. It cannot be insulated from the world's troubles; it must be *engaged* in the world's troubles, actively working to resolve issues. A relevant church speaks to the heart and soul of the human condition.

"These days, we are inundated by the presence of social media and other forms of instant communication: Facebook, Twitter, Skype, texting, e-mail, and all the rest. They all increase the capacity of people to be connected and to communicate with one another 24/7—but these mediums also create a false sense of relationship. While quantity and immediacy of communication are great, quality is limited. If you've ever been misunderstood while using any of these mediums, you get what I mean."

"All too well," Joe said as he thought about a recent text exchange with his wife, Janelle, that had resulted in the need for him to buy her flowers.

"Often in the church we relate to our communities more like people exchanging text messages than like individuals engaging in a personal conversation over a meal. Social media is a shallow way of engaging with people; it's difficult to determine what is happening in someone's soul. But when I sit across the table from someone or sit with someone in the midst of their struggle or pain, I'm able to hear, see, and sense what's happening with them—and then engage with them at a much deeper level. For the church to be important, it must be engaged with the whole person, not insulated from real life.

"Secondly, in its original Latin, *relevant* means to raise or lift up. So a relevant church raises or lifts people out of their human condition. If a church is going to liberate beggars, if it is going to be relevant to the people it seeks to reach, it can't just talk about problems. Churches have to be problem solvers in the name of Jesus. They must be engaged in helping people find jobs, working to see that kids get quality educations, and creating a fair and just society for immigrants. Relevant churches not only speak to the problems of society but also work to *resolve* those problems."

Joe's mind began to catalog the problems that plagued the community surrounding the Church of the Last Chance. He felt both excited at the possibility of making a real impact in people's lives and apprehensive about the challenge.

"Many churches leave people lame," Pastor D continued, "and many churches struggle and die because they are not relevant to the daily situations of life. Not relevant to kids growing up in a hip-hop, capitalistic, YouTube culture. Not relevant to college students wondering what the future holds. Not relevant to singles who are seeking to discover identity and to establish meaningful, potentially lifelong relationships with others. Not relevant to young families needing spiritual tools to strengthen their marriages and their families in the midst of challenging economic times. Not relevant to senior citizens seeking to solidify a meaningful legacy.

"But the churches that *are* relevant take time to acknowledge and lift the lame people around them in the name of Jesus. Relevant churches lead those who are lame to see that their lives have value. Peter and John did not pass the lame man by—instead, they validated his life while everyone else had validated his begging. When the church starts being passionately and consistently relevant through our worship, fellowship, and service, people will come *running* to the community of disciples."

Pastor D's face lit up as he poured out his vision for relevant churches. Joe settled in, eager to hear more.

"It isn't enough to speak to the human condition, you have to actually *do* something to lift people up out of it. The prevalent human condition may look different in your community than it does in mine. If HIV is rampant in your community, you have to speak to the HIV issue and then raise people up and out of despair. We've got to speak to the education issue, and then go beyond discussion by offering tutoring services for our kids. We've got to talk about sex and not be scared about sex! Shucks, if sex is being talked about in schools, in local hangouts, in music, on television, and on the Internet but not in the church, we have a problem. Where else are people going to get a wholesome and positive understanding of sex than from the church and good family conversations? We've got to speak to the human conditions that tear people down, but then we have to raise them out of those places and position them to see divine possibilities. A church that's not relevant in its community is just a Christian social club. And I don't know about you, but my Jesus did not die and then rise again with all power just to have the church relegated to being a Christian social club!"

"I got it," replied Joe. "I've been to too many Christian social clubs, and they aren't very fun."

Joe put down his pen and selected a muffin from the basket. "If you are going to go to a club, it might as well be fun," he added. Pastor D shook his head and laughed.

We must be ENTHUSIASTIC.

"So, next up is *enthusiasm*," continued Pastor D. "Many people misinterpret or misunderstand this word, *enthusiasm*. We think that it means just being excited about something, clapping your hands, and saying, 'Praise the Lord!' We think that enthusiasm is just about getting our shout on—and then leaving the shout in the sanctuary while we curse somebody out in the parking lot.

"While enthusiasm may cause you to shout, the word *enthusiasm* in its original biblical Greek means much more than that. It means to be possessed by God, inspired by God, and consumed by God.

"It sounds like you are saying we are supposed to be drunk on God," said Joe, checking his understanding.

"Correct. You know the story of Pentecost. The Holy Spirit blew in like a mighty rushing wind, and Peter was accused of being drunk. The reality, though, was that he was not drunk on wine but drunk on or possessed by the Holy Spirit. That possession caused him to do things that no wine could intoxicate him to do. He was able to speak God's word with power, break down barriers and build bridges, and unite people who had once been divided. Those who had needs found their needs met. That is what possession looks like. That is what it means to be enthusiastic.

"Joe, do you remember your first love? How did you behave?"

"Yes, of course," said Joe. "Diane. My life was consumed with having to be with her, talk to her, kiss her, and just do whatever it took to make her happy."

"You got it, Joe. In the same way, when we are possessed by God, we are consumed. When God is the object of our love, we are consumed—not for self-centered reasons—but for kingdom ones.

"When leaders of the church are possessed by God, the church can become possessed by God. And when the church is possessed by God, the church has the power, energy, and inspiration to lead people, communities, and the world from situations in which they are lame—stuck and unable to move—to living testimonies so that we can do all things through Christ Jesus who strengthens us.

"Peter was possessed by God. He said to the lame man, 'Look at us!' Then he fixed his eyes on God. He gave the lame man respect, but then he sought to inspire him through his own life."

Pastor D paused for a moment and then looked Joe squarely in the face.

"Have you inspired somebody with your own life because you were possessed by God? Is your church trying to inspire people to be what God has called them to be?"

"With a name like Last Chance, I don't think so," Joe answered.

"Well, Joe, if you are possessed by God, then eventually, like with Peter and John, the lame people of Last Chance will get up. When you are possessed by God, God invades, infects, persuades, influences, and captures all that is around you.

"God begins spreading hope and healing into the people around you who are suffering and struggling. The angel's words become real to you: 'All things are possible with God.' *All* means *all*. Tumors can shrink in the name of Jesus. Cancer can disappear in the name of Jesus. Migraines can go away in the name of Jesus. Families can unite in the name of Jesus. Feuds can find peace in the name of Jesus. Addictions can be destroyed in the name of Jesus. God can take control. 'Eyes have not seen, ears have not heard, neither has it entered into the heart of man, the great things God will do for those who love him.'"

"So," Joe said, really beginning to catch on, "if I'm following you, Pastor D, when the church becomes possessed by God, the world will be healed!"

"Exactly," Pastor D said with a nod. "Now let's move onto the issue of authenticity.

We must be AUTHENTIC.

"Being authentic means being transparent and honest. When we are an authentic church, people will not call us hypocrites or fakes, and they won't stay away from the church either. Instead, they'll be attracted by stories of our genuine journey with God through life's ups and downs. An authentic church owns the fact that we are all sinners saved by grace, seeking to live in God's favor.

"People are begging for a safe place, where they can share their stuff and not get judged—where they can share the good, the bad, and the ugly. If we're honest with ourselves, we all have good, bad, and ugly."

"Sometimes I feel more bad and ugly than good!" Joe affirmed. "Yet, so often the church pretends that everything is good—that everything is alright—when it's really a hot mess."

Pastor D laughed. "Yes, true enough . . . but when the church *is* honest about its successes and shames, about what it has and doesn't have, an environment of honesty and openness is created where people can tell their stories freely—the joyful *and* painful stories about how Jesus made a way out of no way. When we do this, beggars are liberated, and the world can see that we are legit.

"Young people and folk in the street can tell whether you and me are honest or not. And they will put the word out on you and your church in a minute . . . one way or the other." Pastor D sat back in his chair. "So, what do you think they are saying about you, Joe? And what are they saying about the Church of the Last Chance?"

Joe considered the question for a moment before answering.

"Pastor D," he said slowly, "honestly I don't think anyone is saying *anything* about Last Chance."

"Well," Pastor D challenged, "if you decide to step into REAL leadership, that's gonna change. If it changed in this church, it can change in any church. One of our new members shared a memorable testimony at a recent leadership summit. When someone asked her how she ended up coming to Fellowship of the Used-Tos, she said, 'I came here because I could see that your pastor and you were authentic. You see, I've danced and swung my booty for money on a few stages in my lifetime. And I know a hustle when I see one. But this man and this church ain't trying to hustle nobody—they are really trying to help people, and that's why I'm here.'

"You have *got* to be authentic and honest. You have to be who you are. You will reach many more people for Jesus if you do. My story is not your story, and your story is not my story. My story will reach people that your story will not, and your story will reach people that my story will not. So you've got to tell your story, and I've got to tell mine. If you don't tell it, no one else can.

"Don't come to church trying to put on airs. No one cares about that. What people do care about is how God is at work in your life and how that blessing can help them get through whatever they are going through. You be you. If you are you, in the name of Jesus, *people will respond to God.*"

When was the last time I really told my story? Joe wondered to himself. He knew what people expected from pastors, and could only imagine the pressure to just play the role. But he could see Pastor D was serious about the raw, honest truth.

"Peter is authentic with the beggar in the text," Pastor D continued. "Can you hear him? 'Look, bruh. I ain't got no money. It's a recession. Silver and gold I don't have, but what I have, I give you. I have Jesus. I'm possessed by Jesus. And in my relevance, my enthusiasm, and my authentic concern for you, I give you what I have. In the name of Jesus Christ of Nazareth. In the name of the Anointed One of God, sent by God to forgive us of our sins, to save us, to make us whole again, I command you to stand up and walk.'

"And the man stands up and walks! That is the power of being authentic."

Joe let Pastor D's words wash over him as he began to envision what Last Chance might be like as a real, enthusiastic, and authentic church. But he knew there was one thing still left to discuss: love.

We must be LOVING.

As if on cue, Pastor D began, "Unconditional love desires the well-being of others. Love doesn't care where you've been; love is concerned with what God wants you to be. Love isn't dissuaded by the "–isms" of life. Unconditional love is consumed with trying to give life, bring life, be life—even to strangers and *especially* to those on the margins—so that we can all have life, and have it more abundantly.

"When the church loves, beggars can be liberated. Look at Peter. He desires the lame man's well-being—so much so that Peter interrupts his schedule in order to reach out to help him up. Peter gives him the strength of his right hand. *Lifts him up.* Gives of himself so that somebody else can be blessed. He doesn't know the man, but he wants to bless the man. He doesn't know his situation, but he wants to improve his condition. Love is like that."

Suddenly Pastor D got up from the table and walked over to his desk. He reached out and picked up a small, framed piece of paper and then brought it over to where Joe sat. He handed it to him silently. The paper read:

When the church dares to love . . .
It insists on being multicultural and multiethnic in its makeup whenever
    possible.
It insists on being intergenerational.
It insists on loving people regardless of skin color.
It insists on loving people regardless of dialect or national origin.
It insists on encouraging and supporting people regardless of their sexual
    orientation.

It insists on eliminating systems of oppression and ushering in justice and peace in our midst.

It insists on breaking down walls of classism and seeks to eradicate poverty.

It insists on breaking down barriers and building bridges of hope that not even fights among Democrats, Republicans, and Tea Partiers can stop.

When Joe looked back up, Pastor D said, "I keep this on my desk as a constant reminder of what it means to be a loving church."

"I think I understand what you mean," responded Joe. After a moment he continued, "But it sounds like a lot of work, Pastor D!"

"You're right about that, but it is the work of the church. *It is the work the church is meant to do.* At Fellowship of the Used-Tos we are working very intentionally to show that we love our homeless and transient neighbors, and in the process we are seeking to eliminate poverty. I remember this homeless man, Charles, telling me the story of how he got to Fellowship of the Used-Tos. Charles was talking to a friend of his on the bus when it passed by the church building. Suddenly, the friend told him about Fellowship of the Used-Tos and said, 'You need to go to that church.' When Charles asked why, his friend told him about our vibrant worship services and how we are committed to meeting people's needs. He told Charles, 'They care about people—even people like us.' So the next Sunday, Charles came to the Fellowship expecting to see his friend. He didn't see his friend that Sunday but was so moved by the experience that on the following Sunday he returned to Fellowship of the Used-Tos and joined.

"So, the next week, he ran into his friend on the bus again and asked, 'What happened? I thought I'd see you at church.' His friend said, 'I didn't tell you I went to the church, I just told you that *you* needed to go there!'" Pastor D hollered, laughing just as hard as he had the first time he'd heard Charles tell the tale.

Joe shook his head and chuckled. "It must be nice to be known on the street as a church that loves and cares about people—especially people who aren't usually comfortable in church."

"That it is, Joe. But," said Pastor D seriously, "you *always* have to be working toward that because a couple of negative experiences can ruin that reputation!"

Joe knew Pastor D's words were true. He was saddened to think of how many people might already have written off the Church of the Last Chance because of its less than positive reputation.

Not wanting to wear out his welcome, Joe thanked Pastor D for his time.

"I thank you and thank God for this time we have had together. I realize it is late, and I have a ninety-minute drive home. You've given me lots to think about—and you've given me hope that it is possible for Church of the Last Chance to become more REAL. I'm not sure I know what to do next, though . . ."

Joe paused and then said in a rush, "I'd really appreciate having you as a mentor."

Being REAL comes out of our personal Pentecost experiences. REAL means:

WE MUST BE RELEVANT
* Closely connected and appropriate to people's daily realities
* Dedicated to lifting people up and out of their human condition
* Committed to being problem solvers—not problem admirers, who look at problems but won't touch them with a ten-foot pole

WE MUST BE ENTHUSIASTIC
* Possessed by God, inspired by God, and consumed by God
* Influenced by God, allowing Him to take over everything we do

WE MUST BE AUTHENTIC
* Be transparent and honest
* Testify about what God has done in the midst of our good, bad and ugly

WE MUST BE LOVING
* Desire the well-being of others regardless of who they are and what they've done
* Bring people life so that they might live it more abundantly
* Break down barriers—especially the "-isms"—and build bridges of hope.

Chapter 3
Discerning Call
Wilderness. Confirmation. Action.

Pastor D quickly agreed to mentor Joe. There was something about Joe that reminded Pastor D of himself at that age. Then he gave the younger man his first homework assignment. They set up their first call for June 1 and said a prayer before parting.

As he got into his car, Joe was glad he had the long drive home to process all that had happened. *What a night!* As if the powerful worship and rich dialogue weren't enough, he also had new relationships that he felt would make a real difference in his life and ministry. As Joe began reflecting on his first assignment, he couldn't help but replay Pastor D's words in his mind.

"Joe, I need you to get this straight from the start: as a follower and learner of Jesus Christ, you have a call. People may not like that, but as I'm sure you know, once people sign up to walk with Jesus, they discover that He has great plans for their lives and that He is going to call them to participate in seeing those plans come to pass."

"So," Joe asked, *"you are saying everything needs to be anchored in a call and that everyone has one?"* Pastor D nodded his head in agreement, and Joe continued, *"I think I know what you mean when you say 'call,' but give me your definition."*

"A call is a divine summons to fulfill divine tasks," Pastor D began. *"It's like when your momma says, 'Girl, get over here!' or 'Boy, I told you to come!'*

But with God, it's a divine summons to a particular set of circumstances in which your actions will determine whether or not lives are transformed in the name of Jesus. Nothing in ministry gets done right unless you hear that call and follow it. Everything revolves around this divine summons. Every decision and every move you make should be governed by this call. And so, unless God has called you to do a particular ministry, you shouldn't do it, or you will find that ministry to be a very miserable experience. You will burn out and burn out the people around you even before you begin to see the fruits of your labor. But when you are clear about God's call on your life—and then act on it—you will be a witness to many signs and wonders that will blow your mind.

"To be REAL church, leaders need to respond faithfully to their call, and they must encourage others, empower others, and expect that others will do the same. This creates a culture of call, an environment in which spiritual leaders, directed by God, rise up and passionately desire to do with you what matters most to God. And what matters most to God is for the world to live in a peaceful, harmonious relationship with Him where there is justice and righteousness for all."

"I haven't ever experienced a 'culture of call,'" responded Joe, *"but it sure sounds good and feels right."*

"But let me warn you, Joe, discerning call is an intense process. Just like Moses discovered, once a call is issued, we'll make excuses, we'll try to get out of it, we'll try to convince ourselves that we aren't capable of doing what God wants. We might even tell God no. But if you want to make the right choice about Church of the Last Chance, you need to know whether or not you have been called by God to serve there. And to know whether or not you have been called, you have to spend time with God and discern what God's up to with you. That will entail spending time in the wilderness."

"I feel like I've been in the wilderness for a while now," Joe said.

"That's good, Joe. Good things can happen in the wilderness. Just don't get lost there. Discernment doesn't stop there. If this is what God wants for your life, God will confirm it, and God will position you to take action to lead a transformation the likes of which you've never seen."

Joe glanced at his notes at the next stop sign.

Homework: Discern whether or not I am called to this
ministry. Discernment includes
    1. Wilderness
    2. Confirmation
    3. Action.

Thinking about these three stages, Joe felt compelled to head to the
water, his preferred place to talk with God. He steered his car off the road
home and headed toward his favorite stream of meditation.

As he watched the water crawl over the rocks and wind through the
ravine, Joe thought about where he was in his discernment process and
where God was leading him.

*How long have I been in the wilderness? I think it actually began when I
was a kid.*

Joe's dad had been raised United Methodist and his mom,
Presbyterian. When he was fourteen, Joe heard his call into pastoral
ministry and bolted both denominations at the age of twenty-two after
starting a community fellowship in a rough area of suburbia. Feeling the
need for more structure to prepare him for pastoring, he eventually joined
First Baptist Church halfway through his seminary studies because he had
friends there. The church put him to work immediately!

In three short years, Joe was licensed to preach. Soon thereafter, he
found himself in a season of prayer and meditation because it had become
painfully evident that God was leading him in a different direction. Some
of Joe's closest friends were telling him he had better keep his well-paying
day job, but God was saying it was time to go. There was just one hurdle
to clear: convincing Janelle. After all, Joe was making great money, and
leaving the hospital where he worked would mean a drastic shift in their
family's finances; so, of course, she would have to agree to such a move.

Joe came home one evening and built up the courage to share with
his wife everything that God had put on his mind about ministry, his call,

pastoring—everything. But Janelle knew he'd been called. After all, she was the one who had given him part of his seminary tuition as a wedding present.

Once Joe shared his thoughts with her, Janelle said, "The one thing that I do not want to do is stand in the way of what God is doing in your life. I am with you and will walk with you. All I need is for you to show me a plan for how we are going to make ends meet until you get your first assignment as a pastor somewhere."

But Joe didn't have a plan—not yet. So he entered into a time of prayer and discernment. God gave him a plan. When he shared it with Janelle, she said, "Let's go!"

Joe quit his full-time job in order to devote himself to discovering the vocation in ministry God had for him. *That's when my wilderness got crazy,* Joe thought to himself, remembering that difficult period.

Joe was scared to death about leaving his job. It paid well, and he had always felt confident that he could take care of his family. But now he was about to enter the unknown while placing the brunt of the financial responsibility for their household on his wife. And all of this with a two-year-old and a four-month-old at home. Talk about pressure! It was a scary feeling wondering whether or not they could make ends meet until God brought him to where he was supposed to be.

But within himself, Joe experienced a quiet assurance that the steps he was taking were not his own—but God's—and God would take care of his family's situation. He had reached the point where he fully trusted in God, so much so that the day after he quit his job, Joe and his wife boarded a plane to Hawaii for a ten-day vacation. They used that time to rejoice, to reconnect, and to reflect on God's next steps.

When the couple got back home, their friends and mentors told Joe that he needed to find a job. But he knew what he needed to do. He had to make $600 a month to make ends meet, and he didn't need a full-time job to do that. The initial plan was to earn that through substitute teaching and preaching on the side. But when Joe returned home, God had another provision. Joe's pastor was so enamored by Joe's faith decision that he put him on staff as an Assistant Pastor and paid him a stipend of $1,200 per month. In addition to that, God opened a door for Joe to teach courses in speech communication for $2,000 a semester (almost $700 a month!). During the same period, his former supervisor called and asked if Joe would take on two writing contracts at $3,600 per contract (another $600 a month). Within three weeks after returning from Hawaii, Joe discovered God had taken care of his finances for the transition. And he had plenty of time to pursue the vocation God had identified for his life.

That year brought Joe to the realization that God wanted him to be open and available for Him to send Joe wherever He wanted him to go. A part of that sending included the denomination in which God wanted Joe to serve. Joe was not hung up on denominations, but he knew that he'd have to make some decision about a denomination soon. His divinity school dean had told him during his denominational struggles in seminary, "Brother Joe, you are going to have to sit your boat in somebody's water." But Joe didn't want to have any of it.

What changed him, however, was an interaction with a person on the pastoral search committee at a prominent Presbyterian church in town. She wanted him to consider interviewing for the pastor position in that church. Joe had been Presbyterian before. In fact, half of his life to that point had been spent in the Presbyterian Church. The Presbyterian Church Joe knew was cold, lifeless, and irrelevant to the realities people faced everyday. So without even considering that this particular church was doing powerful ministry in a severely marginalized community, Joe told the woman thanks, but no thanks. When she asked him why, he told her that he wanted to remain a Baptist.

Then the woman said something to Joe that still reverberated in his soul: "I am praying for you, young man. I hope that one day you will realize that it is not about being Baptist or Presbyterian or anything else. It's about reaching lost souls for Jesus Christ in whatever context He calls you. God bless you, Reverend."

As Joe remembered the words she had spoken to him, he sensed God opening him up to the possibility that he might indeed be called to serve the Church of the Last Chance. Humbled, Joe praised God for His patience, mercy, and grace. With a sense of peace, Joe returned to his car and headed home.

When Joe walked in his front door, he tripped over the shoes, coats, and toys that always managed to pile up right by the door.

"I'm home!" he called out in his most cheerful voice—hoping his wife had had a good evening with the kids. As he turned the corner, he was welcomed by his two children, Marie and Mark, who each wrapped themselves around one of his legs. Janelle gracefully got up and kissed his cheek.

"It's definitely your turn," she whispered in his ear, a twinge of weariness in her voice.

"I'm so glad to be back home. I missed all of you," Joe said as he gave his wife a squeeze. "I'm sorry I was out so late. I'll put the kids to bed if you want to take some time to relax." Joe was rewarded with a smile and another kiss. From his time at the river, Joe realized how much his wilderness had impacted his wife, who had committed to be the primary breadwinner until his call thing was fully played out. He was overwhelmed with gratitude for Janelle and that strong faith of hers that anchored their family.

After he put the kids down to bed, and while he was waiting for Janelle to finish her marathon soak in the tub, Joe picked up his well-worn Bible and looked to Exodus chapters 3 and 4 to see what more he could learn about the season of discernment.

Reviewing Moses's call story once again, Joe confirmed the fact that discerning one's call takes people into a season of major wrestling, confusion, and turmoil. God called Moses to lead the people of Israel out of Egyptian bondage. The task was so daunting that it takes almost two chapters of excuse making in Exodus before the reader sees Moses yield to God's summons. The Israelites were in Egyptian bondage. Moses became a fugitive from justice after killing an Egyptian soldier. He fled to Midian, and while Moses was serving as a shepherd around the Mount of Horeb, God showed up out of nowhere. He summoned Moses into His presence and spoke to Moses clearly, concisely, and personally about the ministry He wanted Moses to pursue:

> *[1] Now Moses was tending the flock of Jethro his father-in-law, the priest of Midian, and he led the flock to the far side of the wilderness and came to Horeb, the mountain of God. [2] There the angel of the LORD appeared to him in flames of fire from within a bush. Moses saw that though the bush was on fire it did not burn up. [3] So Moses thought, "I will go over and see this strange sight—why the bush does not burn up."*

⁴When the LORD saw that he had gone over to look, God called to him from within the bush, "Moses! Moses!"

And Moses said, "Here I am."

⁵"Do not come any closer," God said. "Take off your sandals, for the place where you are standing is holy ground." ⁶Then he said, "I am the God of your father, the God of Abraham, the God of Isaac and the God of Jacob." At this, Moses hid his face, because he was afraid to look at God. ⁷The LORD said, "I have indeed seen the misery of my people in Egypt. I have heard them crying out because of their slave drivers, and I am concerned about their suffering. ⁸So I have come down to rescue them from the hand of the Egyptians and to bring them up out of that land into a good and spacious land, a land flowing with milk and honey— the home of the Canaanites, Hittites, Amorites, Perizzites, Hivites and Jebusites. ⁹And now the cry of the Israelites has reached me, and I have seen the way the Egyptians are oppressing them. ¹⁰So now, go. I am sending you to Pharaoh to bring my people the Israelites out of Egypt."

Joe wanted to be sure that this call to the Church of the Last Chance was clear, concise, and personal—just as it had been for Moses. After all, it was for the best that Moses found confirmation of his call before he set out on the journey to free his people from Egypt. If he wasn't clear about his call, he could lead himself and others into some devastating situations. This was important to Joe because, like Moses, he sensed he was about to lead a congregation out of bondage. And the last thing he wanted to do was to lead people from one pit to another unnecessarily.

Joe reflected on his own burning-bush experience. He also pondered a sermon he'd heard not long ago reminding him that ministry cannot be done unless God has visited his ministers and left them "strangely warmed," as John Wesley said. Joe wanted to be sure, beyond a shadow of a doubt, that he'd been summoned to a divine assignment at the Church of the Last Chance. His study on Moses led him to meditate on the New Testament equivalent—Pentecost—and Pastor D's sermon.

In a Pentecost experience, the Holy Spirit, God in us, visits us so powerfully that we experience God soaking, saturating, and filling us with

His presence—so much so that we *have* to respond to what He wants. Joe realized that this was what many churches were missing. He knew that the Church of the Last Chance was missing this and that part of his call would be to restore this divine passion within the fellowship. All of the curricula, the means of grace, the acts of piety, the Bible studies, the new fads for church growth and development—none of them meant a thing unless he and the people he might serve had participated in a Pentecost or burning-bush experience in which God took over.

Joe looked over the notes he had made:

Discern whether or not I am called to this ministry.
Discernment includes
    1. Wilderness
    2. Confirmation
    3. Action.

Moses has a burning-bush experience and in the experience:
    1. God is clear about what He wants Moses to do.
    2. God is concise—in four verses Moses's mission is clear.
    3. God called Moses by name to fulfill the task.

Have I had a burning-bush experience? Have I had a
Pentecost moment? Am I on a Pentecost journey?

Has God made it clear, concise, and personal for me?

As Janelle walked into the room, Joe put his notebook and his Bible away for the night, feeling very grateful for all the blessings God had given him that day.

Chapter 4
Confirming Call

Is it God? Does it have my name written all over it?

What a whirlwind of a week! Between all Joe's odd jobs, sometimes he didn't know which way to turn next. Yet he had a sense of calm purpose through it all, seeking to confirm his call to serve the Church of the Last Chance even though it was a United Methodist Congregation. He was hoping to receive some sort of confirmation during a men's retreat he was attending with one of his childhood friends, Tim. Joe travelled up to the retreat on Friday night feeling a little guilty for leaving his wife and young kids behind. He hoped this would be one of the last nights apart from them in a while.

Joe enjoyed his brief time away but had to leave the retreat on Saturday because he was preaching at the Baptist church the next morning. As Joe was heading out to his car, Tim figured he'd slip in one last question: "So, tell me, Joe . . . where are you now in your call?"

"Well, you remember when I told you I'd reached a point that no matter where God wants to send me, I'd go?" Joe began. "I told you that even if God wants me to be a Catholic priest, I'll go serve in a Catholic church. And then right after I told you that, I got a call from a district superintendent from the United Methodist Church asking if I'd be interested in pastoring the Church of the Last Chance! Believe it or not, I'm still trying to confirm that call and to decide if I should switch denominations one more time. I need to be sure this is what God wants me to do."

Tim laughed one of those laughs that indicated he knew God was up to something. But Joe remained certain that he needed more confirmation. As God would have it, the retreat was about to enter late afternoon worship. Joe slipped his car keys back into his pocket and decided to stick around just in case God had a word of confirmation for him in the worship service.

Not knowing what Joe was wrestling with, but knowing that he would be leaving before too long, one of the retreat organizers invited him to read the scripture of his choice in the service. The first thing to come to Joe's mind was Paul's letter to the Philippians. He read from chapter 3, verses 12 through 14:

> *Not that I have already obtained this or have already reached the goal; but I press on to make it my own, because Christ Jesus has made me his own. Beloved, I do not consider that I have made it my own; but this one thing I do: forgetting what lies behind and straining forward to what lies ahead, I press on toward the goal for the prize of the heavenly call of God in Christ Jesus."*

Joe sat down after reading the scripture and continued to wait for confirmation. He sat through the prayers, the hymns, the sermon—and still, no confirmation.

Right before the benediction was pronounced, the guest preacher for the next morning's service, Rev. Samuel Smith, walked in. His driver had gotten lost picking him up from the airport. The retreat host invited the reverend to the pulpit to say a word before they closed.

Joe's heart, mind, and entire being tuned in as Rev. Smith began to talk: "Tomorrow I want to talk about what it really means to be a Christian. I'm a Baptist, and I've been a Baptist all my life. I've been president of a national Baptist convention. I've been president of a state Baptist convention. I've been president of our local Baptist convention. I've been as high as the Baptists can take me. My granddaddy was a Baptist pastor. My father was a Baptist pastor. And I've been pastoring the same Baptist church for forty-three years. I've been as high as the Baptists can take me."

Then he turned and looked at Joe squarely in the eyes, pointed to him, and said forcefully and passionately, "But I ain't no damned Baptist. I'm a Christian. And wherever God tells you to go serve, go serve!"

While Rev. Smith and Joe didn't know each other at all, it was obvious that he had come with a word from the Lord to clarify Joe's call. In fact, Tim, who was sitting next to Joe when Rev. Smith spoke, shoved an elbow in Joe's ribs so hard that Joe had difficulty breathing. Tim laughed and said, "You need any more confirmation?"

Joe drove home from the retreat clear about doing what God wanted him to do—but still seeking a little more confirmation. When he got home and shared the story with Janelle, she suggested he check out the Church of the Last Chance in person.

The next day Joe drove past the Church of the Last Chance three times before he found it. It wasn't like he didn't know the area. When he was growing up, he had been to the area often when visiting close family friends. Yet today, he kept driving past the Church of the Last Chance, and his GPS kept patiently recalculating and guiding him back to his destination. When he finally drove up to Last Chance, past the unmowed grass, the decaying signs, and behind a tall fence that resembled those surrounding impound lots, Joe felt the bottom of his stomach drop. The dreary, dilapidated structure didn't look like a church. It looked protected, yet forgotten.

After seeing the demoralizing conditions around the church, Joe uttered, "Oh no, God. You definitely made a mistake." But even as he said this, he sensed that God was trying to tell him something.

Joe immediately called Janelle and described the scene to her.

"So what do you think?" Joe asked.

Without hesitation she said, "Go for it!" When he asked her why, she said, "You told me you were called to pastor, and now here God has invited you to pastor. What are you waiting for? *Go for it!*"

Not satisfied with his wife's response—and needing more confirmation—Joe went to see his mother to tell her what had been going on. Somehow she had found out about the church and had already gone down there to visit it on her own.

When Joe asked her what he should do, she said without hesitation: "Baby, it's got your name written all over it."

But Joe still had one last call to make. When he returned home, he dialed Pastor D. After relating to him all the thoughts and events of the past couple weeks, Joe heard himself say, "My wife and my mother haven't talked to each other about the church, yet both of them told me the same thing. It seems clear that God has spoken and wants me to serve this community. They are in desperate need of transformation, and it seems I have my confirmation . . . so, why am I still hesitating?"

"Let's review," Pastor D said. "With any opportunity given to you, you have to ask yourself two questions: First, is God calling me to this place? And second, does it have my name written all over it? When your call is clear for you as a leader, you can then be the catalyst to help others in the pews and the streets, with power and conviction, embrace their own calls. Without a clear call, doing transformational ministry is *impossible. It is only possible with God.*

"Now, we both know that nobody in their right mind wants to go to a church where the grass hadn't been cut in six years, where alcohol bottles and beer cans decorate the church and community grounds, and where other evidence of unholiness abounds. When I came to the Fellowship of the Used-Tos, I found similar conditions. Used condoms and syringes were commonplace; and transient and homeless men and women used our stairwells as bathrooms. Nobody in their right mind wants to go into a situation like the one you're describing—especially not with a wife and two little babies, and where you'll be making a fraction of what you currently make. Nobody in their right mind wants to do that. But when you are of God's mind, you remember, like Jeremiah, that God knows the plans he has for you. Plans not to harm you but to give you a future with hope."

As Joe listened to Pastor D, his stomach started to unclench, and his mind started to clear.

"I feel beyond a shadow of a doubt that God has called me to serve this particular church in this particular situation at this particular time," Joe said. "I feel like my name is written all over it because I grew up relating to this neighborhood and it feels like God is ready to use all my experiences to make a difference for this congregation and this community."

Pastor D encouraged Joe further, "You need to lean into that certainty, Joe. Great spiritual leaders—those who transform people and situations in the name of Jesus—are those who know they've had their calls confirmed. Without great spiritual leadership, congregations and communities cannot be transformed. God sends spiritual leaders, both clergy and nonclergy, to broken communities so that life change happens. God sends spiritual leaders to unpopular places—places that lack notoriety—but are filled with need. God sends spiritual leaders to the corridors of learning, business, government, and corporations where Truth needs to be proclaimed. God sends spiritual leaders to places they may not wish to go, at just the time they are needed, in order to bring hope. If you find yourself in a church of glitz and glitter, where people won't get their hands dirty to help others in need, something's wrong. If you find yourself in a dying church where people are participating in the death march, something's wrong. To get people to march to a divine drumbeat, you will need to lead them to have a burning-bush or Pentecost experience. Then God can uniquely position the church to transform itself and its community. A part of that transformation will always involve helping others discern their own calls and participating in the creation of a culture of call. As one of my mentors used to say to me, 'You're either called or you're crazy—and sometimes you're a little bit of both.'"

After Joe hung up the phone with Pastor D, he fell down on his knees and thought about the prophet Jeremiah, who had felt ill-equipped to do what it was that God wanted him to do.

> *4Now the word of the Lord came to me saying, 5"Before I formed you in the womb I knew you, and before you were born I consecrated you; I appointed you a prophet to the nations." 6Then I said, "Ah, Lord God! Truly I do not know how to speak, for I am only a boy." 7But the Lord said to me, "Do not say, 'I am only a boy'; for you shall go to all to whom I send you, and you shall speak whatever I command you, 8Do not be afraid of them, for I am with you to deliver you, says the Lord." 9Then the Lord put out his hand and touched my mouth; and the Lord said to me, "Now I have put my words in your mouth. 10See, today I appoint you over nations and over kingdoms, to pluck up and to pull down, to destroy and to overthrow, to build and to plant."2*

In that moment Joe asked God to place the right words in his mouth as he had done for Jeremiah.

Soon after, Joe found himself being interviewed by the pastoral search committee at the Church of the Last Chance. It was only when an elder on the committee looked into his face and said emphatically, "You are my pastor!" that Joe finally realized he had the confirmation he was looking for—to face the daunting challenge of leading a dead church and community back to life again.

1. Is God calling me to this place at this time?

2. Does it have my name written all over it?

3. What confirmation have I received that this is where God wants me?

4. How much confirmation do I need in order to act?

Sometimes you need to act and in so doing you get the confirmation.

Chapter 5
Handling the Overwhelm

Prayer. Daily Worship. Support.

"Whew—*it is hot!*" Joe muttered under his breath. It was July 1, his first day on the job as pastor of the Church of the Last Chance. The sun was shining in the cloud-free sky. Though gorgeous by July standards, it was also a scorcher. And Joe was a ball of mixed emotions—joy, anxiety, gratitude, determination, and humility.

On the one hand, he was grateful to find himself finally in the place and position to do what he had been called by God to do, what he was ready to do, and what he'd been yearning to do. This was what he had studied for, prayed for, worked for, asked God for—and he was filled with great joy. Yes, it was a great day!

But on the other hand, as he drove nearer to the deteriorating edifice behind the fence, he began to think about the advice from one of his colleagues, who had said, "If I were you, I'd run in the opposite direction! I'd stay an assistant pastor for as long as I could!"

Joe was scared to death. Butterflies were fluttering around the knots in his stomach. His nervousness came from the sheer magnitude of the task before him. Joe realized that he was now chiefly responsible for bringing a congregation and community into a closer encounter with Jesus Christ. He was now pastor of a congregation that gathered weekly in an extremely challenging setting. His name was on the marquee. The buck stopped with Joe, and the magnitude of the task was getting to him. He felt like a bundle of nerves that somebody had dropped on the sidewalk. As he drove into this part concrete, part pothole, part grass, bottle-strewn parking lot, he was keenly aware of the mixed emotions holding his soul in captivity. *I can't survive with my nerves like this every day*, Joe thought.

Joe's emotional state took a turn for the worse as he unlocked the side door and headed for the sanctuary. He looked up at the leaky roof, complete with water stains, the pukey green walls, and the paint chips dangling from the ceiling. The old, dull, bland pews clearly hadn't been shellacked in years. Dust covered the floor everywhere; no one had swept or mopped in a good while. He tripped on the old, ripped-up red carpet that rolled up under his feet. And hulking before him was the kicker: a miserable-looking, one-hundred-year-old piano with four working keys.

"Where do I start?" Joe said to himself. He took a deep breath and looked to the heavens. The first order of business was prayer.

So he went to the altar, got on his knees, and prayed that the Lord would use him to lead this congregation and community to revival. That was what one of the mothers of the church, Norma Jean, had said she wanted. She'd been there longer than anyone else, and Joe wanted what she wanted.

Scared to death about the extent of the neglect, Joe went to his office and saw a note on his desk asking him to call George McClean immediately. It turned out that George had just been convicted of bank fraud and would be serving a year in prison. He asked Joe to visit him immediately because George hadn't told his elderly parents about his conviction and sentence yet and was afraid that telling them just might kill them.

When Joe returned from helping George, he immediately got a call from another family whose child had been found with marijuana at school. So Joe ran to respond to that crisis. Joe was starting to feel more like a firefighter than a pastor.

Upon returning from that pastoral call, Joe met with the church's seventy-four-year-old minister of music. Joe greeted him with warmth and excitement.

"Hello, Mr. Wilson! My name is Joe Stephens. How are you?"

Mr. Wilson looked at Joe's youthful thirty-two-year-old face and said only one thing before turning away: "I don't like contemporary music."

Immediately after that pleasant exchange, the secretary of the trustee board came in. When Joe introduced himself to her, she wouldn't even look at him or tell him her name. Joe felt a headache coming on.

Before he could get in his car to go buy some aspirin, he got three calls from three different members who all wanted to meet him at the exact same time. Then a drunk man came into the office looking for money. A woman came to welcome him with a plate of brownies (and later Joe would discover that she was interested in him sexually). To top it all off, a broken-down toilet in the basement decided it felt like overflowing, causing new water problems at the church. Joe had been at Last Chance for six hours, and he still hadn't had a chance to catch his breath, let alone organize his office.

When the chaos let up momentarily, Joe ran out to grab something to eat and some aspirin to deal with the headache that had found its way to his temples. When he returned to his office, he took a quick mental inventory: *I have no secretary. I have no computer. I have no piano. I have water issues, a ripped-up carpet, holes in the ceiling, and an old electric typewriter that I have no idea how to operate. I better take a look at the books.*

It turned out that a new computer would have been a pipedream for this congregation, which celebrated if it received $400 in the offering plate on any given Sunday. Joe also discovered in his review of the finances that a preschool was leasing the fellowship hall. Thank God for that because without that money, the church could not have afforded to remain open.

But what scared him the most, more than anything else on that first day, was seeing the huge executive desk in his office. Rising up behind it was a tall, black executive chair. This desk and chair signified that he was the BMOC—Big Man on Campus. The chief responsibility for this multifaceted, challenging, never-a-dull-moment congregation with eighty-five members on the rolls and fifty-five people on average in worship fell squarely on his shoulders.

The first day's challenges were so intimidating that Joe was scared to sit in the imposing chair behind the desk. For him, it symbolized that he was responsible for this mess. Instead Joe sat in the visitor's chair in the corner of the room, unsure what to do. After about ten minutes, he realized that the chair was God's and that he was simply the pastor. Until Joe had fully surrendered to the fact that God was leading this process, and until he submitted to follow God's lead, he didn't stand a chance.

"It seems that your first day sure gave you a taste for what kind of stamina you will need to develop if you are going to successfully pastor Last Chance," said Pastor D on the phone a couple of days later. "A lot of people like to see their pastor run. They'll cheer you on: 'Run, pastor, run! Go, pastor, go! See pastor run! Run, run, run, pastor! See my pastor run!' The first six months of my time at the Fellowship were filled with lots of running, little breathing, when breath was what I really needed. The Holy Ghost breathing fresh life into me every day."

"That's exactly what I needed after my first day—Holy Spirit CPR!" Joe exclaimed.

Daily Personal Worship.

"Ha! Let's be clear, Joe. With the layers of issues before you, you will be overwhelmed unless you start and ground your day with the God who is calling you to chair His transformation movement. You won't have a clue how to manage the ongoing tensions that come with leading a congregation that is gasping for air—unless you begin each day by letting God breathe into you and direct your steps. Daily personal worship must be etched in your soul's rhythm—and your calendar—if you are going to breathe relevancy, enthusiasm, authenticity, and love into your place of ministry.

"Think about Nehemiah. He illustrates a way forward. His first day on the job began with chaos as well. His 'Boyz N the Hood' came to tell him that the neighborhood that had so impacted his life was in shambles and needed to be rebuilt. He felt the urge to go home and do something about it, but he couldn't. Returning home seemed like an impossible dream because he was in slavery and home was at least one thousand miles away. The pain and agony of Nehemiah wanting to help his people, but not being able to, was enough to drive him into mourning, depression, tears, and frustration. He must have asked, 'Where do I start?' The answer? He started with daily worship. Fasting, praying, and offering praise to the God of heaven directed his steps and opened doors for revival to take place. Take a moment to listen to his daily worship, Joe.

Pastor D opened his Bible to the book of Nehemiah and began to read:

O Lord God of heaven, the great and awesome God who keeps covenant and steadfast love with those who love him and keep his commandments; [6]let your ear be attentive and your eyes open to hear the prayer of your servant that I now pray before you day and night for your servants, the people of Israel, confessing the sins of the people of Israel, which we have sinned against you. Both I and my family have sinned. [7]We have offended you deeply, failing to keep the commandments, the statutes, and the ordinances that you commanded your servant Moses. [8]Remember the word that you commanded your servant Moses, 'If you are unfaithful, I will scatter you among the peoples; [9]but if you return to me and keep my commandments and do them, though your outcasts are under the farthest skies, I will gather them from there and bring them to the place at which I have chosen to establish my name.' [10]They are your servants and your people, whom you redeemed by your great power and your strong hand. [11]O Lord, let your ear be attentive to the prayer of your servant, and to the prayer of your servants who delight in revering your name. Give success to your servant today, and grant him mercy in the sight of this man!"[5]

"I get it," interjected Joe. "Nehemiah directed his entire being to God in order to revive Jerusalem, and I have to do the same thing—direct my entire being to God to breathe REAL church into this congregation and community. If I'm going to lead a congregation of change agents, then I have to adopt the discipline of personal daily worship."

"That's exactly right, Joe. The level of daily problems and challenges that leaders seeking to transform struggling congregations and communities face—treating drug addictions, alcoholism, affordable health care, prison reentry, unemployment, job training, family abuse, school system restructuring, gentrification, and on and on—all demand that we have daily time with God.

"But let me break it down even further. Worship is the work of the people to honor the One alone who is worthy to be praised: Jesus the

Christ. Worship happens when we find ourselves individually and collectively summoned into the presence of God. Worship is the most vital and important thing we do, Joe. It enables us to connect and communicate with God in profoundly spiritual and holistic ways. It positions us to interact with God and others in ways that help us build transformative relationships. Everything we do, everything we say, every way we posture ourselves should reflect and position us to give our all to Jesus Christ."

Joe listened intently. He had never heard worship described in quite those terms before. As was always the case in his conversations with Pastor D, Joe was intrigued and eager to hear more.

"We must understand," Pastor D went on, "that the role of worship in our personal lives involves our entire beings—our physical, emotional, mental, relational, spiritual, and financial beings. Worship is more than a corporate event. It is our personal attitude, gratitude, and energy focused on the things of God, not the things of humankind. It is working daily to see that what God wants us to do is accomplished. When I'm offering God daily worth, I am centering myself in God's will for my life on that day."

"What do you do during your daily personal worship time, Pastor D?" Joe interjected.

"Well, for me, it includes a time of prayer, meditation, music, and quiet time. And then I ask God how can I work that day to give Him my best in my vocation, in my relationships with others, in how I handle money, in how I love people unconditionally, and in how I respond to people. *Every day* we need to position ourselves to offer our best efforts to God's agenda—and not our own."

A picture of this kind of daily encounter with God began to form in Joe's mind as Pastor D continued speaking.

"Another piece of daily personal worship involves organizing our days so we're focused on accomplishing the things that are on God's agenda. There are so many things that can distract us from God's plan: phone calls that don't need to be taken, e-mails that don't need to be addressed right away, text messages that throw us off kilter, visits that can be delayed a few hours. We need to be positioned to transfer our praise into accomplishing practical steps that God wants us to take to further advance his plans for our lives."

"Wow—that's way more than I thought! I was expecting you to just talk about a simple time of devotion." Joe was pretty comfortable with the devotional time he had already set up as part of his life, and he hesitated before asking what was really on his mind. "But does all of that other stuff end up making a difference?"

Pastor D laughed. He found Joe's candor refreshing, and for his part, Joe was relieved that he hadn't offended the man he respected so much.

"Yes, Joe. Of course. In this season of my life, the Lord has made it plain to me through my daily worship time that His plan for my vocational life is to preach, teach, write, cast vision, and raise up new leaders at the Fellowship. So, vocationally, if I'm going to give God my best worship, the best of my time needs to be invested in those specific areas. While I do give time to other responsibilities that come with my job, if I don't give my best time to those five 'first things,' I'm not giving God the worth that my daily worship demands.

Joe's ears perked up at the mention of a term he hadn't heard before. "What do you mean by 'first things,' Pastor D?" he asked.

First Things.

"First things are the primary things that God has positioned you to be responsible for. We each have a role to play in the body. God has gifted and positioned us each to play specific roles in that body—if you don't do them, they won't get done the way God wants them done. I'm sure there are a lot of things that you do well, Joe, but they may not be your first things; they may be your second and third things. But if you are doing your second or third things instead of your first, two things happen: your first things don't get done; and you get in the way of someone else being able to do their first things. In both cases, you are interrupting God's divine flow."

Joe pondered what this might mean in his own life and then asked, "Do these first things change over time?"

"They may, Joe, depending on where God leads you. This is another reason daily worship is so important. It helps you stay in sync with the Holy Spirit."

"That makes sense," Joe replied.

"In like manner, through my daily worship, God has given me instructions for my personal and family life. In this season of my life, God has made it clear to me that I need to eat right, rest well, exercise regularly, and have fun. With regard to my family, I need to focus firmly on loving and caring for my wife, Nia, my children, and my mother who is approaching eighty. The Lord has revealed in my worship time that I can offer him my greatest worth through simplifying my life, staying focused on first things, continuing to move forward—and not getting sidetracked by things of the past—and daring to trust Him throughout the whole process."

"I think I understand what you are getting at," Joe interrupted. "If I neglect to worship God daily, then I grow disconnected from hearing and receiving His seasonal plans and purposes for my life. I am wasting my time, and, even more importantly, I'm wasting God's time, and even deeper, I am allowing the devil to interfere with the growth of the kingdom of God."

Joe was thoroughly convinced. He knew that he had to worship daily. It had become clear to him how much of an important role it would play in giving his best to Christ and accomplishing God's purposes for his life.

"So many leaders in the church are cheating God today, Joe, because we are offering God lackluster or nonexistent daily personal worship. Either we really don't understand what worship is or we think that worship is confined to what happens on Sunday morning or what happens in reading a five-minute devotion. To make matters worse, when we cheat God out of worship, we can become so consumed with our own personal ambitions, desires, and ways of living that we become lost and grounded in self more than in God. In fact, many churches and communities are dying today because of this."

"But it seems so counterintuitive that church leaders wouldn't be engaged in connecting authentically with the God of possibility and hope. Why do you think that is?" Joe asked.

"I believe it is because we get stagnant and overwhelmed. We go to bed feeling pressure, wake up in the night feeling pressure, and wake up in the morning feeling pressure. All that pressure often causes us to neglect the discipline of daily worship. Our minds are focused on getting tasks accomplished so that we won't feel so weighed down. We open our e-mail and get bombarded with more and more crises and tasks. The key—and the struggle—is letting go of all those pressures and letting God minister to us in the midst of the pressure. We must wait on our daily marching orders from God before we do anything. It might just change your task list, but it will definitely keep you from extreme weariness and burnout."

Joe's own experience was telling him that Pastor D's words were true.

"I was in a turn-around workshop once," Joe said, "and we were asked to break up into smaller groups to consider steps we might introduce to hold our leaders accountable to some pretty basic spiritual disciplines. It was really minimal stuff like praying for fifteen minutes a day, participating in an accountability group, worshipping weekly, and things like that. One pastor in my small group said, 'My people want to hear that God is telling me what to do. I can't lie to them. God isn't saying anything to me. These days, prayer is just going through the motions for me. It isn't a spiritual discipline.' Most of the pastors in the group agreed. I couldn't believe what I was hearing!"

"It is a crisis of epidemic proportions," Pastor D responded. "When 97 percent of clergy in your denomination don't expect God to move in worship[4] . . . Houston, we have a problem! Without spiritual disciplines, including daily personal worship, leaders find themselves so far from God that they aren't sure God is still speaking. When I have run across pastors who have gotten to this point, I strongly encourage them to find people to help pull them out of the hole—spiritual advisors, prayer partners, mentors, other pastors, and the like.

Do it before getting out of bed in the morning.

"If you ever find yourself in the trap of overwhelm, start by doing daily worship before you get out of bed in the morning. Start small. Start with even five minutes and work your way up to fifteen minutes—and then work your way up to an hour. Ideally, you won't get out of bed until you are clear about what your marching orders are from God. Get those orders before you allow any of your daily pressures to take over."

"I don't know," said Joe. "I wake up every morning with a list of things I have to do in my head. I'm not sure I can do this."

"You may have to train your mind to let go of the lists so that you can listen for God," Pastor D offered. "For me, finding the right music helps a lot. For others, a piece of art can serve the same purpose. Meaningful ritual can allow us to go deeper, faster. Find what centers you, Joe, and use it every day.

Pastor D continued, "One of my mentors, Jack Davidson, used to hound me about the importance of rising early in the morning to have quiet time with God. He insisted—and would later convince me—that this time of the morning was critical for being able to carry out God's call on our lives. He would stress that this was the time when we could listen to God without distraction, when we could receive God's marching orders without being interrupted by alarm clocks, radios, television, phone calls, and movement. He ended up offering to call me every morning at 5:00 a.m. so I could have this time. Unfortunately, most of the time, I would take his call and go back to sleep. But the moments that I rose, and still rise, are the most powerful moments with God that I have."

"So, Pastor D, are you gonna call me?" Joe asked, not sure whether he was actually serious.

"Do you want me to?"

"Let me think about that, Pastor D," Joe laughed. "But you have convinced me of the importance of daily personal worship."

"Great! Then your homework assignment between now and when I come to visit you at the Church of the Last Chance, is for you to make daily personal worship a habit. Let me know if you get stuck."

As Joe hung up the phone, he felt grateful and expectant. He was looking forward to prioritizing time with God—that sounded like a homework assignment that he should do for life.

Daily Personal Worship:

What is it: Spending time each day giving worth to the One who alone is worthy to be praised and letting God breathe into me and direct my steps.

Why do it: to get out of the trap of overwhelm, prevent burnout, get in sync with God's plan, and stay focused on my "first things."

How to do it: first thing in the morning
    a. enter into a time of prayer, meditation, music, and quiet, and
    b. ask God to order my thoughts and actions to give Him my best for that day.

HOMEWORK: Make daily personal worship a habit.

Chapter 6
Getting Familiar with Context

Biblically. Historically. Demographically. Relationally.

The first few days of Joe's new daily personal worship routine were great. Then, little by little, life interrupted it. Joe felt a little guilty when, in an email about his upcoming site visit, Pastor D asked how he was progressing with his daily worship.

Joe toyed with the idea of telling Pastor D that he was having success with it. After all, some daily worship was better than no daily worship, right? Then he remembered one of the first things Pastor D had stressed: the need for total honesty and transparency in the mentoring relationship. It didn't make any sense to request mentoring, if you weren't going to tell the whole truth. Joe let Pastor D know that he was struggling to fit it into his morning routine. After some back and forth, the two determined that what threw the whole thing off was whether or not Joe got up in time to add this new early routine to his schedule.

Joe discovered that he had to create a routine each night to close out his day. The routine included planning his top three actions for the next day and getting to bed by 10:30 p.m. Some days he found himself planning his top three actions at 3:00 p.m. because he knew he would be at church in the evenings until 10:00 p.m., which would leave him no time at the end of the day to plan if he was going to spend some quality time with Janelle and the kids and still make his new bedtime. Being disciplined required much more planning than Joe had thought it would. As a backup, Joe placed a Post-it note on the mirror in his bathroom that asked a simple question: "What did God tell me to do or focus on today?"

Time flew by as Joe began building relationships with people in the community and congregation, and started slowly cleaning up the debris and decay in and around the church. Before he knew it, he was greeting Pastor D in the Church of Last Chance's parking lot, ready for their first official meeting.

Joe was excited and nervous as he led Pastor D around the church. As he pointed out various rooms and projects that were underway, Joe was keenly aware of how much there was left to do. By the time they got settled in his office, he felt a bit exhausted.

"Well," Pastor D started, with a broad smile and laugh, "it looks like you won't run out of things to do for a good little while. Just keep asking God to order your steps, and it will be fine! What have you learned about yourself from doing daily personal worship?"

"It felt a little weird to be managing my time that carefully, but it was worth it," Joe admitted. "I have come to appreciate the clarity and calm energy that come out of my daily time with God. I really feel the difference when I allow God to order my day rather than allowing the urgencies and pressures to order it. I'm glad you helped me figure out what else I needed to rearrange in my life so that I could add daily personal worship as a consistent practice."

"I'm glad that worked for you, Joe," said Pastor D. "Daily personal worship will fuel and protect you during the course of our work together. Now it sounds like you are ready for your next piece of homework: getting to know your context. But first, tell me . . . what have you learned about your congregation and community so far?"

"Well, I've learned that people in the church aren't expecting much, and they aren't doing much either," Joe began. "I'm getting the sense that I was sent to conduct a funeral. The programmatic ministry is dormant. There are no consistent Bible studies or Christian education experiences. Choir rehearsal is the one activity that takes place weekly, and it was really only for those who liked classical, Euro-American, British, "high church"–style music. I keep getting phone calls from pastors from other churches asking if they can come and have worship services for their congregations in our sanctuary—as if we don't even exist! Of course, I said no. We need revival, not tenants! Youth ministry only happens when a musically gifted college student is home and pulls together a youth choir. The Sunday school is struggling to survive. The administrative board is weak and laissez-faire. There are people in positions . . . but the positions and the people aren't doing any consistent, real ministry."

"Is that all?" Pastor D chuckled.

"Actually, no," replied Joe. "I've also learned that over the past ten years, the church has almost closed three different times and was almost sold on two other occasions. Its long history of part-time pastors has made it difficult for the church to grow. On top of all that, it seems as if the district superintendent is about to make the Church of the Last Chance a two-point charge. In the United Methodist Church world, when a church becomes one of two or more churches under a single pastor, it often signifies the beginning of the death march for a congregation. I'm starting to see who in the church is accelerating that march—and who wants to be part of a revival."

"So, you've certainly learned a lot about the church in your short time here," Pastor D replied. "But what have you learned about the community? You must know your congregation's context in order to be able to push the right buttons for a REAL church to emerge. If you think about your relationship with Janelle, you know what I'm talking about. In order to build a fruitful relationship with her, you had to learn which buttons to push and which ones to avoid—which buttons created excitement or a positive response, and which buttons created anger or a chilly response."

"Those were some interesting lessons," Joe said with a smile, "and sometimes I think I'm still discovering them! One of my mentors taught me the value of programming my own buttons. He told me to have certain phrases ready to go at the press of a button: 'Yes, dear.' 'You were right, and I was wrong.' 'I don't know what was I thinking. Next time, I'll ask you first.'"

Pastor D laughed boisterously.

"And even so, sometimes you have to be reminded to say those things, right?" Pastor D teased.

"Have you been talking to my wife?" Joe retorted, joining in Pastor D's laughter.

"I can see you know all about button pushing when it comes to your wife. Do you know what buttons to push that will create excitement for your congregation and for your community?" Pastor D asked, taking the conversation deeper.

"I'm getting to know certain individual's buttons, but I couldn't say what the congregation's or the community's buttons are. Our community has been in transition for many years now. Your urban setting, and our more outer suburb, semirural setting have some things in common. We have a growing immigrant population, some of whom are citizens and some of whom are not. We have pockets of poverty next to places of privilege, as people keep moving further away from the city."

As they continued speaking, Pastor D began to do what he did best—teach.

"Joe," he said, "to get a better handle on your congregation's buttons, I would encourage you to look at three different stories in Scripture: Ezekiel and the valley of dry bones, Nehemiah and the broken and burnt walls of Jerusalem, and Jesus with the lame man at the pool of Bethesda. Each portrays a *sitz im leben*—a 'setting in life'—that may be helpful to you as the spiritual basis for how God could use you to lead transformation. If you take time in your daily worship to study these scriptures, God will use them to show you your reality and to give you biblical directions for revitalization.

Biblical situations, complications and resolutions.

"The great preacher James Forbes talks about breaking down any biblical text by knowing that there are three dynamics at play: a situation, a complication, and, by God's grace, a resolution. In seeking to revive a dying congregation and its community, you've got to take some time after your daily worship to examine the situations that your congregation and community find themselves in, the complications they face, and the potential resolutions God has in store. Let's start with situation. What situation do these three scriptures have in common?"

"Well, there's definitely a common theme of disconnection, disenfranchisement, discouragement, defeat, disappointment, and dis-ease," Joe offered. "The picture in each is of a marginalized community in need of transformation, much like mine."

"Good!" Pastor D exclaimed. "Tell me more."

"Well, Ezekiel's community is represented by the valley of dry bones. Ezekiel is God's prophet and represents God's church. The valley of dry bones represents the street or the community. The dry bones represent human lives in the street that have obviously been disconnected from having life and having it more abundantly—lives in the community that, because of personal sin, societal oppression, and other factors have become dry and lifeless."

"Excellent, Joe. Keep in mind that many pastors and lay people are working, ministering, and living in communities with people who are dry and lifeless across the diverse spectrum of life. Now tell me what you know about Nehemiah's situation."

Joe thought for a moment before answering. Finally he said, "Nehemiah's marginalized community is represented by the broken and burnt walls of Jerusalem. The walls represent the community; but they also represent lives—lives of men and women, little boys and little girls. Lives that are broken, suffering, and struggling. Lives that need to be made whole. Because of personal sin and societal oppression, they have become vulnerable to and defenseless against injustice, institutional racism, and wickedness in high political and socioeconomic places."

Pastor D nodded and indicated that Joe should continue sharing.

Moving on to Pastor D's third example, Jesus at the pool of Bethesda, Joe said, "Well, the lame man who Jesus approaches is sitting in a marginalized community, which, in John 5, represented both the street and the sanctuary. There were five porticoes or five porches—so they were in the street. But they were in the sanctuary as well because *Bethesda* in the original Greek language of the New Testament means 'house of grace.' Many people get up and go to the house of grace every Sunday."

Pastor D interjected, "I'm sorry to interrupt, but look at this house of grace in the text. There are multitudes there—all invalids. They are suffering from diseases and disabilities. In the condition they're in, they are in-valid. There are blind folk there, which means they can't see—they have no vision. And where there is no vision, the people perish. Where there is no vision, congregations perish and communities perish. If you and me have no vision, we perish. There are lame and paralyzed people at the pool. They can't move. God is like the rap star Ludacris, trying to tell them, 'When I move, you move, just like that.' But, like the Church of the Last Chance and its community, their condition is complex. So complex they can't do, won't do, or struggle to do the will of God in their lives. Who do you think these people are?"

The picture was becoming clear in Joe's mind, and he answered, "They are unchurched folk, dechurched folk, detached folk, church folk, clergy, and everybody in between. They are dry and broken, vulnerable and defenseless. Broken and burnt. Too many of our people are not whole. They struggle with the challenges of living in this day and age."

Joe thought for a moment. "That does seem to speak directly to my situation," he affirmed.

"Yes, it does, and we aren't finished with the texts yet. In each of the biblical stories there is a complication. Do you see them?"

"Ummm, well, in Ezekiel 37, not only was the valley full of dry bones. There were 'very many' in the valley. Not only were the bones dry, they were '*very* dry.' In Nehemiah, not only are the walls broken and burnt, but the people are in great trouble and shame. And those with the strength and resources to do something about it are in exile, absent from the community . . ." His mentor's point was beginning to crystallize in Joe's mind. "You know, Pastor D, some of the people who can lead the needed transformation at Last Chance are present physically, but seem to be in exile, mentally, emotionally, and/or spiritually. At the pool of Bethesda, the focus was on a lame man who'd been in a marginalized state for nearly forty years."

"Excellent, Joe. You've got to analyze the situation and complication in your community in the same way you've done with the scriptures. You've got to understand the history of your church and community so that you can more easily position it for revival. The old adage is true—history does repeat itself. If you don't know the history of where you are, you can make unnecessary mistakes or dig even deeper holes that make revival even more difficult. Unfortunately making errors when there is already a need for revival could lead to death before you even get off the ground."

Pastor D rose from his seat and gestured toward the door. "Let's go for a ride and talk about congregational and community context," he offered.

"Sure," said Joe, excited to continue the conversation. "I'll drive."

As they walked to Joe's car, Pastor D began helping the younger pastor to unpack his context.

Age and major life events of the congregation.

"So, how old is your congregation?" he asked. "You need to know how old your congregation is because events in time often impact a church's identity and culture. For example, the Fellowship, as an organized body of believers, was founded in 1832. It was originally founded by white families with roots and ties to the rural South. When I did some research, I discovered the church had a deep relationship to slavery and Civil War history."

Fortunately, Joe had done a little research of his own and had a decent handle on his church's history.

"From the 1800s up until about forty-five years ago, our area was rural farmland. This congregation is the same age as the formation of the new township," Joe reported. "It was started by a church down in a neighboring town that wanted to provide a place of worship for people who were moving into the area. It got off to a great start because of the energy of one of the founding members who had deep pockets and big ideas. Trouble started when the founder and the pastor assigned to the new church didn't see eye to eye. Eventually, that conflict split the congregation, and the founder left with many key leaders in tow."

"It sounds like you have a very fresh history in which much healing still needs to be done," Pastor D remarked.

"You're probably right about that," replied Joe "but do you think I need to start there?"

"Well, just make note of it for now, and let's continue to unpack your context," Pastor D encouraged. "Can you pull into the shopping center so I can get a feel for the culture in your community? And are there any favorite local hangouts here?"

"Local hangouts . . ." Joe began, "well, to be honest, I don't actually know where people in the community hang out. This shopping center is where my wife and I do our grocery shopping, though. Really, I've been so busy trying to get to know my congregation and deal with the disrepair of the building, I haven't even thought about the heartbeat of the neighborhood yet."

"I understand where you are, Joe. And I understand how difficult it is to walk into a place that is gasping for air and how easily all of your time and energy can get consumed there. Part of your assignment for next time is to find out where the local hangouts are. Go there yourself and get a feel for the place. Introduce yourself to the managers and shop owners. Let them know that you are new in town and that you'd like to get to know them and that you'd like to have some meetings with people from the church at their establishments."

Pastor D's last comment surprised Joe. He had never thought about having church meetings outside of church. He also wasn't sure how that would help.

"What does that have to do with turning around this church?" asked Joe, almost afraid to hear Pastor D's response.

"It means everything! This congregation will be built through relationships that you and your congregation forge with people in this community—but *you* have to take the lead in that. You can't expect or require people in the congregation to do it without your leading by example. Furthermore, if you aren't actively engaged in building relationships in the community, you won't have the community on your mind constantly. Instead, you'll only focus on the congregation inside of the walls and forget that the much larger congregation is in the community."

Pastor D grew more animated, as he always did when discussing one of his favorite topics.

"People have to know who you are on the street, Joe," he explained. "That will make you and your church that much more relevant in the community. For example, one of the first stops I made when I got to the Fellowship was to the popular dry cleaners across the street from the church. I met the owner and his employees, and I began taking my laundry there.

Immediately, it connected his shop to our church, and soon after, some of his employees began worshipping at the Fellowship. Much to my surprise, the owner of the dry cleaners started mentioning our congregation in conversations he had with other community leaders who frequented his shop. Conversations like these get you known in your community and cause people to be curious about what's going on in your church. Frankly, Joe, most pastors and most churches don't invest quality time doing this—and because of that, they never understand their context and many private, political, and community leaders ignore those congregations and deem them irrelevant.

"It's so much easier to send out flyers and postcards to let people know what you're doing, but if they can't connect a face or a relationship to that information, those flyers will probably end up in the circular file. Relationships are key."

"I get it, Pastor D. Building relationships and investing in local community businesses will grow the circle of awareness about the congregation," said Joe, checking his understanding.

Demographic dynamics in the neighborhood.

"You got it!" Pastor D exclaimed. "Now, tell me about the demographics of your community. Who's here? What color are they? What do they look like? How much money do they make? How old are they? Are they single, divorced, married? Are they Catholic, Muslim, unchurched? What are the demographics? Has there been any gentrification in your congregation and community? Who are the marginalized people in your area? What do they look like?"

The sense of calm that had momentarily fallen over Joe was hastily snatched away as Pastor D's words once again reminded him of the work that lay ahead.

"You've got a lot of questions, Pastor D!" he said.

"That's because you need a lot of answers if you're gonna turn this thing around, Joe."

"Well, I don't have many answers yet," Joe confessed. "I haven't had time to do much of anything except put out fires."

Pastor D affirmed Joe by saying, "I understand. When you start trying to revitalize a struggling situation, a lot comes at you, fast and furious. But let me suggest that you carve out some time to do two sets of demographic studies of your neighborhood. First, you and your people need to do what I call a 'windshield' demographic study—that is, establish a one- to two-mile radius around your church building and do some drive-bys and walk-throughs. Drive around and take notes for yourself based on the demographic questions I just asked you. Then get out of your car and walk into the stores and restaurants, and around the residential areas. You and your congregation may know some of the details already, particularly if they live around the church. But much of it will be completely new to you, or you may see it with fresh eyes.

"Secondly," Pastor D. continued, "get a *professional* demographic study prepared for you. Try a company like MissionInsite or Percept. Or your denomination might provide this service to you for free—just ask. But once you get these two studies done, you can compare notes and get a good idea of what's happening around you. This is critical for you to do effective community ministry. Oh, and while you're at it, Joe, take a trip to the planning office in town to see if there are any development plans for real estate in your designated study area. If a new shopping center or gas station is slated for an area near you, you need to know about it. It could impact your people positively or negatively."

"Okay, I got you . . . Man, this is all very interesting," Joe said as he rounded the corner and made his way down a residential street that, like the Church of the Last Chance, appeared to be in decline. The homes were hidden behind weeds and overgrown shrubs. Rusted-out gutters and railings were in full view.

As Joe continued down the street, Pastor D asked, "Hey, man, have you been here before?"

Joe replied, "Sort of . . . it reminds me of the three biblical texts we just talked about!"

"You got that right, Joe."

"From what I understand, this is the older part of our area. With all the recent growth and development that has the rest of the community looking more like a suburb, this part of town has been neglected. I haven't been here before," Joe said.

Pastor D said, "Good, let's pull over. We can do a walkthrough while we talk about one other aspect of community context."

Joe pulled over, and the two men stepped out the car to stretch their legs and continue the tour on foot.

As they walked down the sidewalk, they passed by two run-down homes. Shingles were peeling off the roof of one home, and busted-out glass decorated the windows of the other. A group of kids played in the street in front of the houses, not seeming at all disturbed by their surroundings.

The kids zoomed by on their bicycles, and Pastor D called out to them, "Hey, what's up, y'all?"

One girl replied, "Nothing . . . just having some fun before we have to do our homework." She looked up at Pastor D with a puzzled expression. "Who are you?" she asked.

Pastor D smiled and said, "I'm a friend of this man. This is Pastor Joe, and he is the new pastor of the Church of the Last Chance a few blocks from here. You heard of that church?"

"No, sir. Never. We don't go to church unless my grandmother comes to town. Then she takes us."

"Well," Pastor D said, "I want you to meet Pastor Joe. He'll probably be back to talk to you and your parents about how the church can help support your community. You guys can play a big role in that, you know."

Pastor Joe greeted them warmly, and as they pedaled away he shouted, "See you soon!" One of the kids looked back and waved his hand in reply.

"Wow, I've never done anything like that before," said Joe, turning his attention back to Pastor D. "Is that what you meant by a walkthrough? I can't imagine my people doing that—and, frankly, it might take some time for me to get comfortable with it." Joe hated to admit that, but he knew he could share with Pastor D in confidence.

"Confession is good for the soul, my brother," his mentor replied. "Just remember that ministry is often uncomfortable—especially when you are seeking to transform a congregation and a community. But you have to think of yourself as the hands and feet and mouth of Christ to this neighborhood. Allow the image of what Jesus would do to be bigger than your own sense of what's appropriate. Once you model it, your people can get it. It is important to model how to do a walkthrough in a way that leads to real interaction with the people in your community. And it's okay to start slow. To begin with, as you are doing this windshield and walking tour, take some mental notes about how you and your congregation can reach the people you meet."

As they continued to walk, Joe noticed a park at the end of the block. "Do you mind if we sit down for a minute so I can take some notes?" he asked. "This is all a little overwhelming!"

"I bet it is," Pastor D laughed. "But let's do it. Take a minute to think about it, and then why don't you share with me what you've learned so far about how to discover your congregation's context?"

The two men made their way over to the nearest park bench, and Joe sat down and began writing almost immediately. Every now and again he would stop and look up, deep in thought, before hunching over his notepad again. Finally, a few minutes later, after taking a deep breath and looking at his notes, Joe began laying out the picture that was coming together in his mind as Pastor D listened carefully and nodded. The older man was pleased to see how much progress his young friend was making already.

"That's right, Joe," Pastor D affirmed. "And just as we talked about the major life events of your congregation, it is important to do the same for your community. For example, in my situation, the Fellowship was established in an all-white community. And the members at that time believed that one could be Christian and own slaves at the same time. At one point the church had 1,200 members. The immediate community around us was known as Vinegar Hill, one of a few "free black" settlements located in the middle of this white community. In fact, Joe, two-thirds of the property we own now was purchased from a black woman in 1855. Our community remained all white and significantly Jewish until the 1960s when the civil rights movement led to white flight in our neighborhood. Joe, that's significant because there was a time when people who looked like me weren't even allowed in the neighborhood.

"I got a good history lesson while talking with a retired AME Zion presiding prelate who requested a tour of our church one day. He was seventy years old and had been pastoring in the city for fifty years. I remember him saying to me, 'Son, when I was your age, I wasn't even allowed in this neighborhood. Being black, there were only certain places in the city where you were allowed to go, and this neighborhood—and this church—wasn't one of them. If you came to this neighborhood, you had better be just passing through or have a darn good explanation for being here or the police might take you away.' That was our neighborhood for many years—but when Dr. King was assassinated in 1968 and with the riots that followed, the exodus of whites really took off. On top of that, the civil rights movement provided more economic opportunity for blacks, and black folk began moving into our community at an accelerated pace.[5] By 1976, the year the United States celebrated two hundred years of independence—and I'm using that term loosely—the Fellowship, became a small black church of roughly thirty-five members and had its first black pastor appointed on a part-time basis.

"Today, our community is about 80 percent African-American and black with a recent influx of Africans, West Indians, and even more so, Latino families into the neighborhood. With regentrification as a major reality in our city, we are experiencing whites coming back to the neighborhood little by little. You need to know the history of your neighborhood because it will shape how you do ministry in your community."

Joe nodded his head. He knew Pastor D was right.

"I don't think our story is that dramatic," Joe offered. "But our young community did experience some major events that have had an impact on demographic and socioeconomic realities here.

"The planning for the town unfolded fairly rapidly, which attracted professional, dual-income families; and many contractors experienced a boom because of all the construction. But then, the real estate crash hit in the early nineties. Here in Hopeville, the number of foreclosures began climbing, slowly at first, and the folks moving into the neighborhood were more blue-collar types. It seems that somewhere around the second construction bust in the 2000s, a tipping point occurred. After that we saw an increase in the divorce rate, an increase in single-parent households, a decrease in the average household income, and an increase in alcohol abuse. Of course, the combination of that economic reality, combined with the internal battles in the church, led to membership decline. At least that's what my people tell me."

"That's good information for you to know," Pastor D said approvingly. "It sounds like you have figured out some of the reasons for your membership decline—the why and the how long. You mentioned earlier that the church was in danger of closing several times, right?"

"Actually, I think they had to fight hard to get another full-time pastor. Now if we can't figure out how to increase membership in the near future, we may be facing a merger or closure."

"I see you are thinking strategically, my friend. That kind of thinking is essential for the work that we do. You have to keep in mind that a congregation's memory is long. If they have had to fight denominational, community, or government officials to stay open, then seeds of mistrust have been planted, and they will directly impact your work. Remember when we talked about healing earlier? This might be some of the healing that you need to make happen. If you don't know yet, trust me, you will know shortly."

Pastor D took a deep breath and slapped Joe on the back. "Well, we've covered a lot today, haven't we?"

Joe nodded his head in agreement.

"Remind me of our schedule for the rest of the day, would you?" Pastor D asked.

"Well, we have a dinner scheduled with the lead team for seven thirty tonight, but that's pretty much it," Joe answered. "That's in just a couple of hours. Let's head on back to the church and take a break before then."

"That sounds good to me, Joe."

On the walk back to the car, Joe started to see the beginnings of the revitalization process at the Church of the Last Chance. What had first appeared to be overwhelming, he now saw with a glimmer of hope.

Pastor D seemed to be reading his mind. He said, "Just as God had other plans—plans for resurrection and transformation of the church I serve—God has plans for transformation of the church you serve. But you've got to do your homework. You've got to study the history of your congregation and community so that you know how it impacts your present reality.

"It's exactly what we talked about earlier: situations lead to complications. But in God's mathematics, there is *always* a resolution. For Ezekiel, the valley of dry bones came to life again. For Nehemiah, the people rebuilt the walls of Jerusalem. The lame man at the pool of Bethesda in the Gospel of John, got up, took up his mat, and walked. Your resolution is coming. Stay encouraged!"

We can learn about context from:

1. Biblical examples such as Nehemiah and Ezekiel as well as the stories of Jesus. Each contains a situation, a complication, and a resolution

2. Age and major life events of the congregation

3. Demographics of the neighborhood (walking, windshield and census-based research)

4. Discovering local hangouts and building relationships with people in the community

Chapter 7
Knowing Where Leaders Are

Be. See. Do.

"Pastor D, thank you so much for helping me to better understand context and the steps that will help me connect with people in our community," Joe said as he slid behind the wheel. "I'm actually starting to feel energized by the whole experience and am looking forward to sharing it with my core group."

"That's great," Pastor D replied, "but I'll tell you what, I'm also looking forward to dinner with your core team because I'm hungry! Are you hungry?"

"Yup!"

Joe had a picked out a nice restaurant for dinner. As he rolled into the parking lot, he spotted some of his leaders heading into the lobby.

"That's James, my council president right there," Joe said, pointing to a tall, thin man wearing a sports coat. "He is co-owner of a construction company that has managed to make it through the recession. Julie, his wife, heads the patient accounts department at the local hospital. The two of them are the biggest givers in the church. People have told me that, without them, our church wouldn't have the money to stay open."

"That's helpful," said Pastor D. "Listen, before we go into the restaurant, can you tell me a little more about the rest of the group?"

"Sure," agreed Joe. "In addition to James and Julie, you'll meet Pamela.

She truly has a servant's heart. She stepped in and handled all of our administrative needs as soon as I arrived as pastor, even though she consults with company presidents in her day job. She has become one of my most trusted leaders and has been a great sounding board for me in the early stages. She is also a prayer warrior. I rest easier knowing that anytime I ask her to pray for something, she does.

"Finally, you'll meet Gary and Monica. Gary has been a member of this church longer than anyone. He practically bleeds the Church of the Last Chance. I really believe he'll do anything for us to become a thriving congregation. In fact, he often shares his dreams and visions of what he sees God wanting us to be. Monica is Gary's daughter. She's twenty-two and just recently moved back home. She seems to be really interested in starting some sort of young adult ministry."

"Sounds like you have a great core here," Pastor D commented. "Do any of them live near the church?"

"Pamela lives here in Hopeville, but James and Julie live in the next town over. And Gary has recently moved back here as well," explained Joe.

"Well, my stomach is growling," Pastor D said. "Let's get this show on the road."

The two pastors emerged from the car and headed toward the restaurant, a local spot called the Eatery. It was clear that Joe had selected some of the people attending the dinner because of the positions they held in the church, and had chosen others because he thought they might truly be long-term spiritual leaders for the congregation.

When they arrived in the lobby, the only leader missing was Gary. When the hostess asked if the group wanted to wait for him or be seated right away, Julie was the first to answer.

"Gary is always late," she said, with a hint of irritation. "Let's go ahead and be seated. We may even be finished with our appetizers before he gets here." Her husband nodded in approval.

As they approached the table, Pastor D was curious about how the seating would be handled. He didn't have to watch too carefully to see how things shook out. As soon as they were near the table, Julie began instructing everyone on where to sit.

"Pastor Joe, I think you should sit at the head of the table, and James at the other end of the table . . ."

In the blur of instruction that ensued, Pastor D noticed that Julie positioned herself as close to Joe as possible. Interestingly, Julie tried to remove Pamela from the hub of activity, but Pamela graciously found a way to avoid that.

As the menus were being distributed, James said to Pastor D, "You've *gotta* get the breaded tilapia—it's the best thing on the menu."

Pamela intervened, saying, "James, maybe Pastor D wants to try something else." James pressed on with the rationale for his tilapia recommendation, and Pamela gently pushed back. The others laughed at the minor scuffle that was unfolding, and Pastor D soaked in the dynamics being played out in front of him.

Soon after the group had placed their orders, Gary arrived at the table and, with much enthusiasm, exclaimed, "So sorry I'm late! The traffic was awful tonight." Everyone but Julie and James smiled and nodded in agreement.

"Glad you could make it, man," Pastor D said.

After Gary's order was placed, Joe cleared his throat and addressed the table.

"I want to thank each of you for making room in your busy schedule for yet another church meeting. I realize that I ask a lot, and I really appreciate you for allowing me to do that. Tonight I am so pleased to introduce you to someone I know you are going to enjoy. I've already raved about Pastor D and about my experience at the Fellowship of the Used-Tos. Pastor D has pastored the Fellowship for almost twenty years, providing the pastoral leadership necessary for transformation to occur there. The Fellowship used to be much like the Church of the Last Chance is today—but where God has led them is remarkable. Pastor D and I spent part of today walking around the neighborhood and talking about how important context is to our ministry. Tonight, he wanted to meet you and talk about some of the things that we might be doing over the course of this coming year."

"Thanks for that," Pastor D said warmly once Joe had wrapped up. "You all probably realize how fortunate you are to have been given such a great leader! I am happy to be with him—and with you—so that you might not make the same mistakes I did when I sought to turn around my congregation and community."

Pastor D laughed to himself as he recalled those early days, and the table joined in, chuckling quietly and shaking their heads as they imagined what those struggles must have been like.

"I'd like to walk you through a process to help us get on the same page," Pastor D continued, "but before I do that, I'd love it if each of you could remind me of your name, share how you became a member of the Church of the Last Chance, and tell me what keeps bringing you back each week."

"My name is Julie, and I'm on the finance committee. Both James and I have been United Methodists our whole lives. One of the first things we do when we move anywhere is join the United Methodist church closest to our home. It helps us get to know people and our neighborhood faster—and we just feel it's the right thing to do."

Julie's husband spoke up next.

"I'm James, and I am chair of the church council. I agree with everything Julie said and would add that I think we need to do a better job of letting people who are moving into the area know about our church—in case they can't find it."

Next the group turned their attention to Gary.

"You know I'm Gary," he said. "I don't serve on any committees, but I do sing in the choir every now and then. I grew up in this church. My parents were members, and I remember when I could walk to church from our house. When I moved back to the area after college, I couldn't imagine going anywhere else. What brought me back then, still brings me back today—the people here are like family. They are faithful and really care about you. I don't want to see this church die because it means a lot to me . . . and I think it can mean a lot to the community, too." He paused for a moment. "I'm ready to do whatever we need to do to make that happen."

"Thanks for volunteering, Gary. We'll definitely take you up on that," said Pastor D.

The young woman seated beside Gary spoke up next.

"Well, you heard my dad. I really didn't have a choice about where I went to church because it would break his heart if I went anywhere else! But, I realize that if I'm going to be fully happy coming back each week, I'm going to have to do something to get more people my age here. I'm hoping that Pastor Joe will be willing to make the church feel more related to what me and my friends are going through."

She folded her hands in front of her. After a second, she blurted out, "Oh! My name is Monica, by the way." The group laughed warmly, and then Pamela, who was the last to speak, introduced herself.

"My name is Pamela. I live here in the neighborhood but was invited to Church of the Last Chance by a colleague when I first came to town. I keep coming back because I feel God needs me here. Even if it is just helping with the church bulletins each week, I love to feel useful."

Pastor D nodded. "Thanks so much for sharing," he said kindly.

"It helps to know a little bit about your experience," he continued. "What I'm hearing is that some of you are really connecting with the church because of your tradition and others because of relationships you have, and some of you because you feel a sense of being called into ministry here.

"I would like to ask a few more questions to learn a little about what you see and feel about your church, your community, and where God is calling you to operate within both," Pastor D clarified. "And I'd like each of you to describe who you think the Church of the Last Chance is for."

Of course, Julie was the first to answer. "I think our church is for people who are looking for a United Methodist church," she explained. "For people who want to instill those values in their families and society. I think it is awful how our young people and politicians are behaving."

James said, "I agree with Julie and would add that we need people who understand that financial stewardship is important. Without people like that, we will continue to struggle to pay our bills."

Gary said, "I think the Church of the Last Chance is for families and for people who need a family . . . maybe for those in Hopeville who are suffering in one way or another. At least I'd like it to be that."

Pamela said, "While I agree with everything that Gary said, I think it is for sharing the Good News of Jesus Christ with those outside the church and helping grow the faith of those inside the church. After all is said and done, aren't we supposed to be about saving souls?"

Monica said, "I like what Dad and Pamela said, too. I hope our church is for people in the community—including kids and young adults—who are in need of hope and God's grace."

Joe looked at Pastor D to see if he expected him to participate in this round of discussion. After his mentor nodded, Joe said, "Well, while I think the Church of the Last Chance needs to be about making disciples of

Jesus Christ for the transformation of the world, it needs to be for everyone in our community. The experience I had today made me realize that we must be about reaching and growing the young people and their parents. Our community's young people seem to be begging for a place that cares for them in a way that Twitter and Facebook alone cannot."

"So," Pastor D prompted "when you were listening to each other's answers, did you notice that some were describing things geared toward church operations, while others were focused on those who are already members, and some of you described issues that stood outside of the four walls of church?"

He noticed lots of nodding heads, so he continued.

"This happens all the time. It is the reality of many churches. We get stuck when those considered outside the church aren't a part of the church's daily reality. When the primary socializing you do is with the people in your church, you may start to forget what it is like for those who aren't in the church. Another place of stagnation happens when there is an artificial separation between social justice and what Professor Doug Bailey of Wake Forest University School of Divinity calls 'soul justice.'"

Noticing the puzzled looks on the faces of most at the table, Pastor D went on to explain.

"If justice is the absence of oppression, *soul* justice is ridding ourselves of things that harm or oppress our souls—those lifestyle issues that can hamper or destroy us. The evangelical church oftentimes proclaims this while it ignores social justice. Social justice seeks to rid a community of practices that would keep a group of people or a segment of society down or disenfranchised. The liberal church often focuses on social justice while ignoring the deep issues of the soul. The key is to create an atmosphere where both thrive—where the soul is nurtured and the church yields itself to God to rid society of the '-isms' that divide it."

"I believe some in the church pray too much," said James. "We need to do more *acting* than praying."

"That's actually a great example of the split between soul and social justice," Pastor D replied. "I would argue that we need as much prayer as we need action, and sometimes more. To repair the breach, a congregation needs to operate within the Holy Spirit for the good of their communities. Since a congregation is made up of people, the starting point is always personal. A simple process that works for both individuals and congregations to get unstuck and back into flow with God's plans has been developed by ARE—A Renewal Enterprise.[6] The three steps in the process are: first, be who you are; second, see what you have; and third, do what matters to God.

Joe took a moment to jot these down in his notebook.

> * Be Who You Are,
> * See What You Have and
> * Do What Matters to God

At that very moment, the food arrived, and Pastor D proclaimed, "Obviously, what matters to God at this very moment is that we eat!" Once the food was distributed and grace had been said, everyone happily dug in.

James was the first to change the conversation back to the business at hand. "When you say 'be who you are,' isn't that just giving people an excuse to not change or to behave badly?"

"I can see why you might ask that," Pastor D replied, laying down his fork. "But it is about people and congregations recognizing who they are *gifted and called by God to be*. You've actually provided a perfect transition. Let's explore what 'being who you are' might mean for Last Chance. Tell me a little more about who you are as a congregation. Not about what isn't working and not what you wished you were, but about your giftedness or the things that make you special. I even want to hear about any specialness that you haven't found a way to use quite yet."

Pastor D turned to Gary. "As the long-timer here, why don't you give us your perspective?"

After thinking for a moment, Gary responded thoughtfully, "Well, one thing that makes us special is that we don't give up. No matter what has happened in our community, it seems a group of people still fight to keep our church going. I guess that speaks to another thing that makes us special—we are loyal."

"I think that we are a church that operates like a family . . . different ages, loving—and in your business!" Monica added, half joking.

"With the addition of Pastor Joe, I think we are now also inspirational and teaching biblical truths. Can we use something like that—even if it is relatively new, and about who the pastor is?" asked Pamela.

"Sure, you can use it," Pastor D encouraged. "But if for some reason the pastor changes before having the time to create a culture that demands that quality in a pastor, you would have to revise the list." Pamela nodded.

"Anything else?" Pastor D asked. Now that the group had warmed up, new answers popped up quickly.

"We have family roots in the community."

"We respond to needs that we become aware of. A couple years back, Mary's brother's family lost everything in a fire, and we were able to send them clothing and cash within forty-eight hours."

"We love music. In fact we love it so much we sometimes take time during worship to learn a new hymn or song we don't know."

"I see Pastor Joe writing down your comments," Pastor D noted. "Perhaps periodically at lead team meetings you could read through the list and add things that you start to notice. Positive things that guests point out or that are mentioned by the community are things to be especially aware of. For now, this list will give us a sense of some things that distinguish you.

"So, let's move on. Now, I'd like us to spend a few minutes considering what assets you have to work with in order to grow the ministry. An asset could be a relationship with an individual (like the principal of the elementary school) or organization (nonprofits or for-profits with capital and/or influence). You can list things that you haven't yet developed—just let me know which is which. If I asked you to *see* what you have that might be developed and then used to serve your purpose, what would you say?"

"You know our community was really hit hard by the economic recession," James pronounced. "Our unemployment rate must be among the highest in the nation. I'm not sure if we have any actual assets at our disposal. Not only do we need to work hard to get enough money in the offerings to keep the lights on, but the needs in the community far outweigh our ability to meet them."

As James spoke, the group could feel a sense of hopelessness start to creep in, and Pastor D knew he needed to change the tenor of the conversation.

"Do you remember the story of the feeding of the five thousand? In Mark's version we hear Jesus tell the disciples, 'You give them something to eat.'[7] Essentially, Jesus is telling the disciples that the resources they need are in the very community they are serving. Likewise, I'm asking you to list out the resources in your community—available to you for God to work *miracles* through."

And just like that, the hopelessness that had been building itself into panic and despair seemed to vaporize. In its place emerged a rich conversation about potential relational assets.

"I graduated from Battlefield High School. I could imagine creating stronger ties there."

"I think we need to start younger than high school too. Surely we can think of people who have inroads to George Washington Elementary School and Rosa Parks Middle School."

"The Parkers—they own this restaurant—they're friends of the church. They know a lot of people!"

"I'm friends with the commissioner of the Columbia Youth Sports League."

"Yes, and we've had some positive interactions with the town manager and the police department, too."

"And let's not forget our collaborative relationship with the Columbia Pantry!"

Pastor D looked on enthusiastically.

"Well, you have created a great starting place!" he affirmed. "We will be talking more about how to go about building strong partnerships in the next couple of months. In the meantime, can you think of any assets within the congregation itself?"

Joe was very pleased with how his team was working now. He captured their conversation in a few bullets. He couldn't help making notes beside some items.

See What You Have:
- Willing Members (but not enough of them)
- Talented Musicians (but limited music)
- Trust
- Inspirational shepherd (really?)
- Being creative (where?)
- Using resources at hand
- Faithful (Is this a code word for something?)
- Location (need better signage)

All this got Joe thinking about how to make better use of these assets. He also thought about whom he might assign to take responsibility for following up with some of the potential community partners.

Pastor D interrupted his thoughts. "It seems that when we actually *see* what we have, possibilities become more clear. But the last question I have for you tonight can wait until after we order dessert!"

Pastor D was glad to see how some members of this core team really fed off each other's ideas and energy wonderfully. He also noted that Julie had fallen strangely quiet in the discussion of assets.

After dessert arrived at the table, Pastor D asked the final question he had alluded to.

"We are to behave in alignment with who God has created us to be and use the resources God has made available to us in our communities. In order to surrender ourselves and those resources to God, we need to clarify what matters to God and commit ourselves to doing that. So, given what we've talked about thus far tonight, what does the Church of the Last Chance need to do that matters to God?"

Again, the group didn't hold back.

"I think it is to make disciples and bear fruit through living as disciples: inviting the community to follow Jesus, and sharing the good news of salvation."

"I think what matters to God is for us to reach out to the community in as many ways as possible."

"How about growing a deeper relationship between us and God and us and each other? Don't you think that matters to God, too?"

"I agree with everything everyone else has said, but I'm thinking of something different. I think multigenerational mentoring groups matter to God because they are a particular way we can extend our family style into the community for God to bless."

"You know, when I think about where we are and where we've been, I think God wants us to bring about healing in the congregation and the community."

"Wow," Joe said, "you all have named some really powerful stuff. I could see most everything you mentioned really mattering to God, but that last one really caught my attention."

Turning to Pastor D, he asked: "How specific should we be in terms of the various places we hear God calling us to do that healing?"

"You are right to be asking that question. It is too soon now to try to get specific. At this point we are going to treat these three categories as vision containers that you will continue to add to over the next year or so. At the end of that time, we will use what you have collected *through discernment* to inform a vision for the future."

Pastor D looked around the table. "I hope you all realize what a great opportunity you have to lead the transformation of the Church of the Last Chance," he said.

Joe couldn't contain his enthusiasm. "This is a fantastic opportunity, and I for one am grateful to be a part of the team to work with God in making it happen!"

Joe couldn't imagine doing this work alone. Looking around the table it was clear that everyone but James and Julie was clearly grateful and hopeful too.

"You are now entering a time of discernment," Pastor D said as he prepared to give the homework assignment. "It includes daily worship, prayer, and testing your understanding through action. So in the next five months, here are three things I want each of you to do: First, worship daily—Pastor Joe can fill you in on what that entails. Second, keep track of your be-see-do revelations; and third, bring one new person a week to worship who doesn't currently have a church home.

"Do you have any questions?"

Julie asked, "How are we supposed to bring one new person a week to worship? I don't know if I know anyone who isn't going to church."

Pastor D smiled at her. "You'll have to get out and meet some new people then, won't you?"

Lead Team Homework for the Next Six Months:
1. Develop the spiritual discipline of daily personal worship

2. Keep track of be-see-do revelations

   a. Be who you are

   b. See what you have

   c. Do what matters to God

3. Bring one new person a week to worship who doesn't currently have a church home

Chapter 8
Creating a REAL Worship Culture

Encourage. Expect. Extol.

"This has been a great day," Joe said as he drove Pastor D back to the church. "The community tour, the conversation about context, and then the meeting tonight with my leaders—it's all been very enlightening. I am so eager to work on getting us better connected with our community while we work to transform our congregation. I think the be-see-do framework will be helpful as we continue to discern God's preferred future for us."

"We have covered a lot of ground today," Pastor D said approvingly. "Is there anything else on your mind before I leave?"

"Well, there is one thing . . ." Joe hesitated. "I had hoped we could talk about how to resurrect my deadly worship experience." They had reached the church by then; so Joe swung into a parking space, and the two men walked back to his office.

"Hmm . . . Worship is a very complex and important part of transforming your congregation, Joe" Pastor D said. "Tell me about your first few worship services here, and we'll see what aspects of the worship culture need to be addressed first."

The invitation unleashed a river of concern within Joe, but knowing that he could trust Pastor D, the young pastor took a deep breath and dove in.

"Well, I hate to say it, but I discovered that I inherited a worship *mess*. My first Sunday here—I'll never forget—it was a beautiful day outside. I was anxiously anticipating how many people would be present, considering it was the holiday weekend and the fact that the new pastor was starting. Frankly, I was hoping for a packed house, but I didn't really know what I would face. What I came to was probably the most *boring* worship experience I have ever been a part of.

"I truly cannot remember a more lifeless worship experience," Joe continued, his face looking as sad as the experience must have been dead. "It was so quiet you could hear that raggedy grass outside grow. I was preaching as best as I could, but the faces looking back at me were completely expressionless or tuned out. In the middle of worship, the minister of music stood up to teach a new hymn—they called it the hymn of the month. I thought I was in choir rehearsal!"

"Ha-ha!" Pastor D laughed sharply. "I nearly fell off my chair when James mentioned this as an example of their love of music. *Choir rehearsal in the middle of the worship experience?* I can't even imagine that. I understand the need for a music ministry to sing and teach new songs that are relevant to people's lives, but teaching it in a way that isn't worshipful, *completely* misses the point."

"That's exactly what it felt like—worship missed the point," agreed Joe, chuckling at the memory.

"Sometimes in ministry, you gotta laugh to keep from crying," Pastor D said, expressing just what Joe was feeling.

"You are right about that," Joe responded. "So, anyway, on top of that, I was told by the lay leadership that I had no more than fifteen minutes to preach, when I was used to preaching at least thirty-five minutes. Everything we did was spelled out in the bulletin, and if you didn't have the bulletin, worship didn't make sense!

"There was no authenticity, no life, no vibrancy there. The service was so uninspiring that people began sleeping. Even choir members were sleeping. Afterward, a friend of mine came up to me and said, 'Man, you have a major reconstruction project here.'"

"Sounds like you were overwhelmed that Sunday," Pastor D commented. "I remember my first Sunday at the Fellowship of the Used-Tos. I couldn't get out of church fast enough, I was so overwhelmed."

"Exactly!" Joe exclaimed. "I began questioning God and asking if I was where I was supposed to be. For hours after the service, I repeatedly asked God, 'I know this is where I'm supposed to be, so why doesn't it feel like it?' There was no place in the worship service for the Holy Spirit to breathe. Everything was regimented and controlled. The music did not resonate; it was so structured and dry. People mumbled the hymns, and the organ drowned everything out.

"I came to this church not knowing exactly what to expect, but knowing that it would be challenging. In fact, it has been. Now I find myself in a context where people seem more concerned about getting out on time than they are about experiencing God," Joe said. His exasperation was clear.

Pastor D looked intently at Joe as the new pastor's frustration continued to build.

"I came home from worship that first Sunday discouraged and depressed. I had only been there three days, and I already felt defeated," said Joe. "I had preached my butt off and no one seemed to care. That afternoon, I sat on the couch with Janelle, and I cried like a baby in her lap. I said to her, 'I know this is where I'm supposed to be—but why doesn't it *feel* like it? I know this is what God wants . . . why does it have to be this way? That church is dead.'

"After I had pulled it together a little bit, Janelle asked me, 'Why are you crying? What did you just preach about—what was the title?'

"I said, 'Keeping Your Eyes On The Prize.'

"She said, 'Okay. And what were your three points?'

"'A call to self-denial. A call to self-sacrifice. A call to self-determination.'

"Then she looked at me and said, 'Well, there you have it. Sounds to me like God has confirmed that you are where you are supposed to be. Keep your eye on the prize. Get down to business.'

"Is your wife a prophet?" Pastor D asked Joe. "Sure sounds like she could see the situation you were in, but also see beyond the situation all the way to the hope that is down the road. She sounds a lot like my wife."

"Yeah, sometimes I remind her that God has gifted her mightily and that there is some profound ministry that she needs to be doing," Joe commented.

"She really helped get me through that day." He added, sheepishly, "And, unfortunately, she has had to do it every Sunday since."

Pastor D felt bad for Joe. The young man's struggles reminded him of his own experiences when he had first started pastoring at the Fellowship. He knew he had to let Joe know that he wasn't alone and that there was hope.

"Interestingly enough," Pastor D said, "I had a very similar worship situation when I started at the Fellowship."

"I can't believe that," Joe said. "What happened?"

Preach and teach the truths of transformation.

"Well, after the second deadly worship service at the Fellowship, God confirmed for me that worship could be a way to transform our congregation. More specifically, during my prayer time, God revealed that if we changed our culture of worship, God could lead us out of our mess."

"Really? How did that change what you did? Inquiring minds want to know!" Joe chuckled as he spoke, but it was clear that behind his laughter lay an intense interest.

"Well, I was scared to death to come to worship the following Sunday. I didn't want to relive the same experiences from the weeks before. Man, my situation was so bad, you could hear a rat pee on cotton. I was so intimidated by the situation that I didn't show up to church until ten minutes before worship was about to start.

"When I got there, the choir was at the front of the church. I was supposed to assemble with the choir for the processional. But I came through the side entrance instead and ran into one of our dear members, Mrs. Lillian Flowers, who had been deeply worried for the entire week that I wasn't coming back to the church. In those early days, she'd already become my adopted church mother. You need a good church mother, Joe. She will bless you in times of need. And I'll never forget her saying to me, with a smirk on her face as I came in, 'Morning, Reverend. Glad you decided to come back!' I looked at her, forced a smile, and said, 'Yeah, me too.'"

Joe laughed as Pastor D continued.

"So I came to the second worship service, still devastated by the lack of life in the previous one and overwhelmed by all the difficult work that needed to be done. The irony didn't escape me as I announced the title of the sermon I was about to preach: 'Why Can't We?' The sermon was structured around a series of questions designed to open doors of possibility and to face issues and doubt head on:

"Why can't we revive this congregation?

"Why can't we revive this community?

"Why can't we eliminate the demonic forces that keep us down and defeated?

"Why can't we build up this broken building?

"Why can't we clean up this place that is so dirty?

"Why can't we create a ministry that blesses broken people and that gives people hope in the midst of hopelessness?

"Why can't we dream?

"Why can't we vision?

"Why can't we work to see that the hopes and dreams we have for our families and communities come to pass?

"I was closing out the sermon, and I kept repeating the litany of 'Why can't we?' And then I said—before Barack Obama ever uttered it—'Yes, we can. We can do *anything* we want to do. We can do all things *through Christ Jesus who strengthens us.*'"[8]

"That will preach!" said Joe. "Do you mind if I steal it?"

"Funny! Just give me 10 percent of your love offering," Pastor D joked back. "But be careful with it. I haven't told you the rest of the story. It was while I was laying out all the things that could be done in Jesus's name, that an eight-five-year-old woman by the name of Bessie Tillman leaped up from the back pew. And what she did next took us all by surprise. Mrs. Tillman pushed aside the one lady that stood between her and the aisle, and began running, jumping, and dancing up and down the aisle, screaming, 'I'm a witness! I'm a witness!' For the last five minutes of my sermon, she was running up and down the aisle screaming and praising God and shouting, 'I'm a witness! I'm a witness!'

"Are you serious?" Joe asked. "I've never heard of anything like that before."

"I'm serious as a heart attack," Pastor D said, gazing out the window, fixed in the moment. "Everyone looked at us like we were natural fools. Here was this fiery thirty-two-year-old preacher with spit flying out of his mouth and sweat streaming down his face proclaiming what God can do with us and through us if we would just trust Him. And here was an inspired, respected, running-and-screaming eighty-five-year-old Liberian woman who was encouraging the congregation to realize that we could, by God's grace, revive the church in the name of Jesus.

"Later on I learned that Mrs. Tillman knew firsthand the devastation of Liberian civil war and revolt. She knew what God could do even in the midst of the devastation of governmental and societal oppression, abject poverty, death, and the worst kinds of abuse—children having their limbs cut off, the most horrible violence—can you imagine? But she knew we could do it. God sent her shouting that day as a reminder and encouragement to me and all who would listen that even in a dead place like the Fellowship and its community, God could bring us new life."

"Well, we don't have any Liberian women here, and none of my people shout," Joe responded. "I will think we've made huge progress when people start nodding their heads in agreement rather than in sleep. So," Joe began reading from his notes, "other than 'preaching on a series of questions designed to open doors of possibility and to face issues and doubt head on,' what else are you suggesting I do?"

"Well, I'm suggesting that, given your context, you adopt the position that worship is the best place to start your congregation's transformation process. It is the only existing event you have that causes people to gather and have any conversation about God or church. So, just as understanding context is the place to begin in order to better reach the community, worship is the place to start if you want to transform hearts."

Pastor D sat quietly for a moment, giving his words time to sink in.

Gather a team.

"There's so much more that I need to share with you about creating a worship culture that leads to transformation, but it's getting late. Tell you what—let's talk after you preach this sermon you are about to steal from me. When are you planning to preach it?"

"This Sunday! Is that too soon?" Joe laughed. "I can't wait much longer."

Pastor D cracked up. "Okay, call me Tuesday night at seven thirty, and we'll go from there. In the meantime, between now and then, identify one to three people who share your heart for worship and plan for them to join us."

"What if I can only find one?"

"Don't worry about it," Pastor D answered. "If it is only you, me, and God, that's enough. My Bible says, where two or three are gathered, God is in their midst."

With that, the two shook hands and embraced. As Joe started turning off lights and locking up for the night, he thanked Pastor D for sharing his wisdom, his friendship, and his sermon idea.

Worship is a great starting point for transformation:

1. Preach and teach as many in the congregation as possible on core Truths required for transformation (e.g., Why Can't We? Sermon—10%?).

2. Model what the spiritual disciplines of worship, prayer, Bible study, and giving look like.

3. Gather a team—even two or three—to help make REAL worship happen.

Chapter 9
Teaming to Transform Worship Culture
Called. Equipped. REAL.

Joe was amazed by what happened as a result of Pastor D's sermon outline. Not only did heads start nodding, but he found two people who actually shared his heart for worship.

Kate, a young newlywed, came up to him before church was over to congratulate him on preaching a great sermon.

She said, "If you keep this up, we'll be bursting at the seams in worship—and I'd like to help make that happen."

That was a no-brainer for Joe, and he immediately invited her to join his call with Pastor D. The second person was David, a thirty-seven-year-old pharmaceutical salesman and father of two who had nodded his head in agreement during the sermon and smiled at the conclusion. These small signs hadn't escaped Joe as he preached, and he called David that same afternoon to learn more about him and to discern if worship might be a part of his passion or giftedness. David had been in worship every Sunday since worship started and seemed to be pretty well connected to the regulars.

That Tuesday night, once Kate and David were both settled in his office, Joe exclaimed, "Thanks so much for joining me for our first ever worship team meeting!"

Kate and David smiled. They were both happy to be included, although David grew a bit anxious at the mention of a "team."

"As I mentioned to you individually," Joe went on, "we are going to focus on creating a worship culture that helps us transform the sanctuary and the streets. I'm so grateful you've both agreed to join me in making that happen."

It was not quite seven thirty yet, but in his excitement, Joe decided to go ahead and call Pastor D anyway.

"Hey man, what's happening? How'd it go Sunday?" Pastor D greeted him.

"We had a good day! I didn't have any Mrs. Tillman running down the aisles, but there were heads nodding," Joe said. "I've really been looking forward to talking to you tonight. I'm going to put you on the speakerphone because I've asked Kate and David to join me on this call so that we can talk about how to develop a strong worship culture at the Church of the Last Chance."

"Good," said Pastor D. "Kate and David, it is good to meet you, albeit by phone. Hopefully we'll get a chance to meet one another in person soon. Let me ask the two of you, how was the sermon on Sunday? And," he said with a chuckle, "don't hold back just because Pastor Joe is listening!"

Kate and David laughed—as did Joe, a bit nervously.

"Pastor Joe did a fabulous job," Kate replied. "To me it was the best sermon he's preached since coming to us. The sermon was so good that I told him afterward that I wanted to help him in the transformation of our church."

"I was moved," David added. "There's been a bit of a buzz travelling through the congregation since Sunday . . . people are asking why we can't be a stronger church than we are. I'm excited about being a part of making us stronger through worship."

"Fabulous," said Pastor D. "That's great to hear! Joe, it sounds like you owe me 10 percent, but we can talk about that later on. David and Kate, that's an inside joke between me and your pastor."

"You're a funny man," Joe said.

"I am?" Pastor D replied in fun before shifting the conversation. "David and Kate, I'm sure your pastor has already shared with you his desire to transform the worship experience at Last Chance. From your comments a minute ago, it seems as though you share his desire."

They both affirmed that.

Pastor D continued, "You guys get to help lead worship that will change the lives of multitudes in your area. We were created to worship God, and worship enables us to experience and connect with the God of transformation. Congregational transformation often begins with a revival in worship.

"In this day and age, we are seeing more and more people connect to a church through mission projects, in many cultural and ethnic contexts— and more importantly in *your* context—but worship still remains a primary place of meeting. A place where people can experience a sense of belonging, a sense of God's power, and a sense of safety in the midst of life's impending dangers. In my context, we affirm what Toni Morrison described in her best-selling novel, *Beloved*. The main character, Sethe, speaks of the need to get to the 'clearing' to worship. The clearing was the one place where she and those in her community could go, be themselves, discover God, and affirm their identity without having to worry about what others said of them. There are other cultural—and subcultural— groups that feel just the same."

"What do you mean by 'subcultural groups'?" Kate interjected.

"Culture can get defined a lot of different ways and depending on how broadly you define it, there may be subcultures within it. For example, youth could be considered a subculture of the larger congregation. So from a worship point of view, developing worship that is relevant to youth would be connecting to that subculture in a way that is different from the way you'd connect to the predominant adult culture.

"But regardless of who is worshipping, vibrant, spirit-filled worship is the engine of each church's ministry because corporate worship is the largest unified and unifying gathering of the body. This is not to say that worship is the only way to reach new people, but it is often the best place to start putting in place what I call REAL DNA."

"What's REAL DNA?" asked David.

"DNA is what gives us our identity, right? In our bodies, DNA exists in each cell in our body and contains our genetic blueprint. Well, from a church point of view, REAL DNA yields a church that is R-E-A-L—relevant, enthusiastic, authentic, and loving. Every part of the church—from hospitality to Bible studies to meetings to worship—has this genetic makeup. Worship is the work of the people who gather to honor the One who alone is worthy to be praised, Jesus the Christ. So, to transform our communities and congregations, we've got to view worship as one of the most important things we do. Not only does worship invite us into the presence of God—where the impossible can become possible—but the worship time itself offers an opportunity for teaching, connecting, and demonstrating to the congregation and broader community what is *REAL*. But let me ask you this: how would you define *real?*"

"I don't know, because our worship has been more surreal than real," Kate said. "I'm not always sure that what happens in worship is related to anything we do in our everyday lives. Is that what you would call relevant?"

"We'll get to that," said Pastor D, "but you are on the right track."

"And I was gonna say that our worship doesn't feel like a living expression of love directed toward God or one another. I could imagine our worship would be real *and* transformational if it did that," David added.

"I agree with Kate and David—and would add that it is definitely not enthusiastic," Joe commented.

"It sounds like you have identified the root of your problem," said Pastor D. "Let's work together to identify how you might move this problem into the possibility of having a dynamic worship culture."

Kate interrupted with another question. "What do you mean by 'worship culture'?"

"A *healthy* worship culture is an atmosphere that honors God and allows people to draw near to God through all of the various elements of worship: singing, praying, preaching, giving, sharing, and the like. This atmosphere cannot be manufactured; it has to grow from the very hearts of the people gathered so that those gathered expect God to show up," Pastor D replied. "But let me go back and answer your earlier question, Kate. You asked what I mean when I say 'relevant'?"

"That's right," Kate replied. "What do you mean?"

Relevant Worship

"Kate, a church is relevant if it has the ability to speak directly to people's self-interests and common human conditions as they relate to the culture and times in which we live," Pastor D began. ""A church is also relevant when it has the ability to lift people from despair and give them hope. Entire books have been written about how to make worship more relevant to your community, to seekers, and/or to younger generations. But with that said, there are simple ways to make your worship experience immediately relevant.

"One way would be for Pastor Joe, if he doesn't already, to use practical, nonchurchy language to speak to people's daily realities in his sermons. For example, if I am preaching to you, I need to be able to speak your language, talk your talk, sit where you sit, feel what you feel, walk where you walk—so that the teachings of Christ might be plainly understood. It sounds like he did a good job with that this past Sunday."

"He sure did," David affirmed.

"Well, that means that Pastor Joe might be getting a better idea of who's sitting in the pews, who's in the community, and what they're up to."

"His 'Why Can't We' sermon seemed relevant to me," Kate said, "not just because it plainly described important things at church, but because I was able to take some of the points and use them at work during a difficult meeting."

"Pastor Joe, you obviously hit some chords that were very deep and personal in your sermon," Pastor D continued. "And you did so by speaking language that transcended church and included community—so much so that you've got two people on the phone with you now, who you didn't know were with you prior to Sunday."

"You got that right," Joe said.

"Another way to create a relevant worship atmosphere is to have music that resonates with the congregation and community that you serve. Singing hymns of the month that no one has heard and that no one cares about just won't cut it today. On the other hand, if your community listens to Eminem and Jay-Z, or for that matter, Alicia Keys or Lady Gaga, using lines from Frank Sinatra and Jackie Wilson songs will not cut it. You need to be able to demonstrate in word, deed, and music that the gospel applies to their everyday lives *now*—not just in the good old days.

"If the music is out of touch with the community, people will not come. Or if they do come, they won't return. Music is a vehicle that has the power to draw people closer to God. And when the style of the music matches the various cultural preferences of your congregation and community, then you have the ability to lead people to closer encounters with God."

Joe jumped in immediately. "Well, you saw during our tour that there is a significant contingent of people from different ethnic groups. They are heavily influenced by their indigenous culture as well as the current culture. So, are you saying that for our congregation to be drawn closer to God through music in worship, we have to use traditional hymns that are significant to their faith *and* also use electric guitars, steel pan drums, and other percussion instruments and rhythms from their culture to touch their souls?"

"That's exactly what I'm saying, Joe."

"All this sounds great to me . . . but how do you do this in a congregation where people are so stuck on one type of music that is so out of date that it outdates them?" asked Kate.

"Every congregation has to wrestle with your question," Pastor D said. "And decide if it is going to take the necessary risk of upsetting some long-standing, deep-pocketed members for the possibility of reaching many more souls for Christ. Congregations that take the risk position themselves to flourish. Congregations that don't . . . well, they accelerate their own death march. It's that serious. It is important that you seek to educate your people as you are moving forward. Then you'll develop allies along the way and not unnecessary enemies. But you have to do *something*—and not just with music—but with the totality of the worship experience.

"A third piece of advice I would leave you with is that you've got to allow relevancy to permeate the entire liturgy. 'Liturgy' simply means the placement of music, prayers, offering, sermons, and the like in worship. Seeking relevancy means that sometimes our prayers in worship need to be spontaneous and not just written in the bulletin. Seeking relevancy means, for example, that if I haven't seen someone at the Fellowship for a while and suddenly they show up in worship, I take the time to leave my seat, embrace them, and ask 'How are you doing?,' instead of demanding to know, 'Where have you been?!'"

"I can't imagine what that looks like. And I definitely can't imagine people in our congregation going off script," David shared honestly.

"If Pastor Joe leads it, it can happen. After all, he is the chief worship leader in the church. So, let's say healing and forgiveness are sorely needed to bring together your congregation; then Pastor Joe can use the sacrament of the Lord's Supper as an opportunity to build unity amongst factions. He can share the bread and the cup with members of those factions standing with him publicly. He can speak to a divided situation and teach about what the table can do to unify. Personally, there are times when I have evoked public figures who have harmed others or committed public gaffes while drawing the congregation to the communion table. When I do that, I'm inviting them to a seat at the table with us even though they are not physically present. This gives us the power to forgive them even as we are being forgiven ourselves."

"You are giving me fresh revelation," said Joe as visions of possibility raced through his mind. "I see it clearly. Relevancy like this will draw people to Jesus and our congregation like a magnet. And this is the kind of relevancy in worship that leads to congregational transformation."

"Just so I'm clear," said Kate as she reviewed her notes, "we can do three things to make our worship culture more relevant: sermons that speak to people where they live, music that captures the hearts of people on the streets, and liturgy that has room in it for speaking to people where they are."

"You got it!" Pastor D answered. Then, transitioning to the next topic, He said, "Joe, you commented on the lack of enthusiasm in worship. Can you speak more to that?"

Enthusiastic Worship

"Sure. In our services, there's just no excitement—no joy," Joe began. "There is nothing that makes me want to come to or come back to the worship experience."

Joe turned to Kate and David, "Pastor D has explained to me that enthusiasm in its original Greek is *enthousiasmos,* which means 'inspired or possessed by God.' Peter and the disciples at Pentecost were so possessed by the Holy Spirit in Acts 2 that people around them thought they were drunk. But they weren't drunk with wine; they were intoxicated with the presence of God. And their intoxication in worship that day led to three thousand souls being saved. If we were possessed by God, then people would want to come back to the worship experience because excitement and joy are contagious."

"Exactly," Pastor D responded. "As you create a culture of enthusiastic worship, it should move worshippers toward experiencing the in-dwelling of the Holy Spirit—and position them for God to use them in any capacity He chooses. Enthusiasm is something that needs to get into the DNA of our congregations and has to be present in worship. Enthusiastic worship is more than simply lively worship or lively responses to something that happens in worship. It is worship that inspires people to the point where God can possess them and then use them for transformational purposes.

"I think from time to time about John Wesley. He was famous for preaching long and enthusiastic sermons. It was not uncommon for him to preach three hours at a time. Try that today, and you might be preaching to empty pews!"

"Don't get any ideas, Pastor Joe!" said Kate.

"Yeah, 'cause you won't hold onto me for long," added David.

"I agree with y'all—I'd be gone, too," Pastor D retorted. "But Wesley was also renowned for saying, 'I set myself on fire so that someone else will burn.' It reminds me of Kirbyjon Caldwell, pastor of Windsor Village Church in Houston, Texas. He is famous for saying, 'No one is coming to see an icehouse freeze. But everyone will show up to watch a building burn down.' In other words, we need to create a worship experience for God and others that is so rich in enthusiasm that it becomes contagious to those who come in contact with it."

"Yeah, but how can we create such an experience?" Kate queried.

"First of all, enthusiastic worship gets into the DNA of the congregation when people in the congregation are practicing daily personal worship.[9] David and Kate you will need to learn about what that means from Pastor Joe as soon as you get a chance. The practice of daily worship leads to God taking possession. When that becomes the case, it is natural for us to come to the corporate worship experience ready to express joy—because enthusiasm is being possessed by God, and joy is the outward expression of that possession. It's like being given a gift that you love—as soon as you get it, you can't help but reveal to others the gift you have and your joy in it."

"I'm guessing you have a specific definition for joy just like you did for enthusiasm, right?" David asked.

"You're right! Joy is the outward expression of praise and thanksgiving to God because of the inner possession of God and because of the knowledge of His victory over every adversarial activity that seeks to deny us from being at one with Jesus. It is living with the unfailing confidence that God grants victory over any and every obstacle seeking to rob us from living in harmony with the Lord. We express this confidence with excitement and spiritual ecstasy."

"That gives a whole new meaning to 'Joyful, Joyful We Adore Thee,'" said Kate. "I love this—but don't you think it's unrealistic for people who come to worship to be at that place?"

"I don't think it's unrealistic at all," Pastor D replied. "You need to raise your expectations and identify leaders who model enthusiasm and who are natural worshippers. Thanks be to God, Pastor Joe is one of those leaders. Otherwise, the congregation would have problems. I'm not talking about style, though; I'm talking about substance. Congregations often model the behavior of their pastors and key leaders. So if a church yearns for enthusiastic worship, the chief worship leader, who is the pastor, needs to be possessed by God herself or himself. If the pastor and key leaders are possessed by God, the style of worship is not the issue. It's what God *produces* from your possession."

"Wait a minute," Kate said. "Pastor Joe, do you expect that David and I will worship enthusiastically?"

"You have some great questions, Kate," Joe replied. "I do expect that as you walk more closely with God through your daily personal worship that you will find God taking deeper possession of you and you will bring that to worship."

"As I've travelled around to many churches," Pastor D interjected, "I've learned that dead people attract other dead people, just like enthusiasm breeds enthusiasm. If a key leader is unenthusiastic, perhaps that leader needs to step down. Hear me clearly on this: I'm not talking about a frustrated, discouraged key leader, because all of us will have moments of frustration and discouragement. I'm talking about being *unenthusiastic*. If a key leader is not enthused about who God is, what God is doing, what God can do, and what God is doing in his or her life and the lives of others right now, then key leadership is not for him or her. That person might be doing more harm than good to the kingdom of God simply because he or she is not properly positioned to serve the kingdom.

"It is important that you create a critical mass of key leaders on fire for Christ so that the congregation isn't successful at throwing water on the pastor and key leaders in their efforts to contain what looks to be a dangerous situation—a spreading fire. It is imperative that you all keep burning. The only way you do this is through sticking to the discipline of daily worship and finding a core group of people who can help you keep God's fire burning in you. As long as you keep burning, you will experience transformation in your worship service. You have to encourage your congregation to understand that if they are not willing to catch fire—if they aren't willing to be fully possessed by God—eventually the church will die.

"More and more, I've noticed church buildings that used to contain thriving congregations now housing restaurants, cafes, nightclubs, bars, and condos. I imagine this repurposing of church buildings happens because the people refused to allow God to possess them. Woe unto congregations that have a greater passion for being religious social clubs than people who lead hurting souls to life change in Jesus Christ."

"All this talk about fire and enthusiasm reminds me of what I say to the kids I coach in little league: get fired up!" said David. "I was just thinking that if it is easy for me to do that while mentoring, why can't I do it in worship?"

"David, you are right on point," said Pastor D. "And that leads me to one more thing about enthusiasm. You have to arrange your liturgy so that the worship service can breathe with enthusiasm. When I was young, my father used to love to build fires in our fireplace. He taught me to roll up paper and go outside to find kindling wood. You put the kindling wood on top of the paper and dry logs, properly positioned on top of both."

"Yeah, my dad taught us to do the same thing," Kate said. "Some things are universal!"

David laughed, "Then you know, too, that green wood doesn't burn!"

"You got that right!" Joe chimed in.

"Well, in our fireplace, I'd light the fire, and we would have raging fires that would keep the basement warm," Pastor D shared. "However, Dad also taught me that two other things were critical to keeping the fire burning: the poker and the bellows. The poker was important because it enabled me to reposition the logs, particularly if they shifted so as to cut off airspace between logs. If that happened, the fire would die. We need pokers in worship. Because in any worship experience, there are things that threaten to kill the fire. Your worship leaders need to be prepared to see that this does not happen.

"In the same vein, you need to have bellows. The bellows blow air into the fire so that the fire has the proper amount of oxygen and can burn with greater intensity. In my initial experience with the Fellowship, our liturgy had no space to breathe. The logs were too close together. For that matter, no one had even bothered to light the fire in the first place. So I had to light the fire, grab a poker, and operate the bellows—often all at the same time. This is less than ideal, which is why it's important to identify leaders who can help you tend the fire."

"Pay attention to your worship flow. Look for where the fire burns brightest and for those places where the fire dims. Poke around where necessary to create a balanced flow for enthusiastic worship to catch hold and burn. Additionally, grab your bellows to create necessary transitions between elements in worship. If you do these things, corporate worship will get so good that you won't want to leave. And even the clock watchers will lose track of time!"

"In order for us to poke and give air, we have to be sure we have a strong enough fire first, right?" Joe asked.

"Absolutely. But if you keep leading, modeling, and adding leaders who model like Kate and David, you'll be ready for the bellows and the poker and everything that comes after that," said Pastor D.

"I must say," he added, "I found it interesting that when we began this conversation, none of you mentioned the authenticity needed in worship. You mentioned the need to be relevant and enthusiastic, but without authenticity, worship will not be REAL. As a matter of fact, some people use *authentic* and *real* interchangeably. And if they sense that your worship expression lacks sincerity, you've got problems."

Authentic Worship

"So, can I ask a question?" Kate asked.

"Of course you can—you've been asking them all night long!" Pastor D said.

Kate laughed. "What do you mean by authenticity? I'm not sure my definition matches yours."

"Authenticity means simply being down to earth, honest, and forthright. People are begging for a safe space and place to be who they are and to be able to express who they are—the good, the bad, and the ugly. When people come to your worship experience, they need to know that they can be themselves comfortably and not be judged for who they are, what they say, what they look like, or what they smell like.

"Creating space like this can be uncomfortable. Asking people to be transparent can produce tension. But congregations that invest in this critical element of worship culture discover tremendous growth and maturity. And they find God moving in profound ways within the worship experience."

Joe could tell from the look on David's face that he was growing increasingly skeptical.

"But how much transparency is required?" David pushed back. "I don't see how or why I should share stuff with people I don't trust or don't know well enough to know what they will do with it."

"Enough for people to know that you are sincere," Pastor D replied immediately, "that they see you walking your talk and talking your walk. Different levels of transparency will come with different levels of spiritual maturity and relationship building. As people become more possessed by God and develop deeper relationships with one another, greater transparency will be required to go even deeper."

"Yeah, but how do we begin to develop a culture of authenticity?" Kate asked. "We are nowhere near transparent. The folks at Last Chance would rather hide stuff than disclose it publicly. Add to that the fact that many of our older members were taught to hold things in and not to express their feelings publicly. So, how do we crack this? I don't really see how it's possible."

"It *is* possible!" Pastor D exhorted. "Remember, you serve the God in whom all things are possible! So, the question we have to ask is *how* does it happen? Well, first of all, leaders must tell their stories—the good, the bad, and the ugly. People are more inclined to hang around when they hear the pastor and others in leadership talk about their struggles openly. They are persuaded to keep coming to worship when they hear people testifying rather than 'testi-lying.' There's a difference between the two, and people can discern them very quickly."

The group laughed. Pastor D had a lingo all his own.

When the laughter had died down, Pastor D continued, "Testifying happens when people share a test in their lives in which God has brought victory. We often call this testimony—a life test has become a triumph. When testifying happens, lives are changed; people are encouraged; multitudes find strength to keep moving forward even in the midst of their present trials. They are inspired to know that even in a test, God at any time can show up with a blessing.

"At a recent watch night service, for example, a member stood up and said, 'I want you to know that I used to smoke crack. Over the past five years God has taken the taste of crack out of my mouth. And I just want to stand to give God praise for what He has done.' 'Testi-lying,' on the other hand, is a story about God that is empty of God's personal action in that person's life. When somebody gets through testi-lying, you have no better sense of who they are or who God is in their lives. You often end up frustrated because you realize the person who has been talking has been faking and has just wasted your time. In extreme cases, you may even feel manipulated."

Joe interjected, "So, you are telling us that authentic churches are filled with people who are not afraid to talk about how they have fallen and how God has lifted them back up?"

"Yes—exactly!" Pastor D proclaimed. "This should happen in the context of the sermon and should also be heard through the lyrics of the songs that are lifted in praise to God. The more authentic you are with others, the more you create possibility for others to share more authentically. You can tell that you're in the midst of an authentic worship experience when you hear stories of how God has turned bad times into good ones, not just from biblical times, but in everyday situations *today*."

David felt himself getting back on board with Pastor D's vision of authenticity. "I am starting to see the need for building our group of core worship leaders," he said. "We have lots of modeling to do."

"It takes time," Pastor D said. "And speaking of modeling, let me give you another piece of advice: relax your dress code. Encourage people to wear what they want to wear as an outward and visible sign that people can come as they are. If folk want to get dressed up in suits and ties and fancy dresses, encourage them to do so. But if folk want to wear jeans and T-shirts and tennis shoes, don't discourage it. Many people who are considering church—some for the first time—often make dress an excuse for not coming. This is especially true in poor communities where money for nice clothing simply doesn't exist. It is also true in communities where homelessness is a real issue. And it is common in communities where golfing, sailing, and other outdoor activities are a way of life.

"At the Fellowship of the Used-Tos, we started doing this out of necessity in the summertime by having casual summers. Now it has become commonplace to come as you are. I have found that, when people are comfortably dressed, they are more cheerful and approachable. This is especially helpful for newcomers. Furthermore, I'm better able to connect with the congregation. I haven't worn a robe or preached from the pulpit in eleven years. I wear everything from suits and ties to African garb to T-shirts and shorts to football jerseys in worship. While some people are thrown off by this, the vast majority embrace it because it allows *them* to be *them*."

"You are kidding me," said Joe incredulously. "Is a dress code really that important?"

"I know it is for my kids. If I didn't have to argue with them to get into their dress shoes, they might come every week with me," David affirmed.

"There is one last idea I would like to share with you to create an authentic environment in worship," Pastor D continued. "Kate, I have a question for you."

Kate laughed and said, "Yes?"

"Do you all pass the peace in your worship service?"

"What is that?" Kate asked. "I'm trying to visualize our bulletin. That doesn't sound familiar . . ."

"You know, it's when we turn to the person in front of us and the person behind us, and shake their hands, and say, 'Peace be with you.' And they reply, 'And also with you,'" David reminded her.

"Ohhhhh, okay," Kate said.

Amused by the exchange, Pastor D said, "If you want to create an authentic worship culture, you need to pass the peace and mean it. I know I'm in an authentic church when I'm greeted warmly, sincerely, and intentionally. Not with the standard 'peace be with you' handshake, but with joyful handshakes, hugs, and kisses that are accompanied by smiles and words that let me know that I'm valued. A colleague of mine from Phoenix joined us for worship with her husband once for the very first time. After we passed the peace, she was left standing in tears. Later on, she emailed me commenting about how moved she was by the authenticity of the service. She said, 'You guys had me by the third hug.'"

Loving Worship

"Joe, you've been a little quiet. I hope you don't let all of this overwhelm you . . . I know it's a lot," Pastor D empathized.

"I have been quiet, but it's just because I've been taking notes and letting it all soak in," Joe answered. "I must admit it is good to have some more concrete ideas for how to change the nature of our worship. Some of those ideas will be easier than others to implement, though."

"Good, just let it soak in," Pastor D said. "You will find God providing the simple steps you need to take to make all of this happen in your context and in good time. After all, your context is not mine, and mine is not yours. But if you let all of this sink in, God will give you what you and your congregation need to become REAL for your people."

"David, you mentioned earlier the absence of loving God and one another in the beginning of this conversation. We've talked about creating a relevant, enthusiastic, and authentic worship culture. Each is critical to the overarching process. But just as important to the previous three is the last part: your worship has to be loving."

"A church is loving when it unconditionally desires the well-being of others regardless of race, class, gender, age, ethnicity, nationality, or sexual orientation. A loving church points to Jesus and lives out his expression of love to all people, particularly the poor, the marginalized, the outcasts, and the downtrodden of society. I'm sure that describes some of the people in the community you serve here, right?"

"Right," all of them said.

"Good," said Pastor D. "Remember, loving churches are consumed with the unity of the body and do not allow divisive behavior to rob them of their purpose. When there are conflicts and disagreements, loving churches seek to draw near to Jesus and to influence others to come into His divine presence. That's where common ground is found and where truth can prevail."

Just then Joe chimed in, saying, "You know, I have always believed that the one place where people ought to be able to feel love and to express love is in the worship experience. Many people have gone all week long not being loved. Instead they've been harassed, yelled at, neglected, isolated, fought with, talked about, used, and defeated. They come to church searching for a different experience, hoping to find God and His love manifested amongst His people. So the necessity of building a worship culture where God is honored and where people can experience God's love is paramount. After all, God is love, and we are commanded to love God with all our heart, mind, soul, and strength and to love our neighbors as ourselves."

"I agree Pastor Joe," David interrupted, "but I just don't feel that enough love is being expressed in our congregation. That is particularly noticeable in the worship experience. Pastor D, how can we make sure love invades our worship?"

"Well, first, I would encourage each of you to focus your energies on what can be, not on what is," Pastor D challenged them. "I want to give each of you a primary task to make it more possible for a love invasion to take hold at the Church of the Last Chance. Pastor Joe, you have the first assignment: make love the *centerpiece* of the proclamation coming from your pulpit. You control that; you can dictate that. As the pastor, when you preach love in relevant, enthusiastic, and authentic ways, love can begin to invade the environment. Love needs to be the foundation of all that we teach. Grounded in that teaching must be the desire for the well-being of others. For as the scripture says, 'God is no respecter of persons.' Jesus calls us to be ambassadors of love and to make followers and learners of Him by teaching His principles of love in word and in deed. As the pastor, you've got to be the one who sounds the clarion call for love in all you do, and people need to see you practicing what you preach.

"This next assignment is also for you, Pastor Joe," Pastor D continued. "Love needs to be at the heart of your *prayers* in worship, and you are the one who is responsible for making that happen."

"Understood," Joe said.

"There are two particular types of prayers: congregational prayers and individual altar prayers. The word *altar* literally means slaughter. It was the place in Old Testament times where burnt offerings were sacrificed so as to persuade God to forgive us of our sins. Sin prevents us from being well, and it prevents us in many cases from desiring others to be well. So if sin can be slaughtered, love can prevail. So, if the altar call and the altar prayer are used as opportunities to slaughter sin and interject love, people can arise from the worship moment feeling renewed, revived, and refreshed in love. We do this at the Fellowship of the Used-Tos, and I would encourage you to pray about how that might be incorporated at Last Chance."

Pastor D continued, "We also interject love in other types of prayers. Sometimes we will partner people together in prayer. Sometimes, instead of reading a printed prayer, we ask people to partner together to share one thing that you want the other person to pray for you about right then and there on the spot. This allows perhaps even a total stranger to demonstrate their desire for your well-being through prayer. Furthermore, it allows for a new relationship to be developed.

"David, your assignment is to collect a hot-topic list so that preaching and prayers in worship might be pointed toward breaking down barriers and building bridges in the congregation and the community. If we are contaminated with the '-isms' of life, we need to begin intentionally dismantling them with love."

Kate confessed, "I get a sense that there is a lot of healing that needs to take place in this congregation. People have been hurt because of rifts in our town, past relationships between pastors and the congregation, family feuds and conflicts, failed and fake attempts at reconciliation . . . There really needs to be a healing spirit in our church before we forfeit our last chance. I'm starting to see how this REAL culture will really help us make progress."

"Much goes into the healing process, but," Pastor D stressed, "don't underestimate the power of preaching and prayer. Through preaching and prayer, we can build loving bridges of opportunity that heal and restore relationships that are key to family, church, and community harmony. This attitude of love in the church needs to spill out and spill over into our neighborhoods through ministry to people from all walks of life."

"Kate, I haven't forgotten about you," Pastor D teased. "Your assignment is to do a REAL worship culture assessment. I will email Pastor Joe a checklist of items[10] for you to use as a starting point for your inventory. Don't try to get an A all at once. It should be worked on over time. It seeks to measure more detailed components under each of the four areas in addition to those things we talked about today."

"It's funny that you started answering my question before I even asked it! I was going to ask if there were simple ways we can measure how well we are doing at creating a REAL worship culture," Kate asked. "Will that checklist answer my question?"

"The checklist is even more detailed than what you are looking for," Pastor D answered. "I think the simplest way to measure the impact you are having on the culture is to use your new members or participants as a barometer. At the Fellowship of the Used-Tos, we ask each person who attends our new member orientation class to describe why they came back to the Fellowship. If everything you do is tied into creating REAL culture, you should hear those cultural elements creeping into their comments. For example, the top three reasons new members give for coming back to the Fellowship center around relevance, enthusiasm, authenticity, and love.

"People say things like, 'Pastor is down to earth, and he preaches in a way that I can apply to my life. He shares his struggles—never comes across as holier than anyone—and testifies to the power of God in his life.' That's relevant and authentic. Others will say, 'I feel the presence of the Holy

Spirit in the place—that God is up to something. Worship is exciting.' That's enthusiasm. Someone else might say, 'I feel genuinely loved by the people.' At least one person mentioned the experience of being hugged genuinely at least seven times before worship ended. That's being loving and authentic."

"I got it," Kate said. "We haven't had any new people in a while, so even having some new folks sitting in the pew will let us know that the culture is improving!"

"Amen!" Pastor Joe responded. He looked up at the clock and said, "I'm so grateful for the time we've spent together tonight. It's so clear to me that we've got to be relevant, enthusiastic, authentic, and loving—particularly in our worship. REAL worship culture is created through intentionally embedding relevance, enthusiasm, authenticity, and love into key worship components: preaching, prayer, music, offering, passing of the peace, and the sacraments.

"And," he continued, "I'm especially grateful that God sent Kate and David to accompany me on this journey. I couldn't do it all on my own!"

"And you won't and don't have to!" David exclaimed.

REAL Worship Ideas

Make worship relevant:
1. Sermons that speak to people where they live, and lift them up in times of despair
2. Music that captures the hearts of people on the streets
3. Liturgy that has room in it for speaking to people where they are

Make worship enthusiastic:
1. Participants who engage in daily personal worship.
2. Leaders who are enthusiastic, natural worshippers (Position them to model that for others!)
3. Liturgy that has room for the Holy Spirit to breathe enthusiasm into it

Make worship authentic
1. Leaders tell their stories—the good, the bad, and the ugly
2. Dress code that is relaxed and varied
3. Pass the peace and mean it

Make worship loving:
1. Proclamation that makes love the foundation of our pulpit
2. Prayers with love at the heart
3. Assess worship culture

Chapter 10
Inspecting Your Community

Interviews. Demographics.
Mayors. Gifts. Meetings.

Since their last conversation with Pastor D, Joe, Kate, and David had gotten right to work making the worship service at the Church of the Last Chance more REAL. They had success in making the order of worship breathe. Rather than having printed prayers every Sunday, Joe began to assign people to pray every other Sunday. Additionally, Joe's sermons began to take on a more relevant tone—he started preaching sermon series on issues that he knew his congregation and community were dealing with. It was working, and people were inviting others to come participate in worship because of the topics he was preaching on. Worship was showing signs of turning for the better even though Joe knew they had a long way to go—for while progress was being made, chaos was beginning to rear its ugly head.

"So, how is worship going at the Church of the Last Chance?" Pastor D asked as the two men opened up the mentoring call. "I sensed a tremendous amount of energy in you, Kate, and David on our last conference call, and I'm curious to know how things are proceeding."

Joe, having already anticipated that Pastor D would ask this question, decided to be very blunt. "We see signs of hope, and we are encouraged—but we are in the midst of some serious music ministry wars."

"What do you mean?" Pastor D asked.

"We've stressed the need to include contemporary selections amongst our music offerings," Joe began. "As we talked about with you, for our music to be relevant it needs to speak to the people we seek to reach in our community. And it needs to minister to the people who are already here. As you can imagine, this has created an uproar. Our minister of music, Mr. Wilson, only likes to play high-church, traditional music. He has a loyal faction in his choir that doesn't want to change, yet there is also a significant group of people who want to broaden our musical horizons. So, Pastor D, we have a lot of tension. And the tension is keeping me up at night to the point where Janelle is getting very worried. How do I get through this?"

"By running in the opposite direction!" Pastor D joked. "No, I'm just messing with you. Believe it or not, you are in a great place. I'm sure it doesn't feel that way, but this is a positive thing. When you're growing in a healthy way, you're going to create tension—this is *good* tension. It's like a parent having to buy a kid new clothes because his body is growing. It's better to have to buy new clothes than to have a child who isn't growing.

"The bad tension is what you want to avoid. Bad tension comes when people's concerns are not heard, when people are not invited to participate in the growth and development of community, and/or when people aren't being treated with love. What I hear is that you are inviting people to grow beyond themselves and to reach people who are starving for the gospel. That involves change, and as Mark Twain put it, 'The only thing that likes change is a wet baby.'"

"Mr. Twain obviously hasn't tried to change my son's diaper," Joe interjected. "'Cause there are times when he really doesn't want his diaper changed."

Pastor D laughed, "I know what you mean. But the way you deal with fussy babies and people who don't like change is through a lot of prayer—both personal, congregational, and intentional. By intentional, Joe, I mean inviting people who you know can get a prayer through to God. They specifically need to intercede with you on behalf of your minister of music and your music ministry as a whole. Ask God in prayer to shape that ministry in any way necessary for God to be glorified and for the lost to be reached. In addition, Joe, ask God in prayer to reveal to you if anyone's season in the music ministry is up and to let you know when transition is necessary. And ask God, in prayer, to send you the people you need to accomplish His will.

"Wow," Joe said. "I've never had to initiate prayer like this before."

"Welcome to pastoral ministry, my friend. As you lead your congregation in prayer through the good and the bad, you will find your congregation leaning on God in prayer for all things. That will be the foundation of your church's transformation.

"In addition," Pastor D continued, "the way through this music ministry storm is by preaching and teaching about the love of Christ, the importance of unity in the body, and the fact that there are a variety of gifts—but one Spirit. You may even need to get more specific and teach about worship and even the role of music ministry in a congregational setting. It would do you well to do some extra study in the books of Leviticus, First and Second Chronicles, and First Corinthians. I would guess that most of your folk have never learned about the aspects of music ministry and the points of unity in the midst of diversity that these scriptures address. As you preach and teach this, your congregation will learn that the growth you are advancing is not for selfish motives, but for the good of the church and expanding the kingdom of God. You may lose a few people, but as a mentor of mine told me, for everyone that leaves, at least three to five more are coming. Does that help you, my brother?"

"Does it help? You better believe it helps!" said Joe. "The load is a little lighter now." He sighed and then continued, "My fear has been that we have so few people at Last Chance that we can't afford to lose even one. Yet if that one is getting in the way of us becoming a REAL church, it is far better to lose that one and have God send us the three to five people who either get it—or at least don't get in the way!"

"You got it, Joe. We will be praying with and for you as you move through these music ministry growing pains. And, just a note of encouragement for you: we had a similar issue at the Fellowship, and God brought us through. If He did it for us, He can do it for you.

"Now, is there anything else regarding worship or any of the other homework assignments?"

"Not really . . . but . . . " said Joe, hesitating, "Well, I am sensing some disconnect between James and Julie and me. The conflict seems to be stemming from the fact that they have pretty much been in control of this congregation for years. I sense that they are beginning to push back on sharing leadership with others. But I'm not sure there's anything to do right now. I'm just paying attention to and waiting for God's guidance."

"Good move. You are thinking and discerning very wisely, which says to me that you must be investing good time in daily worship. Keep it up, my friend," Pastor D encouraged, "and remember that when someone's season is over, it is over. When it is time to start a new season, it is time to do something new.

"So, are you up for us talking a little more about getting involved in your community's transformation?"

"Absolutely! I was hoping we could spend some time there. It will be a relief to think outside the Last Chance box—literally!" Joe shared.

"I feel you," Pastor D replied. "Now tell me, what's happening in your community? Have you taken any time to inspect it?"

"Well, some," Joe said, "but we've been so focused on trying to develop a REAL worship culture at Last Chance that we simply haven't had time to do much of anything in the community."

"Understood," Pastor D said. "Ministry gets crazy like that, and the things we want to do and need to do can rapidly slip away from us if we're not careful. Particularly at the Church of the Last Chance, you have had many immediate needs that have demanded your attention—needs that, if you didn't address, you wouldn't have a church! I fully understand that. In fact, as my kids used to say a few years back, 'Been there, done that, and bought the T-shirt!'

"But, Joe, you've grown in your leadership to a point where you are ready to begin thinking, acting, and working like the street is your sanctuary and the community is your church. In fact, this will help you with your worship challenges right now. The more new people who invade Last Chance, the quicker the music debate will subside. It's important that you begin looking at the world as your parish, as John Wesley used to say. To begin doing that, you've got to do a thorough community inspection."

"Yep, since we went on the tour, I have an idea of what's happening around me," Joe said.

"Yeah, I know, Joe, but touring is not enough," Pastor D pointed out. "You've got to get to know your community and let your community get to know you. This does not have to be a complex process—this can be done simply. For example, I conduct prayer services in the gym where I exercise as called upon. I preach and conduct prayer meetings at the family support collaborative down the hill from the church as called upon. Like us, there are other folks in the trenches who need the holistic support of the church to make it through life's challenges.

"Remember, we began talking about that while we were on the tour. You must constantly inspect your community. Get to know it like the back of your hand. If I stop in your community and ask someone if they know your church and what your church is known for, they should be able to tell me—and what they tell me ought to be positive. Your congregation and community need to have a great marriage together. But for that to happen, there's got to be a first date, then many dates afterward, and then an engagement and a *marriage*, not just a wedding.

"Let me tell you a story," Pastor D began. "One of our first dates with our community was with transient men and women. In Columbia, we have a large population of transients. It has been this way for as long as I can remember. However, things are beginning to change. Many people—drug addicts and alcoholics, disenfranchised Vietnam and Gulf War veterans, ex-convicts, those devastated by broken homes—wander up and down the major thoroughfare on which our church building is located. These folks are looking for shelter, food, money . . . any signs of hope and compassion that might relieve their inner pain, sickness, or feelings of failure. In fact, a friend of mine who grew up in the neighborhood calls this section of the street the 'Avenue of the Walking Dead.'

"When I first got there, it was not uncommon for our church to be vandalized and used for drug and prostitution activities. Things really intensified about two years after I arrived. At the street level of our church, there are about twenty windows that look into the fellowship hall. The windows stretch all the way around the church like a horseshoe. Whoever was breaking in would break one window, wait for us to repair it, and then break the next window. After the seventh window was busted, our church leaders finally gathered to figure out what to do about the problem. One woman stood up and said, 'We need to build a fence around this church to keep the vagrants out!' But others spoke up and said that it was time to open our church building to the community. If we opened it, maybe the break-ins would stop. So that night we decided to open our doors and invite the community in."

"We started by inviting the oldest chapter of Alcoholics Anonymous to meet in the church. Then we sent out Harry and Jim, who had heard their call to street ministry while in Bible study. They began inviting men and women from the street into the church for a hot meal, clothes, and Bible study on Sunday afternoons. Not too long after Harry and Jim started on the streets, not only did the vandalism and burglaries stop, but we've been a friend to those on the street ever since. And they have been friends to us."

"Are you serious?" Joe asked. "How long did that take you?"

"Well, the break-ins stopped within a couple of weeks," Pastor D answered. "But don't look at the time factor, look at this as a process. Truth be told, this was the beginning of an entire transformation process that is still going on. We began to understand how vital building relationships with people in the community was to becoming a community change agent. Soon after the break-ins stopped, a tragic community event propelled us into deeper community relationships. A teenager walked into one of the three liquor stores next to our church and was shot by the owner, who thought the boy was going to rob him. The police didn't find a weapon on the boy. And then, when it was discovered that the liquor storeowner was squatting in an apartment complex that had become a crack house full of squatters, it became abundantly clear to us that we needed to increase the number of relationships we had with people in the neighborhood. Here was a major tragedy literally happening under our noses. For us to ignore it would have been to ignore the Gospel and to be irrelevant to our community.

"Joe, a congregation that is not relevant to its surrounding community is irrelevant. Furthermore, the church is the one entity in the community that has been called by God and established by Jesus Christ to be a catalyst for community change and hope for the people. Out of our response to the tragedy, an emphasis on community development and community organizing took root."

"They didn't teach me this in seminary," Joe said.

"Don't be so hard on the cemeteries—I mean, the seminaries," Pastor

D chuckled. "Many of them have seen the light and are beginning to teach about community development. What you need to know is that you need to learn the streets and learn how every community functions. And that begins with you doing your own community inspection.

"You see, Joe, the natural inclination we have when things are broken is to jump right in and try to fix everything that is in front of us. This is natural because the needs around us are so great that oftentimes we don't know where to begin—so we try to begin everywhere.

"But at some point," Pastor D stressed, "you've got to identify the primary place of need in your community and then build from there. As soon as you begin equipping and growing your people, you must begin to frame your strategy for how you are going to take that spiritual energy to the streets . . . so that hopeless people regardless of their race, class, ethnicity, or gender, who are scratching, clawing, and fighting just to live at peace with themselves and others, can find hope—sooner rather than later.

"You and I need to see beyond just the people we serve in the box Sunday after Sunday. We have to be the church to our wider communities, unboxed and unbound. As the pastor, Joe, you've got to model the behavior you want to see. I can tell your lay people the same thing when you come to the REAL Church Revival in the fall."

"Huh? What's that?" Joe said.

"That's our teaching weekend for congregational leadership teams that are seeking to lead a movement of transformation in their communities," Pastor D said. "And I'm inviting you and a team of leaders from Last Chance to be there. There's so much your people can learn from our people that weekend, and you and I will have more time to spend together. How's that sound?"

"Sounds great to me. I will make sure that we are there in good numbers," Joe replied.

"Good," said Pastor D. "I'm gonna hold you to that. You and your people have to model the behavior you want to see. All of you need to get into the community and learn it, inspect it, and see where God is seeking to develop connections. There's an old adage that helps us here. It goes, 'You can't teach what you don't know, and you can't lead where you won't go.' The community expects the church to meet it, greet it, and feed it at its point of need. And if you are not in the place of need with them, whether it is a major or minor need, you won't have any credibility with the people to make positive change happen."

"So, are you telling me that one of the reasons why we are at our last chance at the Church of the Last Chance is because we have turned our backs on our community?" Joe asked.

"Well, Pastor, you are the one to best answer that question," said Pastor D, putting it back to Joe. "And if the answer is yes, perhaps God is telling you that you have one last chance to change this perception."

"Well, I really want to make this last chance count. What do I need to do?"

Revitalization happens when the community and the church come together to make it happen.

"Let me give you a brief overview now, and people will get a deeper explanation at the REAL Church Revival training. You won't be doing this alone. I'll start with the guiding framework and then leave you with four steps."

"Four steps seems manageable," Joe said. "I'm ready!"

"Good," said Pastor D. "But before I get to the steps, you need to understand that revitalization happens when the community and the church come together to make it happen. It can't be the church saying 'This is what the community needs.' No, no—doesn't work that way. It has to be the community in the church and the church in the community that find their common voice and not only speak a vision of hope, but lay out a plan for bringing their dreams and aspirations to pass.

"Some of the people in our congregations live in the community surrounding the church building. But others do not. Regardless of where people in our congregations live, we need to have a book-of-Acts approach to community development. Jesus told his disciples before his ascension that 'you will be my witnesses in Jerusalem, Judea, Samaria, and to the ends of the earth.'[11] What Jesus meant by that is that we need to be his kingdom developers—first in our homes and immediate neighborhoods. That's what

Jerusalem represented. Then we need to spread His mission to surrounding neighborhoods and regions. That's what Judea represented. Then to people who were ostracized, marginalized, and who nobody wanted to be bothered with. That's what Samaria represented. And finally to the ends of the earth, which meant the mission had to be global in nature.

"Once you understand that concept, you are ready to begin identifying the primary needs impacting your community," Pastor D concluded. He paused while Joe pondered this, lost in deep thought.

"In my experience," Pastor D continued, "I have found that the best place to start is with a thorough community inspection. Like *Law and Order* and *CSI*—you've seen these programs on TV before, right?—we need to do a thorough inspection of the crime scene in order to determine the causes and the dynamics at play.

"We talked earlier about the stories of Nehemiah and Ezekiel and the experience of Jesus at the pool of Bethesda in the Gospel of John. Let's return there for a moment. Nehemiah had to deal with the broken walls of Jerusalem. Ezekiel had to resurrect a valley of dry bones. And Jesus, who ministered in multiple communities, found himself at a pool where there were a variety of cases of disenfranchisement and despair. The vast majority of people who worship, live, and minister in many communities, particularly those that show signs of disenfranchisement, see the same things that Nehemiah, Ezekiel, and Jesus saw. What do you think these people can teach you about doing community inspections?

"Well, in a nutshell," Joe began, "Nehemiah inspected the conditions of Jerusalem, the city of peace, his community that needed to be rebuilt. Ezekiel took a moment to survey the valley that he was called to revive. And Jesus placed his eyes on the condition right in front of him. In Nehemiah's case, he took people with him to see what he saw, so that his report would not be the only one heard or seen after he returned."

"You are a fast learner," Pastor D affirmed. "Whenever you go somewhere to learn—whether to conferences, the street, or wherever—you need to take somebody else with you so that when you return, you're not the only one talking. Please understand that community transformation begins when you *and your people* carry back the message."

"Let me give you four steps you've got to take in order to conduct a thorough community inspection.

1. Conduct Relational Interviews

"First, Joe, you and your people must engage yourselves in doing one-on-one relational meetings. I learned this through watching my family interact with our communities in DC, Pittsburgh, Philadelphia, New Orleans, and the Los Angeles and Oakland areas. I also learned the importance of this through immersing myself in various training opportunities related to community development and community organizing, like the Communities of Shalom, which is a United Methodist initiative, and the Industrial Areas Foundation (IAF), which organizes people and money with churches and communities to leverage for power to address social justices issues. One-on-one relational meetings are foundational to conducting a useful inspection.

"To identify who and where you need to begin the one-on-ones, you need to identify a particular area or boundary in which you are going to interview people," Pastor D continued. "For example, you may decide to talk with everybody within a very small radius of your church. Or you might make that radius wider and select people in particular sectors to begin your interviews with, like those in schools, businesses, and associations. As you talk with these people, ask them basic questions to get to know them, as you allow them to get to know you. You'll discover that you have far more in common with the people in your neighborhood than you ever imagined. Joe, you'll also discover names of others in your community who you need to interview. For example, one person I started with was the director of the private school that leased out space in our church. This led me to other educators and leaders in the neighborhood and served as the springboard for my relational meetings in the neighborhood.

Pastor D sipped on some water with lemon as he continued talking. "As I just said, Joe, these interviews provide a time where you can get to know people and allow people to get to know you. In addition, you can take note of people's passions, dreams, and desires—not just for their lives, but also for the communities in which they live. As you get to know people, these one-on-one relational meetings become an opportunity to reach people for Jesus and to develop new members in the congregation as the Holy Spirit guides. But the key factor here is simply building relationships so that community can be formed.

"Ask basic questions such as: Where are you from? How did you get here? How long do you see yourself here? What would you like this community to become? What is your perception of our church? How can we help you or help the community achieve your vision?

"These questions will open the door to conversations that will blow your mind. They'll also position you and the person you are talking with to feel what the other feels, experience what the other experiences, and at some point, begin taking steps to make transformative community partnerships. After each conversation, you need to make notes to help you keep track of what you've learned.

"In Nehemiah's community transformation process, it was through this relationship building that he was later able to inspire the people to do what they collectively needed to do."

2. Understand Community Demographics

"Then, Joe, you need to gather and get to know your community demographics intimately," Pastor D said. "I know I referenced this when we went on the community tour during the site visit. But let me get a little more specific here. While the one-on-one relational meetings provide you with firsthand accounts, you need to research your community's demographics so that you have a broader understanding of the community trends that are taking place in your neighborhood. For example, you need to confirm who is in your community through these studies. You may see it firsthand yourself, but I guarantee you there are a host of people you don't even know about in your community. You need to find out who they are. All of these demographic studies rely on census data, so many elements of the population may not be accurately represented.

"You need to find out how old and young they are, how much money they make or don't make, whether they are single or married, their religious preferences, if any. You need to find out this information and more so that you can have the best handle on what trends in your community must be addressed."

"Okay, I'm following you," Joe said.

3. Identify Your "Mayors"

"And while you are studying your demographics and conducting your one-on-one relational meetings, you will discover who the 'mayors' are in your community. I'm not just talking about your actual mayor or other elected officials, Joe. Obviously you should know who the elected officials are in your community—you will need them and they will need you down the road—but as you are talking with people in your community, you will discover who the real mayors are. These are the people of influence that even the elected officials unofficially report to. These are the people who know your community better than anybody. They know that you are at the Church of the Last Chance even though you may not have even met them yet!"

"What?" said Joe, looking puzzled.

"Yeah, that's right. They know who you are, and you haven't even met them yet," said Pastor D. "These are the people who sit on their front porches, play checkers on the front stoop, hang out in the barber shops, beauty salons, feed supply stores, ball courts, and local hangouts who can tell you everything happening in your neighborhood, when it is happening, how it is happening, who is doing it, who it benefits, and who it hurts. These folks can trigger the start of any project, or they can kill any project. They can put a good word out about your church, or they can influence people to not even be bothered with your church. Church leaders *must* get to know these 'mayors' intimately and seek to win them over to our team—even if they never worship in our churches. Why? Because they can greatly impact the growth and development of our congregations and communities.

"Understand, Joe, that these individuals are powerful people; and they may go to church, or they may not go to church. They may be Christian, Jewish, Muslim, or may not declare any kind of faith. They may be homeless or professional, blue collar or white collar, male or female, gay or straight, they may be gangbangers, drug lords or simply grandmas or grandpas who've been in the neighborhood longer than anybody. They may be from any number of nationalities or ethnic groups. But you've got to get to know them."

Pastor D took a moment to reflect and then continued.

"In our community, there have been only three mayors among many mayors that I've sought to be close to. One is a homeless man named Jim Allen. Jim's mom lives in the neighborhood, but Jim, for various reasons, seeks to spend periods of time living on the street. Jim knows everybody and everything. In fact, when my hubcaps were stolen off my car twice in one month, I asked Jim if he knew who did it. Within a few days Jim knew who did it and where they were. He said, 'Pastor, I found out who stole your hubcaps, but you won't have to worry about them because the police found them, and they're gonna be locked up for a good little while.' Later on, Jim and I developed such a close bond that he appeared to know my every movement. One day I came into the office, and five minutes later Jim showed up and said, "Pastor, I just want you to know that I know when you come in and when you go out. And I want you to know, we got your back.' It is important that you build relationships with people like Jim.

"Another mayor in my area is a middle-aged woman named, Kathy Peterson. For years, she has provided critical leadership for the major community association in our neighborhood. Kathy's influence reaches from city hall to the surrounding street corners. She passionately cares about her community. Nothing is done unless Kathy is consulted. And her word can convince mayors, council members, developers, and leaders of boards and commissions to do the right thing in our community. You need to get to know the Kathys in your neighborhood."

"Still another is an elderly woman, Ms. Green," continued Pastor D. "We don't see Ms. Green as much as we used to, but she's still around. She's been volunteering for years for our community's long-standing Meals On Wheels program, which serves hot meals to homebound seniors in our community. Everybody knows Ms. Green because she sponsors a host of educational programs for the community—particularly for seniors.

Because seniors represent a strong voter block and because seniors have more free time on their hands than most people, they are a powerful force in the community's ability to revive itself. You need to get to know the Ms. Greens in your world as you work with them to develop and redevelop community. Do you follow me?" Pastor D asked.

"I'm with you 100 percent," Joe said.

4. Conduct House Meetings

"Great! Now, you've got to understand that your relational interviews, demographic research, and relationships with the mayors in the community will position you for the next critical step in community transformation: the implementation of house meetings. A house meeting is a gathering of people with whom you have already conducted relational interviews. Gather people around a common theme or issue that resonates with them. The one-on-on meetings you've had will reveal the common theme or thread. The house meeting itself will provide the opportunity for people to begin strategizing about how the issue or need can be addressed. And, Joe, when you do these meetings, or when others in your congregation do them, you want to be sure to bring some of your potential congregational leaders into this process. Oftentimes these house meetings are key to an emerging vision."

"But how do I even put one of those meetings together?" Joe asked. He was feeling a case of the nerves coming on again.

"Here are some things to keep in mind," Pastor D said. "First, don't be afraid to prepare some food. Some of Jesus's best ministry was done around a common meal or other eating opportunities. Second, be sure to bring an easel, flip-chart paper, and markers so that you can take notes and record the main points shared in the meeting. And third, make sure everyone signs in and includes at least their first and last name, phone number, and/or email address so that people can keep in touch with one another, get the minutes from the meeting, and find out future meeting dates.

"These meetings should be no longer than two hours and should be held in a place and space where people feel comfortable. No more than fifteen to twenty people is a good size so that you can easily meet in somebody's home or a favorite neighborhood hangout. The purpose of the meeting is to talk—based on information collected—about shared dreams, visions, and images of what you want the community to become. The meetings are powerful because they enable multiple constituencies to discover common ground."

"Sort of like a friendly, small town hall meeting—or what we'd like a town hall meeting to be, right?" Joe asked, checking his understanding.

"Correct, Joe. House meetings like these position you to attract more potential community leaders and even more congregants. Because many participants in the house meetings may not be connected to a congregation, they'll find yours appealing and inviting because you have taken time to invest in them and their community. Frankly, my brother, many congregations and many pastors are not doing this because this is a lot of work, or because we frankly have never learned how to do this. But I tell you, if you take the time to do it and teach your people to do it, people in your community who have frowned on the church will begin to embrace the church because you are meeting needs. And that's what Jesus did—he met needs!"

"Amen," Joe said.

After their closing prayer, Joe hung up feeling that there was still much that needed time to sink in. But this didn't stop him from continuing to imagine and dream about the great things God was getting ready to do with the Church of the Last Chance.

Revitalization happens when the community and the church come together to make it happen.

There are four steps in a community inspection that will help us understand the causes and dynamics at play.

1. Conduct relational interviews. Ask:
    * Where are you from?
    * How did you get here?
    * How long do you see yourself here?
    * What would you like this community to become?
    * What is your perception of our church?
    * How can we help you or help the community achieve your vision?

2. Understand community demographics.

3. Identify your "mayors."

4. Conduct house meetings.

Chapter 11
Gaining Commitment
Passion. Walk God's Talk. Align.

The dreary clouds hanging heavily in the sky above Joe's head as he walked from his car to the church building accurately reflected how he was feeling. He was heavy, filled with tears that were ready to be released like raindrops from a storm cloud. He couldn't believe how, in one short month, so much excitement around worship and all the eagerness about doing the community inspection could have spiraled downward so quickly. Joe was dreading his call with Pastor D, which they'd scheduled for later that day. He not only felt like he had hit the proverbial brick wall; he felt like the wall had punched him back.

While he, along with Kate and David, had enthusiastically approached the new worship possibilities at Last Chance, the apathy and pushback from other leaders in the congregation was so strong that any momentum that had appeared to be building, now seemed to be lost. Added to that was the fact that Joe couldn't find any leaders to go out into the community with him to even talk about inspection, let alone do one. The young pastor had fallen to his most discouraged point to date. Key people he had thought were with him would not step up to the plate. James, Last Chance's council chair, and his wife Julie were continuing to subtly undermine any signs of the progress that was taking place as they struggled to maintain their influence.

At that moment, the phone rang. It was time for his conversation with Pastor D, and, Joe, sensing that his mentor was on the line, let the phone keep ringing. *Do I really want to go on with this*—or is it time to just give up and forget it all? Joe asked himself. The phone went silent.

He was low. So low that he was considering whether or not he was even the one to lead the process at Last Chance. When the phone began ringing a second time, he contemplated not answering it again. But because of his commitment to his vocation, his appreciation for Pastor D, and a small glimmer of hope that transformation was still possible, he picked up the phone.

"Where you been?" Pastor D said.

"I was away from my desk and didn't hear it ring," Joe lied. "How are you doing?"

"A little tired from yesterday's worship experiences, but doing well," Pastor D said. "How 'bout you?"

"Doing good," Joe answered, trying to cover up his disappointment by forcing extra cheer into his voice. But Pastor D had been with Joe long enough to know that something was not right.

"It sure doesn't sound like it, Joe. Why don't you tell me what's really going on?" Pastor D responded. Joe realized he wouldn't be able to fool his mentor.

"Man, I'm about ready to give up . . . I'm tired of being at a church that is comfortable being dead. I'm tired of being in a church with people who don't seem to notice or care that their church is dead. I'm tired of being in a church where no one wants to lead. And I'm tired of feeling like I'm leading this process all by myself. I'm sick of this church, I'm sick of pastoring, and to be honest with you, the reason I didn't pick up the phone was because I really didn't know if I felt like talking to you today. Not that I don't love or appreciate you, because Lord knows I am so grateful for all you are doing, but I've had a pretty rough time here since the last time we talked."

"Yeah, I can hear from the tone of your voice that you're ready to whip somebody's assets," Pastor D interjected.

"You got that right!"

"Well, Joe, let me assure you that you aren't the only one who has felt this way," Pastor D encouraged. He had certainly been in Joe's situation before, so he knew what he was talking about. "Virtually every leader who is seeking to bring about transformation in their congregation experiences several moments of despair and frustration. In fact, Joe, if you were not having these moments, I would begin to wonder whether or not something was wrong. You have reached the point, my friend, where you are learning who is with you and who is not with you. And you're also learning who's on the fence. It is sometimes helpful to do an inventory of who is with you because it is easy to get discouraged by those who are sitting on the fence or are against you. Let's just take a minute right now to list the people you know are with you."

Joe began to rattle off names of people who had been supportive of him. And then he jumped right into naming those who'd been giving him and others hell—but Pastor D cut him off.

"Joe, you don't need to worry about who is against you right now. You need to focus your energies on who is with you and who wants to experience transformation. As you do that, you will see God open doors of growth and opportunity. Let me ask you a question: How many people do you think you need to have on your side in order to move forward?"

"More than I do now!" said Joe, more than a little frustrated. After a moment he added, "Actually I have no idea."

"Well, in my experience, I had twelve or thirteen out of fifty-five. Those twelve or thirteen turned the church around in a matter of a year because they committed themselves to prayer, worship, and intensive Bible study. Through that process, God spoke. Each person knew the particular areas of the ministry in which they were to serve. You don't have to have a lot of people on your side to make progress. You just need to begin moving whoever is with you toward commitment.

"Now, you can stay mad and angry if you want to. Or you can thank God ahead of time for providing a way for you to gain commitment from people."

"Mad?" Joe asked innocently. "Angry?"

"That's what you sound like. You sound like Elijah after he ran from Jezebel. Remember him sitting in the desert under the broom tree, discouraged, depressed, and depleted of all his energy, telling God that he was the only one left to do ministry? The fact of the matter is, God doesn't intend for you to do this transformation work on your own. In every space and place that God wants transformation to occur, God has already placed people in your midst who will help you. They are already there. You have to find them and lead them to the point of commitment. God will send or raise up who you need and how many you need. You just have to trust Him.

"Let me give you an example from my own experience," Pastor D continued. "After starting to pastor at the Fellowship of the Used-Tos, my wife and I ended up buying a house right across the street from Sam Haskins. It turned out that Sam had a deep passion for gospel music and music ministry. Over time, he began to express frustration about the use of his gifts at his church. Things got so frustrating for him that the church terminated him from serving in the ministry without even telling him! As God would have it, we were looking to broaden our music ministry at the Fellowship. There were a number of people who had expressed a desire to sing gospel music, but at the time, we were one-dimensional in our music offering. We sang hymns and high-church music–that was it."

"Oh, yeah," Joe said. "I get my full dose of that every Sunday!!"

"Well, one day while talking with Sam about how to kill weeds in my lawn, I shared our desire to broaden our music offering—to weed out some of the music that simply wasn't connecting," Pastor D continued. "A couple of weeks after that, Sam started visiting the Fellowship. One day, out of the blue, he walked across the street, knocked on my door, and said, 'You didn't ask for this, but if you need a musician to start a gospel choir, I'd be more than willing to do it. Music ministry is a call on my life, and I simply want to serve God this way. You don't have to pay me. This is my offering to God.'"

"Not too long after that, we had our first gospel choir, and Sam has been playing at the Fellowship of the Used-Tos ever since. Shortly into his time with us, he and his wife walked the aisle, indicating their desire to join the church. He said to me, 'Pastor D, I just want to be clear about why we are becoming church members. We are not joining this church because you are our friend and neighbor. We are joining this church because we see the Spirit of God in you, and we see the Spirit of God moving in this church, and we want to be a part of the movement."

"Remember, Joe, this transformation process isn't about you; it's about God fulfilling His will. You are one of the vehicles—a major vehicle—God is using to make it happen. To accomplish what God wants to see happen in your community, town, and region is going to require that you have a whole lot of help. So, my friend, like Nehemiah in the Old Testament, and like Jesus in the New Testament, you need to identify the people who have a mind to work; you need to identify those who will leave everything and follow Jesus!"

"Thanks for the reminder," Joe said. He was a little embarrassed about his earlier attitude, but at the same time he felt a sense of relief. His conversations with Pastor D had a way of shaking him out of a funk whenever he got into one.

Refocusing his energy, he added, "I hear you saying, on the one hand, that it's not about me and, on the other hand, that there is a role I need to play that I may not be playing well now. Obviously, I need some help! Can you give me the basics about how to get people to be committed?"

"Sure, Joe. First, I want to encourage you to recognize that you are in a good place. You've gained some people's commitment already. The struggles and frustrations you have had of late have simply blinded you to that fact. But take your blinders off and see what God is doing. I can already point to some of the people on your supporters list who have shown you they are committed. Kate and David are two clear examples of that.

"Let's look back at Kate and David's road to commitment. I think it'll inform your understanding about how you might reach others. I'm speaking of a process—an art, really—that, when we model it as leaders and as a congregation, will have people running to demonstrate their commitment to God's mission through you and your church."

"Pastor D, I'm not sure how you are going to get a process just from Kate and David. All I did was preach and notice their reactions. I've been preaching every Sunday since and haven't had that kind of response from anyone."

People have to see, hear, and feel the leader's passion and commitment.

"Watch me," Pastor D teased. "I'll bet Kate and David saw, heard, and felt your passion and commitment. How and where do you think they had the opportunity to do so?"

"Well," Joe slowly answered, "one place would be in church when I preached . . . and probably each time I greeted them and talked with them, too."

"Good, Joe. I would add that they observed you closely in the overall worship experience. People in congregations not only pay attention to you in the preaching moment, but they watch you closely in worship. They look at how you worship, what songs you like and don't like. They watch how you act and react. If they see you worship passionately, it gives them permission to worship passionately. If they see you pray like you mean it—in *and* out of worship—it gives them permission to do the same. They look at the dedication you give to each aspect of ministry you are a part of. When someone who hasn't decided whether or not to commit sees, hears, and feels your passion and commitment—and that of the other leaders— that person is more likely to commit," Pastor D stressed.

"I totally get the part about modeling passionate worship, Pastor D. But I'm not sure what that looks like between Sundays."

"Okay, Joe, let me give you an example. When I went to the Fellowship of the Used-Tos, I was assigned as a part-time pastor. I asked the people, 'What does being a part-time pastor mean?' Does that mean that, when I'm in the emergency room with a grieving family, if my twenty hours are up, I have to excuse myself and check back with them the next week?"

Joe laughed at the thought as Pastor D continued.

"They said, 'No, Reverend! It means that we can only pay you a part-time salary.' But, Joe, I didn't approach the pastorate at the Fellowship in a part-time fashion—I was fully committed and fully present with the people of the Fellowship even though I was only being paid $14,000 a year. I didn't know any other way to approach pastoring God's people. I've always been taught and I've always believed that you've got to give God your best. And so I went into it fully committed. Full-steam ahead. Little did I know it, but the congregation was not used to having a fully committed pastor, or fully committed leaders for that matter. I didn't realize that my commitment to the pastoral ministry had caused me to be ingratiated with them; and in turn, several of them began to return the commitment."

"Are you suggesting I work 24/7 as a way of showing my commitment? I'm not sure Janelle will go for that."

"I'm sure she wouldn't, and she shouldn't. That's not what I'm asking you to do. You have to maintain a balanced life in order to be effective in ministry. The point is they have to see you exceed their expectations—and that doesn't mean more time on your part. What it means is that they have to see that you care, that you love, that you have skin in the game. This distinction isn't about what you do, but it is about how you do it. If you do what you do in a way that causes them to feel loved and cared for by you, they will come along with you. If they don't, they will sit back and watch you do everything. They will become takers, not givers. And frankly, Joe, that's not what you want."

"Yeah. I have too much of that now, and I feel like I'm the all-you-can-eat buffet. It also makes me wonder how I can show I care when the largest, most influential family in the congregation is upset with me."

"Say more about that, Joe."

"Well, one Sunday I really got caught up in the preaching moment, and my minister of music, who is the head of the largest family in the church, couldn't hear me when I asked him to stop playing the invitational hymn. I asked twice, and he didn't stop playing; so the third time, I raised my voice and demanded, 'STOP PLAYING THE ORGAN!' I wasn't trying to be disrespectful, but in the moment, all he and the entire congregation could see was this young, new pastor telling this seventy-four-year-old patriarch and musician to shut up. Needless to say, my minister of music, his family, and 75 percent of the congregation were furious with me and have been angry with me for some time. Even though I apologized and sought to get them to understand where I was in the preaching moment, I think I've lost them."

"Not yet," Pastor D said. "Life is full of peaks and valleys. They may be upset with you now, but if you are there for them in their time of need, they will see that you care even when they are furious with you."

"It's interesting you mention that. This morning I got a call that Mr. Wilson's eldest daughter's husband is sick in the hospital."

"Well then, I suggest as soon as we finish this call, you make a beeline to the hospital. By going to pray with the family, you will show that you love and care for them regardless of what they think about you. That's leadership, my friend. And watch—the word will get out that you came, and reconciliation will soon take place."

"Okay, I'll do that as soon as we finish. I wanted to go visit when I heard, but I figured I was the last person they would want to see. But now I think I understand much better how to show the congregation my passion and commitment."

"Good, Joe. But let's go back to Kate and David to explore the next part of how to gain commitment. Do you think either of them saw the hand of God moving in and through you in such a way that it made them want to respond or make a commitment themselves?"

"Well, yes. It was the day that I stole your outline for the 'Why Can't We' sermon."

"Yeah, you still owe me my 10 percent."

"The check's in the mail, Pastor D," Joe laughed. "So, anyway, when Kate came up to me after the sermon, we ended our conversation agreeing that God must be up to something. And when I talked with David after the sermon and told him what I would like him to do, he said yes. He also mentioned how excited he was to see God finally moving through the congregation."

"So with Kate and David," Pastor D summarized, "God revealed to you two people who caught what you were saying and expressed their desire to walk with you along the journey. Almost equally important is the fact that, when talking with them about an opportunity to step up, you gave God the credit. It is really important to set your congregation's expectation on seeing the hand of God. There were two things I did early on in my time with the Fellowship of the Used-Tos that I think really helped with this."

"Well, don't hold out on me, Pastor! What did you do?"

"I can't even tell you the number of times I quoted the words of First Corinthians 2:9, 'What no eye has seen, nor ear heard, nor the human heart conceived, what God has prepared for those who love him.' I would quote this in an effort to raise people's expectations and hopes in God, and to encourage them to see that God was up to something.

People have to see the hand of God moving in and through you as the pastor and through the leaders of your congregation.

"But I also did something else, which leads us to the third aspect of gaining commitment. I would say to our congregation, 'Together we can get there.' That reminded people that church was not about me, the pastor, but that church was supposed to be a collective fellowship moving in the directions that God wanted us to go. There were a few folk who heard that and decided that they needed to invest in God, in themselves, and in the ministry.

Three people in particular—Jim, Harry, and Vanessa—saw the gracious hand of God moving in and around our midst and signed up for one of our first Bible study classes. It was a profound experience. And let me take a second to say how important it is that your people live out spiritual disciplines in their own lives—but we'll get around to that more in our next call. Both Jim and Harry used to have some horrible habits and shameful experiences they had struggled with in the past. Vanessa had broken pieces of her life that she was trying to put back together again. The Bible study demanded a thirty-three-week commitment of time, study, and energy. And during the study, each of them found God moving in mysterious and wonderful ways in their lives. All three experienced personal transformation and began to hear God's call on their lives to commit themselves to start particular ministries."

People have to see that the collective commitment of many can take the congregation farther than the commitment of a few.

"So, are you saying that they began to see God doing with them what they had seen God doing with you?" Joe asked. "Because it sounds to me like they felt the hand of God personally positioning them to lead people with broken lives to healing and wholeness in Jesus's name."

"You got it, Joe. Jim and Harry soon answered God's call for them to be street pastors; they would hang out on the street corners with the drunks, addicts, and homeless folk and personally invite them to start new lives with Jesus Christ. Vanessa sensed a call that she was to help homeless people find a warm place to stay. Soon thereafter, she started the Fellowship's transitional housing ministry. Sixteen years later, her leadership and labor have caused hundreds of people to encounter Christ and find a warm place to stay until permanent residency can be found. Vanessa, Jim, and Harry encouraged each other and others—like Nehemiah had done. Come, let us rise up and build! And they've been doing it ever since."

"Jim, Harry, and Vanessa's story reminds me of Jesus calling Simon to be one of his disciples," Joe said, before taking a sip from his cup of soda. He tore open the small bag of chips that was his lunch for the day and added, "Not that I'm comparing you to Jesus, Pastor D."

Pastor D said quickly, "Thank you, Joe—'cause I'm not Jesus!"

"I know, I know!" Joe said with a chuckle as he tried not to choke on the chips he was trying to swallow.

"Okay, so, tell me what you have on your mind, Joe."

"Well, as you know, Simon Peter had fished all night long and had caught nothing. It was quitting time, and he was washing his nets. He was ready to get on with the rest of his day, and Jesus said, 'Let's go back out for a catch.' Simon says, 'Master, we've fished all night long, but if you say so, we'll cast out our net.' And when they go back out, suddenly they catch more fish than they can comprehend. So many, in fact, they have to go get a second boat to haul in all the fish. Seeing the hand of God move before him and having witnessed for himself the power and passion of Jesus was enough for Peter to give his commitment to Christ. And it also required collective effort to get all those fish safely to shore."

"Kinda like Kate and David, huh?" prompted Pastor D. "Worship was too much for you by yourself, so God used you to bring along people to help you with the process."

"Ohhhhh, I get it," said Joe.

"Well, get this, Joe. You've also gotta help others see what they can *be* and not just what is. This is a very important lesson in gaining commitment. Didn't you do that with Kate and David?"

"If I did, I didn't know about it. Honestly, I'm not really sure what you mean."

"Okay, let me use the story out of Luke 5 that you mentioned to illustrate my point. As soon as Simon Peter saw the hand of God move through Jesus, he immediately saw how awesome Jesus was and how unawesome and unworthy he himself was. His response was to fall on his knees and cry out, 'Go away from me, Lord, for I am a sinful man!'"[12]

"In other words," Joe interrupted, "I'm not good enough to be in your presence. I'm not good enough to hang out with you. I'm not good enough to lead."

"Right, Joe, but look at what Jesus does. Jesus immediately comes back with the response, 'Don't be afraid.' In other words, don't let that stuff get to you. Don't let your unawesomeness, unworthiness, or feelings of inadequacy get to you. Don't let your struggles with low self-esteem deter you. I'll take care of that. Let me show you that I have something far greater for you to do than just catch these fish. From now on you will catch men. Jesus had to help Peter see that he was not just a sinner, but that he was a sinner *saved by the grace of God*—the God who would lead multitudes of other sinners to experience salvation through Jesus Christ.

"This is so important in gaining commitment from people who God is calling to lead, Joe," explained Pastor D, "because so many people, like Simon Peter, feel unworthy and incapable of doing something mighty for the Lord. And if no one has ever bothered to ask them to do the unthinkable, that further adds to their feeling of inadequacy. I would imagine that as Kate heard your sermon, those walls of inadequacy, or even low self-esteem, fell. She can't stop asking questions now, can she?"

"You're right," said Joe.

"And, with David you asked him to do the unthinkable. I'll bet you nobody had ever asked him to serve in the capacity in which he finds himself now. He's like Simon Peter on the water. You've asked him, and he said yes—but he's got to be a little intimidated and afraid. But possibility and love conquer fear. We offer both when we help people see something greater than themselves. And you and Kate and David will need to do this in order to gain the commitment of others."

"It's like you're in my head and in my church, Pastor D."

"The longer you hang around me, the more I will be!" Pastor D joked.

"And now I'm starting to think I have a better understanding of something that happened here at the church not too long ago. I asked a man named Daryl if he could see himself as a developer of leaders. I'd been watching him in a number of settings at the church and his ability to draw people to a cause was magnetic. He's new to the church, but he said yes. One of the most powerful moments of the first leadership development team meeting—just last week, actually—was when Daryl stood up and said, 'I need y'all to be patient with me. This is the first time in my forty-five years of life and in any church experience where anybody has ever asked me to lead anything, so bear with me. I may make some mistakes, but in the end, we're gonna be alright.' And by the end of the meeting, we knew were not just alright, we were *overwhelmed* by the awesome presence of God."

Leaders see in others what can be, not just what is.

"Yes! What a powerful testimony, Joe! In gaining commitment, leaders see in others not just what is, but what can be. A spiritual leader helps people to see not just what they are presently but what they can become. When I can get somebody to see that there is more to him or her than what is, then he or she is going to be positively persuaded to follow—particularly if I keep pointing to the God who keeps working miracles in our lives."

"So, ultimately, you are saying that gaining commitment is really about getting people to commit to doing whatever God would have them do as a part of this body of Christ," said Joe.

"You, my friend, are catching on quickly," Pastor D affirmed. Realizing how much time had flown by, he added, "But let me do a quick rundown of the fifth and sixth points so you can get on with your visit to Mr. Wilson's family."

"Yeah, you're right about that," Joe said. He had almost forgotten himself in the moment. "But I know I need you to cover those last two points before I go anywhere!"

"Okay, I won't take but a minute," Pastor D said. "If you and your leaders want to gain commitment, you all must give clear calls to action. Now, follow me here—because I'm not talking about vision. I'm talking about giving clear calls to action. We will get to vision before we finish our mentoring time together. It's difficult for people to commit to something that is unclear. When you talked with David about how you wanted him to serve and what was to be done with worship, that was a clear call to action. And when Kate said she wanted to be part of the journey as a result of the sermon, we know there was a clear call to action in the sermon."

"And," Joe began, crumpling his empty chip bag and hooking it successfully into his wastebasket, "Jesus issued a very clear call to action when he said 'from now on you will be catching people.'[13] I get that, Pastor D. But how do you handle people who seem to refuse to follow a clear call to action?"

"Who's on your mind, Joe?"

"Well, James and Julie are. I mentioned before that they haven't been enjoying the deterioration of their singular influence. And it all came to a head the other day when Daryl insisted that Julie no longer keep the church's financial information and checkbook at her house. He asked her to return all financial items and records to the church where they belong. We definitely haven't gained James and Julie's commitment. In fact, I don't think a single one of the points you laid out has stuck with them. They don't want to go where God is leading us. They don't want to be a part of a leadership collective. They aren't seeing in others what can be, and others can't see, hear, or feel their passion and commitment to God's mission. The only passion and commitment they have at this point is to control how money is spent at the church. They actually think that if they control the money, they control the church."

> Remove leaders who aren't aligned or attuned to God's vision for the congregation.

"Joe, it sounds like James and Julie's season at the Church of the Last Chance is about to come to an end. You should prepare for this with the knowledge that the ending of seasons can be a good thing. Good for those who have to leave because they can start afresh, and good for the church because it will no longer be limited by people who are no longer supposed to be there.

"And here's the last thing, Joe: if you want to gain commitment from your folk, say to them every now and then, 'Look, the only thing holding Last Chance back from accomplishing our goals is us!'"

"Say more," Joe beckoned. His experiences so far at Last Chance sometimes left him feeling like the things holding them back were James, Julie, and the Wilsons!

> People realize that the only thing holding us back from accomplishing God's goals is us.

"If you and your key leaders are seeking to gain the commitment of others and are doing everything that we've talked about, the only thing holding you back is you . . . your fears, frustrations, doubts, procrastinations, and other human reactions to change. Time can become another limiting factor."

"Well, I definitely agree with that part," Joe said. "One man told me once that between working two jobs and meeting the obligations of being a husband and a father, Sunday worship was the only commitment he could give to the church."

"Yes, and depending on where you live, the demands on people's schedules can be so intense that the free time people have is given to those things they *must* do and those things that bring them pleasure.

"In Columbia, for example, there is a culture that works 24/7 and seems to build in little time for anything else," Pastor D emphasized. "Add to this the amount of extracurricular activities that growing families are engaged in—soccer, basketball, swimming, what have you—and time constraints become worse. If church and community service do not naturally flow within the culture of the community in which you live, or if they are not relevant to the culture in which you live, gaining commitment will be extremely difficult.

"When you are talking about gaining commitment so that the transforming nature of what happens in worship spills out into the street, you have to have your act together. People need to see where they can connect with your congregation in ways that meet their needs and allow them to grow in relationship with Jesus and the world. Are you with me?"

"I am . . . I am." As usual, another conversation with Pastor D had gotten Joe's wheels spinning. "This has been a really helpful call, Pastor. Thank you."

"Joe, you sound so much better than when you first picked up the phone. Let me leave you with this: Leaders assure followers that they are in it and committed for the long haul. Both the people in Nehemiah's story, and Simon Peter, James, and John were bolstered by the fact that their leaders were making long-term commitments. When gaining commitment, it is vitally important for leaders to communicate that they will be very present in the lives of those rising into new leadership. Be present with your people—especially your twelve game changers. Let them know you aren't going anywhere and that you are with them for the long haul.

"Go forward and do great things, Joe. And get off the phone so you can get over to that hospital and start gaining commitment! Holla at you soon!"

And with that, the two hung up the phone.

What had started as a nightmarish day for Joe, now beamed with possibilities, just as the sun started breaking through the clouds outside. As he began to relinquish his frustrations through prayer and simply encouraging himself, Joe began to feel that this transformation process was becoming more and more possible. He sensed the Spirit of God within him saying, "Oh yes, it is possible. You can do all things through Christ Jesus who gives you strength!"

How to Gain Commitment:

1. People have to see, hear, and feel the leader's passion and commitment.

2. People have to see the hand of God moving in and through you as the pastor and through the leaders of your congregation.

3. People have to see that the collective commitment of many can take the congregation farther than the commitment of a few.

4. Leaders see in others what can be, not just what is.

5. Leaders give clear calls to action.

6. Remove leaders who aren't aligned or attuned to God's vision for the congregation.

7. People realize that the only thing holding us back from accomplishing God's goals is us.

Chapter 12
Soaking Decisions and Actions in Prayer
Priority. Pervasive. Personal.

As soon as he got off the mentoring call, Joe cleared his calendar for the afternoon and headed to the hospital.

As he walked into the health center lobby he prayed, *God, hear your servant when I ask you to please be present with us at the hospital. Not only do I ask for Andrew to receive your healing, but Lord, please help Mr. Wilson's entire family—particularly Sophia—to see You more than they see me. God, allow me to be a vehicle of your comforting spirit. In Jesus's name I pray, Amen.*

Just as Joe finished his prayer, Sophia's face appeared before him. The last time he had seen her, she had been angry and upset because of her father's feelings of humiliation in worship. Joe hoped that this encounter would lead to a more positive ending.

"Pastor Joe! What are you doing here?" Sophia asked. "I didn't expect to see you."

"Well, I heard through the grapevine that Andrew became suddenly ill, and I wanted to check on him and you to make sure everything was alright."

"You didn't have to do that," Sophia said with thoughts of their last encounter in her mind.

"Yes, I did," Joe replied. "At the end of the day, whether we have differences or disagreements or fights or whatever, I'm your pastor. I love you guys, and I desire your well-being. How's Andrew doing?"

Sophia, now feeling somewhat uncomfortable, shared with Joe about her husband's bouts with diabetes. Joe learned that Andrew hadn't been taking his insulin consistently, and it had caught up with him. Fortunately, doctors had assured them that, with a few days' rest, Andrew would be able to return to work.

"That's good news, Sophia! I want to go in and pray with Andrew, but before I do, is there anything that you need? Anything I can get for you or that the church can do for you?"

"No, thanks. We're alright. But I really do appreciate your prayers and your presence. It's really nice of you to stop by and check on us."

Joe went into Andrew's room and saw that he looked as surprised as his wife had.

"Hey, brother, I just came in to pray with you. We can't afford you surprising us like this!" Joe teased. "How are you feeling?"

"A little weak, Pastor Joe, but hanging in there. I didn't expect to see you here. I figured after all the arguments we've had about music that you wouldn't make time for us . . ."

Joe assured Andrew, as he had done with Sophia, of his love and care for them. After the three had prayed together, Sophia walked Joe to the entrance of the hospital. She talked briefly about her family and her dreams and even shared her hopes for the Church of the Last Chance. She embraced Joe before he left and sincerely thanked him for coming by. Her expression of gratitude was so strong, it left Joe surprised.

As he drove home, he reflected on the lesson from Pastor D that he had just lived out. He knew he was on the way to gaining the commitment of at least one, just by showing that he cared.

The next day, instead of going to the office, Joe had breakfast at the popular neighborhood diner. Many of his members frequented the diner and raved about how good the breakfast was. Joe thought it was the perfect place to begin his community inspection. Since Gary had grown up in the neighborhood, Joe invited him to join in.

As they settled in, Gary ordered his favorite—a Western omelet— while Joe ordered toast and tea. Breakfast wasn't Joe's favorite meal of the day, so he started off light.

"Thanks for agreeing to meet me on such short notice," Joe began.

"Not a problem, Pastor Joe. Glad I could make it. And when you told me we would be meeting here, I couldn't wait. This is one of my favorite hangouts," Gary said with a smile. "It brings back a lot of good memories of my grandfather bringing me here as a kid. He'd always order oatmeal, and I'd always get the omelet."

"You know a lot about this neighborhood then, don't you?" Joe asked.

"Yeah, you could say I know a little bit. Except for a stint in the military, this has been home to me for most of my life. The place has changed a lot since I was younger. You could say that I'm a part of the old crowd even though I'm barely fifty. The main industry here used to be farming— I remember milking my grandfather's cows—but with the suburbs expanding the way they have, farmlands are now housing developments. Some country roads now feel more like highways. Fields that I used to run through and watch horses graze in are now populated by single-family homes. In some ways, the community is searching for an identity. A good number of people I knew growing up aren't here anymore. We have a mix of people. Some, like me, who grew up here, people who have been around for a while, and then new waves of folks coming in all the time."

Gary shook his head wistfully. As they continued to talk, Joe could see that the some of the changes taking place in Hopeville had left Gary feeling discouraged. He could also see that Gary's concern for the town and its people ran very deep.

"Gary, it sounds like you can help me and the congregation make some stronger and deeper connections with the community. In my short time here, I've gotten the impression that Last Chance has very little connection with the people who live here. But I've been watching you, and you seem to engage very comfortably with all kinds of people in the congregation. And at least half the people in the diner with us have stopped by to say hello in the past fifteen minutes! I can't help but wonder if you would be willing to partner with me to help our congregation better connect with this community."

"Well, maybe, Pastor Joe. I'm a great supporter of your leadership so far, and I believe you have the passion to lead the congregation to be better. But I guess I have to hear more about what you are actually asking me to do before I commit to anything . . ."

"Of course, of course . . . But you pretty much know the story already! We have no formal connections to the community. We are not connected to any community associations; no neighborhood groups meet at the church; and members aren't asking any community organizations to be a part of what we are up to. If we are going to make a significant difference in people's lives, we have to go beyond our walls and into the community. I am asking you to use your relational gifts to help us conduct a community inspection. The inspection involves identifying the influencers in the community to conduct one-on-one interviews and town hall–style meetings. At the end of the inspection, we should have built some good relationships with key people and also have an idea of where the community wants to partner for change."

Joe saw a light in Gary's eyes that he hadn't seen before.

"I'm in, Pastor Joe," he said. "What do we do first?"

Joe breathed a sigh of relief and began to lay out his plan. As the two men continued to talk and share their ideas, Joe thanked God for linking him with Gary that morning.

Over the next couple of weeks, Gary and Joe threw themselves into one-on-one relational meetings in the community. They met business owners, schoolteachers, police officers, and even the "mayors" that Pastor D had talked about. At the same time, Joe was praying hard for resolution to the James and Julie drama and for God to help him gain the commitment of much-needed leaders. Joe was also pouring himself into worship and the two strong leaders, Kate and David, he was being blessed by. Since his visit to the hospital, the music battle seemed to be at a ceasefire. Even so, Joe woke up one morning with the overwhelming realization that the work they were doing needed supernatural undergirding in order for them to make real progress.

The transformational work before him was so great that Joe knew he couldn't do it by himself or even with the small group of leaders he had assembled. He needed God to breathe into the Church of the Last Chance so mightily that more people would be inspired to join in the work with him. He needed God to send people to support the work that He had placed before him. Simply put, the Holy Ghost was telling Joe they needed a prayer revival in the church.

Initially, Joe said to God, Is this even more work I have to do? I'm too tired to do what I'm doing now. But as he continued his quiet time with God that morning, God revealed to him that if he didn't pray for this, there was no way he'd be able to get done all the things he needed to get done. In fact, without a more intentional church-wide prayer practice, transformation would be impossible.

The first thing he did that morning was to send Pastor D an email:

Good Morning, Pastor D,
Things here are going well, but I woke up with a revelation that we needed a prayer revival in order to really make progress. Do you have any ideas? When is the next time we can talk?
Joe

Two days later, the connection was made. As Joe pulled into the parking lot of the diner that afternoon and saw Pastor D's car already there, a spirit of gratitude washed over him. Walking in and seeing his mentor provided Joe with additional encouragement and reassurance.

"Pastor D, thanks for getting me on your calendar so quickly."

"When the Holy Spirit is moving, you move with it. Let's get down to business."

The waitress brought water and menus to the table as Pastor D began.

"The great opportunity you have as a congregational and community leader, Joe, is the ability to invite others into the wonderful discipline of prayer. But you've got to be engrossed in the discipline before any invitation can be extended. Remember, you can't lead where you won't go, and you can't teach what you don't know."

"I have been really intentional about daily worship," Joe replied, "and I've found that it sets me up in an attitude of prayer for the rest of the day. I wouldn't have made it this far without it!"

"That's great, Joe. You'd be surprised how many pastors don't pray enough or at all."

The waitress approached their table ready to take their order. The two men quickly ordered their food before getting right back to business.

"Before you can call your congregation into a season of revival," said Pastor D, "you've got to live out prayer and model it. As you and your congregation seek to join in the move of God, you and your people must lean heavily and intentionally on prayer. Congregational and community transformation is not possible unless prayer is at the center of what you do. Prayer is the foundation of spiritual discipline!"

"I agree," said Joe. "I have been at my strongest, and I've noticed my lay leadership has been at its strongest, when we've been engaged in prayer together."

"I'm sure you've realized by this point," Pastor D continued, "that not everyone knows how to pray. Jesus acknowledged this in the Sermon on the Mount when he taught his disciples and the crowds how to pray. He taught them the Lord's Prayer as a foundation, and so the basis of modeling prayer for others ought to be in the Lord's Prayer."

"We do that every first Sunday," Joe retorted.

"Good, but are you using it as a teaching moment, or does your congregation go on autopilot?"

"I'm not sure what you mean . . . We say the Lord's Prayer like everybody else does," Joe replied. "How do you use it as a teaching moment?"

"You can use the Lord's Prayer and other types of prayer to fully engage the congregation in the power of prayer," Pastor D explained. "Before we begin praying anything as a group, the worship leader sets the stage for the prayer by emphasizing its importance and encouraging the congregation to engage."

"We aren't doing that right now," Joe admitted, "but it would be easy for us to begin."

"Joe, there are a number of resources you can lean on to learn about the Lord's Prayer and its blessing to us all. *Praying to Change Your Life* by Suzette Caldwell and F.O.C.U.S. by Tyrone Gordon are two books you might want to start with. As you're incorporating the use of the Lord's Prayer and its wonderful facets, you also want to take steps to develop prayer as a discipline in your congregation. That requires teaching and modeling prayer so that it is pervasive, personal, ever present, and a priority. When you focus on those four things, prayer gets into the fabric of your congregation."

When the food arrived, Joe said the quickest grace in history and dug in as if he hadn't eaten in three days. Pastor D nibbled a little and kept pressing forward.

"Dennis Blackwell, a great pastor and friend of mine, really helped me and the Fellowship wrap our arms around this. We invited him one year to lead a prayer weekend at the Fellowship, and he encouraged our congregation to set aside a day of the week at the Fellowship for nothing but prayer. Wednesday is now that day for us. No church meetings happen at the Fellowship on Wednesday, no choir rehearsals—nothing but prayer. Wednesday is a day of intentional prayer: we have noonday prayer and evening study and prayer every Wednesday.

Make Prayer a Priority

"I've seen lives change because of this intentional emphasis on prayer. Kids have overcome cancer, and young people on their way to jail have seen their sentences terminated because of this prayer time. Illnesses have disappeared. Jobs have been secured, and jobs have popped up because of this prayer time. The pastors and staff are an integral part of this prayer time because it's not enough for leaders to call for prayer; people need to see leaders praying and be with you while you're praying. Joe, when prayer is a priority at the Church of the Last Chance, you will see God leading, growing, and using the church to be a transforming agent in the neighborhood."

As Pastor D was talking, he noticed Joe getting more stressed and uncomfortable. He had stopped eating and instead was using his fork to push his mashed potatoes around his plate. Knowing the pressure that Joe was under, Pastor D immediately sought to address it.

"I'm not trying to give you an extra task, Joe. I'm seeking to help you lay a foundation. I want to encourage you to discover that the most important work you need to be doing right now is engaging yourself and your congregation in prayer. Then you will know what each day should look like with respect to work. Then you will keep yourself balanced. Your congregation will discover the same. Then as a congregation, you will know how to move forward and how to live out God's plans and visions for you.

"When we started," Pastor D reminded Joe, "one of your tasks was to put together an intercessory prayer team—a group dedicated to praying for specific people's needs and specific issues. How are they doing?"

"Well," Joe said, "I have a team, but they don't seem to be interested in praying for the transformation of the church. They meet regularly, but they only seem to be interested in praying for the hemorrhoids and lost cats of people they know."

"Hemorrhoids and lost cats? That's great lunchtime conversation," Pastor D said, shaking his head. After a moment he shrugged his shoulders and chomped down on his juicy sandwich once again.

"Sorry to disturb your lunch, Pastor D. I was just trying to paint you an accurate picture of how impotent our prayer team is."

"No prob. Humor is good for the soul. What you are talking about shows why so many congregations are lost, dying, or irrelevant. They have lost touch with the power of prayer. Prayer for them has become mundane, back burner, rote. Locked into speaking instead of listening, and tied down by traditionalism that doesn't allow one to freely communicate with the living God. As a result, the enthusiasm that prayer can produce is missing. In fact, many in these nonthriving churches don't believe that God is still speaking or listening. They also don't believe that prayer changes things— situations, circumstances, realities, attitudes, and so on. It sounds like your people have a limited understanding of the power of prayer and its role in transforming all situations. And you might need to reconstruct your prayer team—but we'll get to that in a minute.

"For now, people in your congregation need to see and feel that prayer is valued and that it is the driving engine for your ministry with and to the world. People need to know and understand that prayer is foundational. You need to provide outward and visible signs of this."

"Aren't we doing that already? Isn't praying in worship an outward and visible sign?" Joe asked.

"It is if it is done authentically and enthusiastically. But even so, that is not enough. There are many different ways to communicate the priority of prayer. Regardless of the vehicles you use to create outward and visible signs, keep these things in mind. First, before Jesus ministered to people in the public domain, he intentionally prayed privately so that God could direct his daily actions and movements. You are doing this already—but you have to be sure your key leaders are doing it, too.

"Secondly, be sure that your outward and visible prayer is designed to engage people wherever they are in their faith journey. It should also encourage them to develop and deepen their prayer life. Too often we allow those who love to hear themselves talk dominate a prayer experience—this can turn off the very people who come hungry to experience a guiding word from God. The great mystic, Howard Thurman, once said that 80 percent of prayer is listening."

"So, if I'm following you," Joe checked, "Your designating Wednesdays as a day of prayer is an outward and visible sign of the priority of prayer in your congregation."

"Yes, Joe. It helps us show the priority of prayer, and it also helps make it more pervasive."

Make Prayer Pervasive

"As I said a minute ago, prayer needs to be at the foundation of everything the congregation does, and it needs to be found in everything the congregation does. But for that to happen, you've got to develop a team of the right people who see prayer as their number-one priority in ministry. You need to prayerfully develop, equip, and empower this team to pray for, teach, and equip every ministry team within the congregation on how to create an environment where prayer informs every decision and expression of that ministry.

"So, would this team be responsible for leading the prayer revival?" Joe asked, hoping that was one thing he could take off his overflowing plate.

"Yes, Joe, but you have to be sure that this team feels your heart—and you have to lead by example. Once you sense your prayer team is with you, be sure you organize the team around two functions: intercessory prayer, for one; and two, empowering and encouraging others to pray. The intercessory function involves praying for specific needs and desires in the congregation—both personal and corporate in nature. On the personal side, every congregation is filled with people who have personal needs: people who are sick, unemployed, struggling in relationships—"

"And don't forget those with hemorrhoids and lost cats!" Joe laughed.

"Please don't remind me! On the corporate side, it is critical that all your ministries and decisions are bathed in prayer: worship, small groups, serving teams, decisions about building, spending, staff, etcetera. Are you with me so far?"

"Yes, but can you be more specific about what each function looks like?"

"Sure, Joe. Part of your team needs to be intercessors spending their time solely on praying for God's deliverance on behalf of individuals, the congregation, the community, and the world. These intercessors need to be people who you know can get a prayer through because their tenacity and commitment to prayer defines their very being. You will know who these people are when you encounter them. They may be the first people who show up at your outward and visible prayer opportunities."

"I think I get it. But that means I do have some work to do. I have to get busy creating Last Chance's first outward and visible prayer opportunity."

"Yes, but that really doesn't need to be a huge undertaking. People who are passionate about prayer only have to be asked once. The other part of your team encourages and empowers ministry leaders to pray and to create an environment where prayer informs every decision and expression of their ministry and lives. People who you may think are great prayer warriors are not always the best teachers of prayer and need to be equipped in how to invite and teach others how to pray. These empowering encouragers need to learn about various styles of prayer, and they need to be daily worshippers who can testify that a variety of methods for communicating with God can produce divine results. We're all different, so we are not all going to pray in the same way—your team and your congregation need to understand that. Also, these daily worshippers need to be able to welcome people who are at beginner levels of prayer in ways that aren't threatening or intimidating. And they have to work with those folks so that they develop rich and deep prayer lives. This function must be simple in nature. If it is too complex or perceived as too difficult, it won't work."

"Pastor D, how do I find those people?"

"In my experience, God reveals them. This whole prayer thing requires divine intervention, and we must depend on the Divine to raise up the right people. You can start by getting the word out that you are looking for people who are interested in doing this."

"Got it," Joe said. "And doing that provides another outward and visible sign of the priority of prayer."

"Absolutely—you've got it. Joe, I know you are already carrying a lot of stress, so don't freak out about what I'm about to say. Establishing this sort of prayer team represents a lot of hard work and discipline. But it will be the greatest investment you make in your ministry. You've got to be very discerning and determined to see this process through. And you have to constantly evaluate its effectiveness. One of the mistakes that we made at the Fellowship was allowing too much time to elapse between evaluations of this important ministry.

"Evaluate prayer?" Joe asked, more than a little confused. "What does that even look like?"

"We evaluate the prayer ministry by gathering responses to some key questions: Are more people coming to pray? Is each ministry making decisions that have been informed by prayer? Are more people praying with others? Are more people becoming prayer leaders? Are there more testimonies about where God is leading people through prayer and how God is answering prayers?

"But, however difficult and labor intensive this effort is, your investment in making prayer pervasive in your congregation is the key to your congregation's transformation and its long-term vitality within the community."

Just then the waitress stopped by with the dessert menu.

"Would you like some dessert, Joe, or is your stomach already upset?" Pastor D asked.

"I think I'll pass," Joe said, holding his stomach. Pastor D said, "I think I won't!" and proceeded to order his favorite, German chocolate cake.

"So, Joe, we've talked about how to teach and model prayer in the congregation by making prayer a priority and making it pervasive in the life of your congregation. Do you have any questions about either of those before we move on?"

"No, I think I get it."

"Okay. Well, as you are moving from this point, you want to engage people in making prayer personal. One of the best strategies in making prayer personal is developing prayer partnerships. Do you have a prayer partner, Joe?"

"I think so, but can you explain it to me just in case I'm missing something, Pastor D?"

Make Prayer Personal

"Sure. A prayer partner is someone who helps you stay focused on God and your spiritual journey. Prayer partners hold each other accountable to God and one another. They eliminate spiritual loneliness and isolation. They keep you from stressing out and losing your mind. They keep each other centered in the Holy Spirit in the midst of the routine, challenges, demands, crises, and trials of life.

"Okay, well then, Janelle and I are prayer partners—we pray together every day. But I think I need even more help."

"It's good you recognize that. You don't need to dump all this church stuff on your wife. You need to preserve that relationship as best as you can without allowing the mistress called church to get in between you. Church can be viewed as a mistress, you know."

"Ha! No doubt," agreed Joe. "Were you listening in on the last conversation I had with my wife?"

"Been there, brother man, done that. We have to have prayer partnerships outside of our immediate family. Personally, prayer partnerships have blessed me immensely. They have saved my life. They help me hold my tongue when I need to and unleash my tongue when I need to. They have helped me know my healing is coming. They help me stay connected to God, to the people I serve, and to the connections that God is calling me to make on that day. They keep me from losing my mind. They help me in decision making. God uses them to impart greater wisdom to me. And beyond that, God opens doors of possibility as a result of these partnerships.

"So, how do I find another one?" Joe asked.

"With great prayer, wisdom, and discernment. Ask God to connect you with the person He wants you to partner. Sometimes, God will send you someone. For example, on the first day of the year, in 2005, I received a phone call at seven thirty in the morning from a colleague, who asked if he could pray for me. I said sure. Afterward, I thanked him. The next morning at seven thirty, he called me again and asked the same thing. This time, in addition to him praying for me, I prayed for him. Little did I know that God was forming a prayer partnership between him and others that has continued to this day. Don't take this God-centered matching process lightly, because in prayer, we become vulnerable and transparent, and we are called to become authentic. In prayer, many of the deepest, darkest, and most private secrets of our lives are exposed. So we ought not pick a prayer partner just to have one. We need to receive a prayer partner that God has chosen for us."

"How many prayer partners do I need?"

"As many as God creates. I have three critical prayer partnerships. The first is with Nia, my wife of twenty-five years. If we're married, we need to be praying with our spouses. It will help strengthen this primary relationship, which, sad to say, is prime for attack. Second and third are with clergy colleagues and small clergy groups. So, seven days a week, I am covered by my wife's prayers and by the prayers of my other prayer partners."

"Wow. I thought you were just going to help me plan a prayer revival, and now I have to make prayer a priority through outward and visible signs, make prayer pervasive through creating a prayer team, and make prayer personal through something like prayer partnerships. It seems like every time I talk to you there's something new I have to add to the list! I hope there's not too much more . . ."

"Take a deep breath, Joe, there is only one more thing for you to make note of, but it is vitally important. Making prayer more powerful within your congregation happens through the discipline of fasting. The biblical story of King Jehoshaphat in Second Chronicles 20 demonstrates this. When King Jehoshaphat was attacked by enemies on every side, he called his people into a time of fasting, prayer, and worship. You have discovered already, Joe, that in the transformation process, the devil is always busy. And sometimes this adversary gets fiercer at particular times. We need power far greater than our own to get through some of these situations. With Jehoshaphat, in the midst of the fast, God answered his prayer. God told his people, 'The battle is not yours; it's the Lord's.' Then God proceeded to destroy their enemies.

Make Prayer More Powerful

"Fasting is a spiritual discipline practiced in Scripture particularly when people needed God to intercede in a pressing situation beyond their control. For example, the man with the epileptic son in Mark chapter 9, needed the disciples to cast out the demon of epilepsy from his son. The disciples weren't able to cast out the demon because they were not practicing the disciplines of prayer and fasting. Jesus said that demonic attacks like these can only be cast out through prayer and fasting."

"Pastor D, I have to admit I've never been in a congregation that fasted, and I haven't studied anything about it either. Is it just about avoiding certain foods?"

"Yes, in part, but it's much more than that too—because fasting without prayer is just starving yourself to death. The discipline of fasting involves denying or depriving ourselves of something we crave, covet, or need. Then we replace that need or desire with a focused attention on God and on listening for how God is going to respond to the situation we are fasting about. Oftentimes, the deprivation involves food. However, nowadays people who are fasting deprive themselves of television, computers, sex, spending money, or any number of things. Prayer is critical to the fasting period, though. Without prayer, we cannot hear from God regarding the focus of the fast."

"Okay, I see," said Joe. Just then, the waitress arrived with Pastor D's German chocolate cake, and as he dug in for his first bite, Pastor D continued to lay out the basics of fasting.

"There are various types of fasts in the Bible. If you are interested in learning more about them, I'd recommend Elmer Towns's book, *Fasting for*

Spiritual Breakthrough. There are various fasting timelines. Sometimes seven days, fourteen days, or twenty-one days. Sometimes even as little as one day or as much as forty days! John Wesley required those in his circles to fast with him every Wednesday and Friday."

"So, how long should we fast at Last Chance? I'm concerned about how long I can make it since it is my first time, and it will no doubt be our congregation's first time," Joe confessed.

"You and God need to determine that. The key to fasting is identifying the situation or circumstance in your congregation and community where you need a spiritual breakthrough into a more blessed and balanced life. I hope you get the picture that transformation cannot take place unless there is prayer and fasting. Certain obstacles in our communities cannot be overcome unless there's prayer and fasting."

"But how can I roll something like that out at Last Chance? It sounds pretty drastic."

"You and your leaders must lead it and encourage others to participate. When we fast at the Fellowship, I always distribute the details of the fast during worship two Sundays before the fast is to take place. On the handout, I include the dates, spiritual focus, scripture, instructions, and resources. If your fast involves food, you need to include directions for people to seek the advice of their doctor because some people in your congregation must eat particular diets or on certain schedules for medical reasons.

"Leading the fast also includes being authentic about what is happening with you personally in the midst of the time of prayer and fasting. When prayer is pervasive, personal, more powerful, and a priority, your church will become a powerful vessel for healing and wholeness in your community."

Pastor D glanced down at his phone with a start. Being as engrossed as he was in their conversation, he had lost track of the time.

"Sorry, Joe, I have to take off. But let's schedule some time for us to talk about how to bring the other spiritual disciplines to life at Last Chance."

"Thanks so much for making time to see me, Pastor D. I have a plan for moving forward, prayerfully. I wish I could put 100 percent of my time here because I do believe God will bless it."

As they were walking to the car, Pastor D said, "Look for ways to start adding prayer in the midst of everything you do and asking God to reveal to you potential prayer leaders. It shouldn't be another task; it should be a natural part of your daily and weekly rhythm."

"Okay, got it," Joe replied. "I'll make two announcements this Sunday: Tuesday will be a day set aside for prayer, and I'll start asking for volunteers who feel compelled to pray for the congregation and the community."

"Sounds like a great start, Joe. We'll talk soon."

Prayer Ministry:

1. Make prayer a priority

2. Make prayer pervasive:

     a. Prayer intercessors

     b. Prayer encouragers and empowerers

3. Make prayer personal (prayer partnerships)

4. Make prayer more powerful (fasting)

Chapter 13
Setting Your Rhythm

Pray. Live in the Word. Sabbath.

That evening, Joe called the head of his prayer ministry.

"Barbara," he began, "you know I really appreciate all the praying you and your team have done and are doing. How's it going? What's currently on your list?"

Joe had a plan and thought he would start by seeing whether or not the prayer ministry could possibly make the changes necessary.

"We are doing well," answered Barbara. "Our list of prayer concerns is about the same as last week. Our sick and shut-in list hasn't changed. And, of course, we still need to pray for peace in all the war-torn areas of the world."

"That's great, Barbara." Joe paused for a moment, unsure about how to proceed. "Listen, I'm wondering if the team has been able to incorporate praying for God to transform our congregation and community like we discussed last time. And I'm wondering if you've heard a word from the Lord about who should be on your team."

"Pastor Joe," said Barbara slowly, "you know, we've never prayed about things like that before." She hesitated and then continued. "We talked about it and decided that since we didn't specifically know what to ask for . . . that we would wait until you had a more specific prayer request."

Joe was glad that he wasn't meeting with Barbara in person or she surely would have seen the grave disappointment on his face. He knew right then that he would have to find a different place for Barbara to serve in order to make room for powerful prayer leadership. He had learned from Pastor D that the best way to transition leaders was to help them discover their giftedness and calling and to allow that to inform where they might serve next.

"Barbara, I appreciate all that you have been doing and are doing for the prayer ministry. But I have a question for you: is this really what you want to do at Last Chance? Do you feel called to it? Or is it just something that you've done for a while and gotten comfortable with?"

The silence at the other end of the phone unnerved Joe a bit, and he felt compelled to explain himself further. Quickly he said, "I'm asking these questions of you and each person who is serving in a leadership position in the church because I want to be sure that each person is serving where God wants them to and not just in a place where there has been a need. Do you understand what I'm saying?"

"Yes, Pastor Joe. But I must admit, I'm a little surprised. I haven't had a pastor ever ask me those kinds of questions."

"Well, time and giftedness are precious, Barbara. And when they are properly invested, everybody is blessed. In my simple observations of you, it seems like two of your strongest spiritual gifts are compassion and serving. Would you agree or disagree?"

"I would definitely agree! You are so right," she agreed. "I care about helping those who are hurting, and I want to do what I can to serve them."

"So, if I suggested another place of leadership for you where those gifts are needed, would you be open to making a shift? Personally, I believe you'd be great at being part of a Stephen Ministry at Last Chance. Have you heard of Stephen Ministries before?"

"I have," Barbara said. "But I didn't think it would be possible to start one here—I didn't think we had the resources. But I'd love to work to get one off the ground."

"Count it done," Pastor Joe said. "Let's plan some time to talk about steps we need to take to make that happen."

Joe hung up the phone feeling lighter. He thanked God for transitioning Barbara to a more appropriate place where she could serve effectively. It was clear she wasn't the right person to lead the prayer ministry. He then prayed, "Lord, in the name of Jesus, for your church, I'm asking that you would reveal the person or persons you want to lead our prayer ministry. If you reveal them, I will act on your behalf to equip them. Please show me the way. Amen."

Throughout the ensuing weeks, Joe felt energized in a very different way. In praying his way through ministry decisions, he discovered God opening doors and giving him wisdom and strength to work through his frustrations. He even discovered God moving him to preach a three-part sermon series on prayer. In doing so, God revealed untapped prayer warriors within his congregation. Each week, the prayer team grew by at least one person. In no time at all, another call with Pastor D rolled around.

"Joe! How ya doin'? What's on your mind, man?" Pastor D enthusiastically greeted the young pastor.

"Much better than the last time we talked. I think we've actually made some progress with our prayer ministry. We had our first meeting of the new prayer team, and I am really excited to see what God will do as a result. I decided to take your advice and actively recruit people for the prayer team during worship. Four people have stepped up, and they each have a passion for prayer that I haven't seen in any of our current prayer team members. And I've been able to successfully transition former prayer team members to other positions in the church where their gifts can best be used. At the first meeting, two of the three people from the prayer team identified that they were encouragers rather than intercessors. I really think we are turning the corner!" Joe said, his voice brimming with delight.

"Praise God! It is great to hear the excitement back in your voice, Joe. How are the other assignments coming?"

"I have been more intentionally praying through decisions we have had to make. One of those decisions was whether or not to put in new flower beds in front of the church. At the end of the prayer, it was clear to me that God was saying, 'Not now.' Ironically, that decision ended up being the straw that broke the camel's back with James and Julie. They have returned the financial records back to the church and are stepping down from leadership. I actually think they will be leaving the church, not because I want them to, but rather because I sense that their season at Last Chance is over.

"But, on a different note, I'm happy to report that worship is gaining some momentum, and we are seeing some new faces each week. And a few more people have stepped up to become really committed leaders! It looks like about seven people will be able to attend your REAL Church Revival training weekend. God has been very good to us."

"That is great! I'm guessing that as you have been soaking yourself and your people in prayer that God has been revealing next areas to be addressed. Am I right?"

"You are totally right, Pastor D. As I was seeking to solve the prayer problem, I actually became convicted that we needed to become much more biblically literate."

"Tremendous! Just as prayer and fasting are essential disciplines for creating an enthusiastic environment where people can be possessed and inspired by God, so is the discipline of living in the Word. As the late Bishop Christopher Jokomo of Zimbabwe said often, 'It's a dangerous thing to worship the God you do not know.' If we are not clear about who is the object of our worship and prayer life, we can easily find ourselves walking down a godless, dangerous pathway.

"But Scripture can further inform you here, Joe. Remember, Nehemiah confessed that the reason Jerusalem was lying in ruins was because it had neglected to obey God's commands. And the psalmist made it very clear when he sang to God in Psalm 119 that 'thy word is a lamp unto my feet and a light unto my path.' If we are going to be agents of transformation, we must set ourselves toward God in worship; we must incorporate the disciplines of prayer and fasting—*and* we have to be grounded in God's Word."

"Hey! Thanks for that confirmation and the usable references. Do you want 10 percent for those too?" Joe teased. "I have just started to sketch out my next sermon series on how to study God's Word. Do you mind if we spend this call outlining it?"

"I think that would be a great use of our time, Joe. It is an amazing thing that Christian people are some of the most biblically *illiterate* people in the world. The very thing that gives us life, the very thing that restores us, and the very thing that revitalizes us, we often ignore. Many of us can recite the twenty-third Psalm. Maybe even John 3:16. But after that, the recollection of what God has told us that offers us forgiveness and restoration, and starts us toward God's calling for our lives is missing. If we are going to be agents of transformation—and be divinely possessed and inspired—we have to get into God's Word and *live* in God's Word.

"'Living in God's Word!' That sounds like a great working title for the series to me!" Joe exclaimed. "I really want to make it easy for people to access God's Word without dumbing it down or dressing it up. While some of our people have family Bibles collecting dust on their coffee tables, I'm starting to wonder whether others even *have* Bibles."

"Good thinking, Joe. We have invited people to take pew Bibles if they need them. Of course, some people are too proud or embarrassed to admit they need one. You may want to consider doing something a creative colleague of mine does: have a stack of Bibles available in the bathrooms. He realized that was the most private environment—and guess what? He was on to something. We had to choose another space because we didn't have enough room in our bathrooms, but his point is well taken. We must make it easy for people to encounter God's Word on a daily basis, even if it means using the latest technology to do so. For example, biblegateway. com is one of many good options. But enough from me—lemme hear your series outline!"

"Okay, well, so far I have three parts: 'Just Read It,' 'Study It in Context,' and 'Do It with Others.'

"The first part in the series would encourage people to simply pick up a Bible (physical or online) and start reading. I was planning on helping folks understand that the Word is written in various literary styles so that they might be intrigued to read a part that they may not have read before. I was talking with one of my leaders about this recently. I was surprised that she hadn't been taught—or didn't remember—that there are different literary styles in the Bible. She seemed excited to learn that some parts are narration; other parts read like a history book and some like law books; others like books of wisdom or books of poetry; and still others like letters written to you or me. And then, of course, there are books that are stories of good news emerging from bad news situations.

"So, the thing I really want people to do after the first part is to simply open up the Word and explore it. I'm hoping that by outlining and describing the types of writing and the authors, it will not only help place some general context around the entirety of the Bible but also encourage people to read from different sections and to appreciate the vastness of the Word."

"That sounds like a plan, Joe," replied Pastor D. "If you'd like, I could send you a sheet we have used to teach people about how the Bible is organized so that you don't have to reinvent the wheel." (see Resource B)

"I'd appreciate that—wheel making takes time! Okay, so the next part, 'Study It In Context,' will illustrate how things taken out of context can be misunderstood."

"Man, you got that right, Joe! There are so many examples of what can happen when we don't take context into account in our relationships, in politics, and especially in how some people use the Bible. Every text is written in context!"

"That's it! And I have several hysterical examples from my own life," Joe shared. "I also plan on using one of the many parables Jesus used to help put context around the misappropriation of biblical truths. I was going to leave them with a list of where they can go to find support material that will help them with reading the Word. I thought of putting together a resource table with devotional books, Bible reading guides, biblical commentaries, and other material that can help with understanding the context of the Bible . . . Do you have a resource list already constructed by chance?"

"I'm earning my 10 percent today!" Pastor D responded good-naturedly. "I'm happy to send you the resource list we use for studying the Bible.[14] There really are some great resources out there. I would encourage you to not be afraid to use your seminary education. Your broader understanding of the contexts within the Bible can shed light on subjects that might be confusing or missed by the people you serve. For example, in a recent sermon, I called upon my systematic theology training as I explained the Trinity. I used the totality of the Bible to explain it. I talked about how Genesis is a book that introduces us to *God* the Father, the Creator of the world. From Genesis through the rest of the Old Testament, we see humankind caught in the sinful trend of covenant making and breaking with God. And so when we get to the New Testament and the Gospels we find God manifesting himself in the person of His Son, *Jesus* the Christ, who saves and redeems those who believe. To do so, Jesus had to die as the penalty for our sin, but also rise from the dead as the symbol of our eternal salvation. He ascends in Acts, but then God manifests himself as the *Holy Spirit*, ensuring that the work of redemption that started in Jesus would continue forevermore through the power of the Holy Spirit living in us. Don't be afraid to use your seminary training to help people."

"Thanks for that encouragement and the example, Pastor D. I'll keep that in mind. So, in the last part of the series, I wanted to emphasize the importance of studying with others. I was hoping to launch more small groups formed around studying the Word. I really believe that great learning takes place in small groups. And where there are small groups centered on learning God's Word, God often speaks profoundly and powerfully into people's lives. My call to ministry didn't come when I was by myself or in a corporate worship setting. My call came and was confirmed in a small group Bible study where I could learn God's Word and where others could speak God's Word back to me."

"Mine too!" Pastor D exclaimed. "It's no surprise that Jesus chose twelve disciples to start his process of spiritual formation in their lives. And it's no surprise that he himself spent even deeper time with three disciples, pouring his Word into them all. It is a real blessing to be able to learn God's Word with others. God's Word becomes even more alive when we study it with others who are trying to learn like we are. What happens in a corporate study environment is that people bring their various life experiences to the Word, and God often speaks life into us through the lives and testimonies of others who have experienced His Word. The saying is true: *no man is an island unto himself.* I would argue that, all alone, no man or woman can learn the Word as God wants us to learn it."

"I couldn't agree more! But, now that you've heard the outline, do you think I'm missing anything? Do you have any more ideas—or resources—I should know about?"

"Well, Joe, I think what you have outlined is great and on time. I'm wondering if you don't want to wrap up the series by giving people practical tips for how to consistently live in the Word. For example, I have found that teaching people how to pray Scripture back to God is a powerful tool. When we let God know that we know what He has already promised in His Word, God provides us confidence in knowing that He will answer our prayers at the right time."

"I think I know what you are saying . . . but I'm not 100 percent sure.

Do you mind giving me an example?" Joe asked.

"Sure. There are times along my life's journey—like I know there are times in yours—where life gets stressful. And it becomes very difficult to sleep through the night. I find that the greatest help God provides me in releasing tension and getting back to sleep is praying His Word. For example, I make Psalm 23 personal as I pray it back to God:

Lord, you said that you are my shepherd. You are the one who watches out for me. You are the one who keeps me on the right path. I need you to be my shepherd right now, in the name of Jesus. You, Lord, said that because you are my shepherd, I shall not want for anything. Lord, here is what I need—then I list my needs. You, God, said that you would lay me down in green pastures that in the midst of all this chaos, you would find me a calm and peaceful place where I could dwell in harmony and love. Please take me to that place now. Even in the stillness of my soul. You, Lord, said you would lead me by the still waters. Lord, please still my troubled soul right now. Lord, you promised to lead me in paths of righteousness for your name's sake. And you promised to restore my soul. Please lead me and please restore me, even right now, in the name of Jesus. You said, Lord, that even though I walk through dark valleys, I'd have nothing to be afraid of. So, Lord, by the power of your Word, would you help me to get through and would you take away my fear?

"Usually I keep going, but you catch my drift. If we pray back to God what God has already spoken, God acts on our behalf and allows us to live in the assurance of his Word. Also, praying the word makes us internalize it in a whole different way."

"Wow, that's a great idea. I've never done that before, but I can see how powerful it would be."

"So, Joe, we've been focusing on creating an enthusiastic environment where people are possessed by God through exploring many spiritual disciplines. We've talked about daily worship, corporate worship, prayer and fasting, living in the Word, and small groups. But there's one more discipline I want to be sure you understand and practice."

"There's always one more with you, Pastor D! What's this one?" Joe asked.

"Rest," Pastor D said.

This took Joe by surprise. With all the praying and fasting and worshipping and reading and assessing that Pastor D had recommended, the last thing Joe expected him to say now was "rest."

"Sabbath rest. It is essential that you and your fellow leaders and congregants commit to Sabbath rest. Scripture is clear that God created Sabbath to be a blessing to humankind. In fact, Watchman Nee, in his book *Sit Walk Stand*, reminds us that God worked six days and then rested on the Sabbath, and that God created human beings on the sixth day. Therefore, God began with work and rested on the seventh day. Humans, however, began with rest; the first day for human beings was the Sabbath day. God was trying to send a message from the very beginning."

"I never thought about it that way. Interesting . . ." said Joe as he contemplated Pastor D's words.

Pastor D continued, "Many people are fractured, broken, and frustrated, and as a result we have broken, fractured, and frustrated congregations and communities. This brokenness can be attributed in part to our lack of discipline around prioritizing Sabbath rest. Simply put, Sabbath is refraining from work or from our normal routine and using that time to rest, reflect, and draw closer to God. Eugene Peterson wrote a book called *Working the Angles*, and he refers to Sabbath as a day of praying and playing. It is not a day off, but a day to break the normal routine and reconnect ourselves to the God of our lives. Taking Sabbath rest recharges us, replenishes us, refocuses us, and redirects us into God's intended plans, purposes, and destinies. It allows us to look back at the accomplishments of the last six days and refocus us for what is about to happen in the next six days. Sabbath gives rhythm to life. Without Sabbath, we become lost and burned out."

"I must admit, I'm not sure what exactly a Sabbath day should look like," Joe confessed.

"Okay, well, let me share with you a lesson I learned with a bunch of my colleagues from a resident rabbi. He taught us how the Sabbath is practiced in the Jewish tradition; because we are Judeo-Christian people, Christians should practice it the same way. He said that the day of Sabbath has various components to it. There ought to be time for prayer, worship, and study. Also, time spent with family and friends doing fun things. There ought to be a lot of eating. Traditionally, feasts are conducted on Sabbath days. And obviously there should be time for rest—sleep. The rabbi also said—he had everybody laughing with this one—that the Sabbath should be a day for sexual intercourse! All the single clergy in the room shouted, "Uh-oh!" And most of the married people in the room had big old smiles on their face and were laughing like crazy.

Joe smiled to himself as he imagined trying to preach on that at Church of the Last Chance. That one might have to wait a couple Sundays.

"The Sabbath should be a day when we cease from the normal working routine," Pastor D reiterated. "A time where we recharge, refocus, renew, reflect, revisit, review, refresh, and reignite ourselves for the journey ahead—or at least for the next six days until the Sabbath comes again. As congregations practice this God-given gift of rest, we find our balance and position ourselves to be powerful agents of transformation in the world."

"But, Pastor D, we live in a hustle-bustle, crazy, mixed-up world! The demands on our time are ridiculous, and smart phones steal so much of our private time . . . How in the world can the Sabbath be practiced? I think that many of my people just don't think Sabbath is practical anymore—particularly when they don't work just one job, but sometimes two or three!"

"My contention is that we *must* have Sabbath, Joe. Even if we need to start with a few hours a day until we can build up to a whole day, just start! Your life will never be the same again.

"With that said, I have to add that there are distant relatives to Sabbath rest that, when exercised properly, can contribute to positive spiritual balance. These include full vacations, mini vacations, time with family and friends, and a commitment to fitness."

This intrigued Joe. He had never connected any of these to the concept of the Sabbath before.

Vacations

"All of us need to take vacations regularly," said Pastor D. "It is amazing to me how many clergy and church leaders do not take vacation or time just to get away from it all. Personally, I'm guilty of going too long in a year without taking time off. Vacation time—to be with ourselves, our families, our friends, and God—is so critical to our balance, our well-being, and our enthusiasm that we must begin to invest in it."

"I do agree that vacations are important, Pastor D, but even if Janelle and I could make the time for one, we sure can't afford one."

"Joe, a vacation doesn't have to be expensive or exotic in order to be a vacation. To do the transformative work you've been called to do, you need to take time off. This is time for us to escape, to vacate and go to places where we can have fun, recharge our batteries, take inventory of where we are, and let God lead us to where we need to go next. This is time for us to just do nothing, think about nothing, and sleep as long as we feel like sleeping. We can take some time to recall what life should be all about. Even if you can only 'vacate' across town, *vacate*. Leave your computer at home, turn off your cell phone, delegate your work to someone else, and chill. It is necessary if you are going to be a catalyst for community transformation. You gotta have balance."

"Don't You Dare" Days

"So, in addition to family vacations, you also need to build into your schedule a 'don't you dare' day. One of my staff members strongly encouraged me to do this. It is a day where no one else can drive your agenda. You and you alone decide what gets scheduled, and you tell others, 'Don't you dare put anything on my calendar.' This discipline helps us keep our balance and be properly positioned for the work that we do. On a typical 'don't you dare' day you might exercise and hang out or escape to the golf course or drive around downtown or read a book or go to the park or just chill with friends and talk trash. Or you might catch up on e-mails or details in your life that are causing you to feel stressed. You should schedule them like you would schedule meetings because if you don't, they won't happen. Sometimes, as clergy and church leaders, we feel guilty about blocking time out like this. But if Jesus himself retreated to the mountains, paused to take boat rides across lakes, and even went on a few impromptu fishing trips, then, it seems to me, if we are going to do effective ministry like he did, we need to plan mini-vacations or catch-up days too."

"I love the notion of mini-vacations. How often do you schedule those?"

"It depends on the month and the quality of Sabbath rest, Joe. If I am in a season of pushing myself, I will schedule up to one per week. If I'm in a season of waiting, I need fewer. However you organize it, the ultimate goal is balance and a sustainable rhythm."

Time with Family and Friends

"So, we've talked about what needs to be done to correct an imbalance with regard to work and rest. But another common area of imbalance is time spent in ministry versus time spent with family and friends. A healthy family is the base out of which we operate as individuals and community. Spiritual leaders—both clergy and nonclergy—strongly invest in ministry. And so often, this ministry takes us away from having quality time with our families and close friends. Before we know it, the precious time that we had to develop strong bonds is gone, and we are left wondering what happened. One of my mentors said to me, 'Your family is your first church. If you cannot pastor your own family, how can you pastor God's people?' He was stressing to me the importance of investing time in family.

"I remember a time when I clearly put ministry before family. I was new to the pastorate, and I was excited about growing the church and the community that I served. I had been married for seven years; our daughter was six, and our son was three. My routine was to get up in the morning, get my kids off to school and day care, go to meetings at church and in the community, come home, pick up the kids from day care, wait for my wife to come home, kiss my wife hello, and then run out to the next church meeting or counseling session. This was a constant and routine habit that only seemed to break on Saturday afternoons when I would completely shut down. During this season of my life, quality time with my wife suffered, and critical time with my young children barely existed outside of the necessities. And while I was close to my family and was often *physically* present with my family, my mind wasn't always there with them.

"I was always thinking about the next thing I needed to accomplish at church. This went on for a good two years. Nia didn't disturb me because she was always conscious of not wanting to interfere with what God was doing in my life. But it all changed one day when I brought my daughter home from day care and with excitement she said, 'Daddy, Daddy! Where are we going tonight?' And I said, 'Well, I have to go to church for a meeting.' She stomped her foot and swung her arm in disgust. Then she looked right at me and shouted, 'You're always going to a meeting!' and stormed away. I knew right then that I had to change."

"Pastor D, God has a sense of humor. Just last night, I had a similar wake-up call with my wife. We were arguing over who was going to pick up the kids from day care, and Janelle said to me, 'Joe, you are fussing about adjusting your schedule for these kids when 95 percent of the care for them is being provided by me. You just aren't around. Church is taking up all your time.' Hearing her say that initially ticked me off. But when I went to respond to it, I realized that what she said was oh so true. At that point, I knew that I needed to make some major adjustments in how I viewed family relative to my ministry. But I'm not really sure where to begin. What did you do?"

"In an effort to support my wife and our family, I began investing more time in my children, Joe. This really took a lot of pressure off of Nia. I was their tutor in the afternoon when they needed me. As they grew older, I committed myself to do the best I could not to miss any of their significant activities like plays, concerts, recitals, and sporting events. Additionally, I made a commitment to having a weekly date night with Nia. I don't always fulfill what I intend to do because 'ministry happens'; however, it is a real priority in my life. My son recently left home to start college, and I'll never forget the card he gave me on the last Father's Day before he left. It wasn't so much the message of the card that got to me . . . it was what he wrote inside. Among other things, he took time to thank me for being present for all of his major events. It doesn't get any better than that."

"This makes me think about something I heard a good friend of mine say," Joe added. "She was trying to help me get a better handle on the family/ministry balance. She took a Bible, opened it to the beginning of Genesis and said, 'In the beginning, I see God. And then in the second chapter, I see a family.' And then she flipped from Genesis all the way to Acts and said, 'But it isn't until I get all the way back here that I see church. Be sure that you take the necessary time for God and your family.'"

"Ha! She does know what she's talking about, doesn't she?" cried Pastor D, with a laugh.

"She is one wise lady!" agreed Joe.

Fitness: Physical and Emotional

"Okay, well, here's the last thing I want to leave you with. It's an essential spiritual discipline if you are going to stay physically and mentally strong: fitness. You are discovering that transforming congregations and communities is stressful work. With the exception of emergency room physicians and heart surgeons, clergy have the most stressful vocations in America.[14] We must exercise or the stress will kill us. We have to burn off the stress somewhere. If not, it will be burned off on our people and communities through anger, resentment, frustration, depression, or even succumbing to sinful vices like drug abuse, alcohol addictions, improper sexual relations, and what have you. Exercise should be a built-in part of your workday. And even if you have to go as far as hiring a personal trainer, do it. We have to take care of ourselves. If we don't take care of ourselves, no one will. And we certainly cannot lead others to healing unless we ourselves are being healed.

"And, in the same way that exercise is critical to our physical fitness, so is the need for therapy for our emotional wellbeing. There are seasons where therapy may be needed to restore balance so that we can be positioned as agents for transformation. If you need to, go to therapy. There is nothing wrong with therapy when you know that your therapist is led by the Holy Ghost. A lot of us have issues that we need professional help to deal with. Some of us have been through *Color Purple* or *Fatal Attraction* situations, *Antoine Fisher* realities, and *Life is Beautiful* circumstances. Some of us need to see therapists, and that's okay.

"I have personal experience with this myself. My daddy died while I was in seminary, and all hell broke loose in my family. I went to see a therapist so that I could sort out my reality. I was tired of my body collapsing, tired of stressing out, tired of being afraid that I was going to die young. It wasn't that I was crazy. Many of us stay away from therapy because we think it identifies us as being crazy; it was that I was stressed out and needed to sort out my issues. In the church, we are often guilty of saying, 'Ah, the Lord will help me.' And the fact of the matter is that the Lord will help us, but we have to position ourselves to receive help. Sometimes we have to put ourselves in therapy so that the Lord can transform brokenness into wholeness. Get to the therapist if you need to."

Joe was caught off-guard by Pastor D's candor. He looked up to his mentor so much that he sometimes forgot he was a human being with struggles of own.

"Man, thanks for sharing your testimony, Pastor D," Joe said. "As Henri Nouwen says, 'We are wounded, but we need to be wounded healers.'"

"You're welcome, Joe. For transformation to take place in congregations and the communities, pastors and parishioners must be catalysts for the disciplines of the Spirit."

"Yeah, I'm learning that more and more everyday, Pastor D. Thanks for everything," Joe said. "I feel like we are really laying a solid foundation for transformation. I think I'm going to cancel my meeting this evening and head home early. There are some priorities at home I need to attend to."

"Good for you, Joe. I'm looking forward to seeing you and your leaders at the REAL Church Revival next month. Until then, keep focusing on planting spiritual disciplines in your congregation. Those deep roots will produce much fruit!"

Spiritual Disciplines

If we are going to be agents of transformation, we must:
1. Set ourselves toward God in worship

2. Incorporate the disciplines of prayer and fasting

3. Be grounded in God's Word

4. Practice Sabbath rest (including vacations!)

5. Create "don't you dare" days

6. Make time for friends and family

7. Care for our fitness: physical and emotional

Chapter 14
Taking a
Road Trip

Questions. Expectations.

"Are you sure you don't want to leave the kids with your mom and join me for the weekend at the Fellowship of the Used-Tos?" Pastor Joe asked Janelle. He was thinking that it would help them stay engaged in ministry together and provide an opportunity for some fun away from the hustle, bustle, and demands of work and home.

"You know I'm always fully supportive of your ministry at the Church of the Last Chance, but I'm not sure it makes sense for me to spend my weekend at the REAL Church Revival. During the week, I work all day and don't see the kids until we are all tired at night. The weekends are my one opportunity to be with them during the best parts of our day. Also, I'm not sure that you'll actually be able to step away from the excitement of what you and the leaders you are taking with you will be learning. Plus, I'm not sure about what workshops appeal to me." Janelle's frustration was clear, but she tried to vent as positively as she could. She continued, "Do you really want me to get more involved in the transformation of the Last Chance? What do you think my priority should be? I honestly can't do it all."

Joe got up from the table and gave his wife a hug. She hugged him back, a thin smile just barely evident on her lips.

"I didn't realize how much you've been wrestling with this choice," Joe said tenderly. "And I'm sorry you're feeling so torn. This was not what I wanted. But let's pray about it and see where the Lord leads us."

That night, as he lay down to sleep, Joe gave God extra thanks for Janelle, his partner in life and in ministry. He knew beyond a shadow of a doubt that whatever decision Janelle made, it would be the right one. His mind then drifted to his fledgling lead team and all the adjustments they must have had to make to get away for the weekend. Pamela would be giving up her hobby time; Gary would be giving up his weekend with his wife as well as valuable time with the youth in the neighborhood; Daryl would be losing income from his weekend job; Kate was surrendering time with her new husband; and Crystal was sacrificing precious moments with her children and all their sporting activities. As his thoughts continued, Joe prayed for their peace of mind and God's protection and blessing on them and their families, friends, and ministries. Like he had done so many nights before, he found himself falling asleep midprayer, overwhelmed by the sacrifices, miracles, and grace that seemed to be woven into the fabric of life at Last Chance.

Joe woke up ready to roll, yet thrown off balance. He had dreamt that no one showed up to meet the van that would take them to the event at the Fellowship of the Used-Tos. In the dream, all of his leaders had experienced sudden conflicts that prevented them from attending. Joe had driven to each of their homes to try to convince them to come; and at each home, he found fresh crises and tears. When he awoke, Joe shared his dream with Janelle, and she immediately prayed for Joe and his team's protection. One thing both of them had experienced was that Satan does not like it when a church rediscovers its purpose as an agent of God's mission and begins to focus to that end.

After the prayer, Janelle said, "Joe, I had a dream last night, too. I don't remember all the details, but I did wake up with the idea of asking my mom to watch the kids for part of this weekend. If you and I had date night on Friday evening like we usually do and then I was back home after the workshops on Saturday, I would still have a whole day to spend with the kids *and* I would also be able to learn more about leader development—something that seems to keep coming up for me lately."

"Wow, that would be great!" Joe beamed. "It looks like at least two people from Last Chance will be at the REAL Church Revival! God is good!"

"And you know what the Word says, 'Where two or three are gathered . . .,'" Janelle added, offering one of their more popular refrains. "I will meet you and your team up there. I have a few things to do before seven tonight!" And with that, Janelle got busy.

After getting the kids up, washed, dressed, and fed, Joe dropped them off at pre-school a little late. He couldn't resist spending a bit of extra time with them since he wouldn't see them again until Sunday night. After putting in his gym time and visiting some Last Chance folks who were in the hospital, Joe pulled into the parking lot of the church and was pleasantly surprised to see some folks already there. "Thank you, God!" Joe whispered as his worry began to subside.

"Hey, Daryl!" Joe waved happily as he pulled in next to the van. "How are you doing today? Looking forward to the road trip?"

"Hey, Pastor Joe," Daryl replied. "I wasn't sure I was gonna make it this morning, but everything is fine now."

"Thanks be to God," Joe responded. "What happened?" As Joe was listening to Daryl recount a crisis at work followed by a freakish accident that his mom had been through, Joe couldn't help but think about his dream.

"Come on, let's pray for your mom's situation and the computer virus plaguing your job," Joe said. "And can we add anything else?"

After the prayer, Joe smiled, as Daryl was visibly relieved. His ministry at the Last Chance really did keep him on his knees, and for that, he was grateful. Pastor D had been right when he'd told Joe that prayer was the main ingredient he would need to help others and himself stay in the will of God. And like Daryl, Joe was beginning to feel much better. God had everything in control. And everything was going to be alright.

As the leaders arrived in the parking lot, each one shared details of the bizarre circumstances that had led up to that morning. After everyone was gathered, Joe shared with the team the dream he'd had the night before. He praised God for making a way for the team to overcome all of the stumbling blocks Satan had put in each person's way. He thanked them for their commitment and extolled them for their faith. Then he got everyone focused.

"As we are driving up to the Fellowship of the Used-Tos, let's review everyone's assignment and gather all of the questions we want answered while we are up there. Pastor D really wants this to be a time for each of us to learn about how to strengthen each our critical ministry areas and then apply what we receive to the Last Chance in a way that makes the most sense. Since we'll all be in different workshops, I thought it would be helpful to begin sharing expectations and questions now so that we have what we need to create our ninety-day plan."

The group nodded in agreement, and everyone piled into the van. Those who had packed more than one bag discovered that Gary had a solution—extra belongings soon found their way back onto the laps of those who had brought too much! Gary climbed behind the wheel and started singing, "Ninety-nine bottles of beer on the wall . . ." in his most boisterous voice. Some joined in; others just shook their heads and tried to remember how long Joe had said the drive to the Fellowship would take.

After they began the journey, Joe turned to the group seated in the van behind him and said, "Janelle will be joining us up there and will be sitting in on the leadership development workshops. Daryl, why don't you share with us what you see as your assignment there? Then the rest of us will pitch in our thoughts and ideas."

"Okay, great! That means Janelle will be in the workshop with me. It always helps to have another set of eyes and ears," said Daryl. He looked quickly over the notes he had in front of him and cleared his throat.

"Well," he began, "it seems to me that we need more people to step up and get involved. Too many of us are wearing multiple hats and getting a little burned out. Once we get past that hurdle, I think we need help figuring out how to develop the three kinds of leaders we seem to have—those who do too much, those who do too little, and those that don't even know they are leaders! Since we really don't have a leadership development process, I'm a little worried that it will take us a long time to implement one. I hope they have simple ideas we can use without having a full-blown process in place."

"I agree with everything you've said," Kate chimed in, "but can I ask a question?"

That was met with a round of laughter and some groans from the other leaders in the van. Since she had joined the newly formed lead team, Kate's "Can I ask a question?" had become legendary.

"This may seem basic, but I think it would be great if they could tell us what a leader is and how we can recognize a potential leader." Her suggestion was seconded by the entire van. Joe smiled to himself and thought about what a difference Kate's spirit made to this team. Not only did her presence lower the average age by quite a bit, but her questions kept things simple and clear.

"Does anyone else have a question they'd like Daryl and Janelle to get answered in the leadership development workshops?" Joe checked.

"Yeah, it would be great to know if they have a particular way of training people to assume particular roles required by our denomination," Pamela offered. "It seems some of our problems are created because people don't really know what is expected of each particular role—especially the ones the denomination requires."

"Great. Anyone else?" asked Joe. Hearing nothing, he got ready to move onto the next group.

"Well, thanks, Daryl, for your willingness to bring leadership development to the Last Chance. It will be exciting to see what God does through us once we have even more leaders leading! Now let's hear from Gary and Pamela, who will be attending the community development workshops. What questions are you two looking to get answered?"

"Do you mind if I go first?" Gary asked.

"Not at all," Pamela replied.

"Thanks, Pam. Well," Gary began, "it seems like we have already begun doing some of the community inspection stuff, although I'm really looking forward to experiencing the tour and picking up tips for how to engage community partners. The bulk of my questions are around the 501c3. With this economy—and with our size—it seems like a stretch to start a nonprofit organization. So, I guess my main question is about starting a 501c3. Should we be doing that now?"

"I have a similar concern," Pamela continued. "And my questions have to do with determining the best course of action so that we maintain our identity as a church even as we engage with community organizations. I don't want us to become a political action group or just another issue-based organization and lose our focus on spreading the Gospel!"

"Those are great questions!" Kate responded. "May I ask another?"

"Of course," said Joe amidst the standard laughter and moans.

"I want to know how exactly we are going to convert all the information from the interviews and meetings into next steps. Who is responsible for what? And how do we share what we learn with the congregation and the community in meaningful ways?"

"We have that under control, Kate," Pamela said. "Don't worry about it."

Joe always appreciated Pamela's can-do attitude, but he felt it was critical to step in and remind her and the rest of his team that ministry takes teamwork and how important it is that they as leaders don't try and do everything themselves.

"Well, Kate's question reminds me of the point Daryl made earlier. We need to recruit some more leaders to your team so you aren't responsible for doing everything," Joe reminded her.

He was finding it difficult to balance the need for affirming leaders with encouraging them to share their ministry more broadly. Pamela was an incredibly effective and reliable leader. She was good at delegating tasks, but she wasn't growing any leaders to replace her. In fact, she seemed to have a team that simply waited for instructions from her. This was something Joe would need to talk about with Pastor D during a mentoring call—it definitely wouldn't work as a topic shared with the whole group.

"Kate, you and David will be attending the worship planning workshops with Mr. Wilson who will be joining us up there," Joe continued. "I know for sure that you have some questions that need to be answered!"

"Well, I feel we've made a lot of progress in worship," Kate said, starting with a statement and surprising those waiting for one of her famous questions. "My questions are more about the actual planning of worship. It feels like we don't have enough planning time. Getting the logistics right on Sunday seems to take all of our energy. And sometimes it seems as though we are on autopilot. We have little time for discussing improvements, let alone creatively planning for the future. I also have a question about who should be on the worship team and what their job descriptions are."

"Yes, me too," added Gary. "And I would like to know if our new order of worship is still in line with the standard order of worship put forth by our denomination. I'm also wondering about what kind of music the Fellowship of the Used-Tos recommends. I am concerned that we are moving too far away from the hymnal standards."

Joe focused hard so that he wouldn't roll his eyes. He knew that messing with people's church music was major. And it blew his mind that some people actually believed that God would be offended by any song that didn't originate in a hymnal and that wasn't passed down from generation to generation.

"Gary," said Joe, seeking to offer an olive branch, "the music changes have been to keep the music more relevant for people who don't have a church background. I'm not challenging your question, but I would be interested in hearing what community-minded folks would have to say about music. I'm wondering if you could ask that question in one of your community development workshops."

"Well, I could try," Gary said, backing down and reflecting on the Pastor Joe's question. "I do have a difficult time applying what happens in worship with what is happening in the street. Thanks for the reminder."

"So, does anyone else have a question you'd like answered in the worship workshops?" Joe asked. He was finding this process interesting because it was giving him a chance to hear exactly where people were in the journey toward change.

"I would like to second some of what Gary was talking about," Pamela added. "Tradition is important, so if we leave too much of what people are used to behind, we risk losing people who have been in church for a long time."

Joe decided not to comment on that since he could tell Pamela was still not sure about how to take the last bit of feedback he had given her. Instead, after making sure David didn't have anything new to add to the growing list of questions, he decided to move on.

"Okay, so, that leaves Monica and Crystal, who will be attending the discipleship workshops. Ladies, what questions are you seeking to answer?" Joe encouraged.

"We were actually a little confused about some of the workshop descriptions," Crystal began. "Initially, I thought discipleship was going to be primarily about Christian education. But, from the workshop descriptions, it looks like we will be focusing on restructuring and repositioning ministries to play their part in the discipleship formation journey. Most of my questions are about whether discipleship is different from Christian education—and if it is different, then what is it?"

Joe wasn't surprised to hear the Sunday school superintendent's question.

Monica picked up where Crystal had left off, adding, "If all ministries are supposed to be about making disciples, then how do we help those that don't see themselves that way to change what they are doing or how they are doing it? And that leads me to a question for this team: which of our existing ministries would you say are making disciples and which are not? And who are we missing—in addition to younger adults?"

You could have heard a pin drop. Joe didn't want to be the first to respond, though. He wanted to see how the old-timers reacted.

Pamela was the first to break the silence.

"Well," she said, speaking slowly, "I think we should be very careful about judging our ministries and even more careful about who and how any interventions are done. We don't want to give the wrong signals to leaders who have sought to be faithful servants through all our ups and downs.

"Maybe a question for you to ask during the workshops is around this very topic. For example: 'How do you know if a ministry is helping the congregation make disciples? And if they aren't, how do you address that with them in a loving and respectful way?'"

Joe was impressed by how Pamela had channeled her initial reaction into two simple, thoughtful questions.

"It seems reasonable to gain clarity on those two questions before we apply those answers to our church," Joe guided. "Right now, we are only a few minutes away from the hotel. Hopefully we will have enough time to provide one another with answers at the end of all our sessions tomorrow, and then, from those we can formulate a ninety-day plan. If you think of more questions you have for various workshops, you can get those questions to the appropriate persons in the morning. We have thirty minutes to unload and freshen up at the hotel before heading to the Fellowship for registration and opening worship."

Gary drove up to the hotel and parked, and the team unloaded and headed for the lobby.

For twenty of the next thirty minutes, Joe found himself praying that God would use this time to form the leaders into a transformation team for God's purposes. He then prayed for Janelle's safe journey, freshened up, checked his messages, and headed back out to the van.

Chapter 15
Training with a Purpose

Team-based. Learning Tracks.
90-Day Plans.

"Worship last night was unbelievable," Kate said as she and the rest of the leadership team walked into the Fellowship of the Used-Tos for the first full day of the REAL Church Revival. "The praise, the preaching, the singing, the interaction of prayer. All of the elements of worship came to life for me in ways I've never experienced before. It was awesome."

"Yeah, it was the first time I've seen you questionless!" David teased amidst good-natured laughter.

"I've got plenty of questions today, though. When we get back to Last Chance there are going to be a number of things we need to change and new things we need to implement based on what I experienced last night. You aren't surprised are you?" Kate teased back.

"Not one bit. I'd think something was wrong with you if you did otherwise," Pamela answered.

"Pastor Joe, is this what you experienced when you came here several months ago?" David asked.

"You got it. It's one of the many reasons I'm so grateful that we've been able to interact with and learn from the leadership at the Fellowship of the Used-Tos. I don't know about you all, but I'm really looking forward to all this day has to bring."

Gary added, "If the workshops today are anything like worship was last night, we'll be able to make some really good things happen at Last Chance!"

The team continued talking as they grabbed some breakfast and sat down to wait for the kickoff of the day. The room was filled with teams from various churches who seemed equally excited and eager to be right where they were.

Joe was moved by the warm hospitality he and his team had received, just as he had been on his first visit to the Fellowship. There was almost a tangible joy and warmth in the room that wasn't fully explained by the registration process or the delicious breakfast.

The boisterous chatter began to subside once people saw Pastor D approach the microphone.

"Good Morning, everybody!" he said, his characteristic grin playing across his face. "How are you? I trust you rested well last night and are ready for God to bless us with a powerful day today." The buzz in the room provided confirmation.

"How was worship last night? Did you all enjoy it?" Pastor D asked the room.

"Great!" someone shouted. "Moving," someone else said. "I've never experienced anything like it," another person called out.

"Is it always like that?" Kate asked.

"Well, we do the best that we humanly can to give honor and glory to God every time we gather. Sometimes we do better than other times, but what is most important is that we've created a space in worship for God to do what God needs to do. But, let me not get ahead of myself! I know that Carol, Steve, and Glen will get into how to do that in your congregations during their time with you in the worship track. Raise your hand if you are signed up for that track. You can look at your nametag if you need a reminder."

Some people raised their hands immediately; a few others looked at their nametags; and still others looked at their pastors. Eventually, about a fifth of the room seemed to be sure that they'd be in the worship track.

"Well, we have a great day lined up for all of you today—a lot of great content and instructors that will help you bring new life to the sanctuary and the streets in your communities. But before we break out into our different groups, let me give you a brief overview for the day.

"We talked last night about the importance of being relevant, enthusiastic, authentic, and loving. Well, today we are going to take a look at how we *manifest* that in the congregation and community in ways that bring about transformation. We're going to share with you the good, the bad, and the ugly of implementing all these ideas. We do not pretend that we know everything or that we have it all figured out. You will see our successes and our failures—our good sides . . . and our trifling sides. And that is because we profess that we're not perfect. But we believe the Holy Spirit has revealed some powerful things to us, and we are seeking after the will of God as we do our part to expand the kingdom of God here on earth.

"For us here at the Fellowship, we believe that a REAL church revival in the sanctuary and the streets has to express itself in several ways. We've broken these ways down into ministry tracks and asked you to come here in teams so that ultimately those tracks come together in one unified plan with each role clear and coordinated with the whole.

"I'm going to run through the different tracks now. Each track has three workshops, and I'd like the leaders for the workshops in that track to stand up when I name your workshop. We hope you will participate in each of the workshops within your chosen track because each is essential to the overall success of that ministry area. Once everyone on your team has gone through their individual tracks, you will have time to debrief together as a team and then plan out your next ninety days.

"Since we started with worship last night, we'll start with worship this morning. The following workshops make up the worship track. Workshop one is 'Creating a REAL Worship Culture.' In this workshop, you will learn critical and effective steps for developing a positive and powerful atmosphere for worship. Workshop two is 'Core Four Design & Plan!' In that workshop, you'll develop practical, relevant tools for designing and planning worship on a weekly, monthly, and quarterly basis. Last but not least, workshop three is led by our HUGS ambassadors, and it is called 'Radical Hospitality and Beyond.' That workshop will discover how to create a worship experience that reaches people before, during, and after worship.

Pastor D laughed as Kate's hand flew into the air. "Yes, Kate?" He'd been introduced to her inquiring mind on that conference call they'd had with Pastor Joe and David way back when.

"What's a HUGS ambassador?" Kate asked.

"You'll find out in that workshop. For those of you who aren't going and are curious about it, be sure to ask your worship-track teammate."

"The next track is the discipleship track. Workshop one is 'Simplify Your Structure and Clarify Your Steps.' You will be led through a process of reorganizing your ministries so that REAL discipleship can happen. Ideally you will leave this session with clear, simple steps to follow as you look to implement your own plans back home. Workshop two is 'Connecting New People in Ministry: How to Bring People to and through Your Process.' Discipling people is a process! This workshop will show you how to effectively move more people to and through your process for making learners and followers of Jesus Christ. And workshop three is 'Ministry Boot Camp!' In the boot camp, you will experience a replicable planning model that enables your local church ministries to create strategic roadmaps for growth within your congregation and community. Each team here must have someone attend this track because discipleship has to be at the core of your transformation process. If you don't have a process in this area, any momentum you create will come to a screeching halt.

"The third track is all about leadership development. John Maxwell is famous for saying that everything rises and falls on leadership. And he's right! If you have the right leaders in the right places, ministry can flourish. The wrong leaders—anywhere—will cause you to have nightmares. At the Fellowship, God has recently given us a wealth of people experienced in organizational and leadership development. This is a blessing that we are happy to share with you. Workshop one is 'Increasing Leadership Capacity.' You'll learn how to increase your personal leadership capacity through becoming REAL FAT! Kate, before you ask what that means, let me encourage you to ask Monica to tell you when she finds out. Workshop two is 'Developing a Leadership Passport.' In that workshop, you'll find out how you can expand your congregation's leadership capacity through developing an ongoing, effective process for leadership development. The final workshop is something that all of you will want to know about. It certainly has been an issue at the Fellowship over the years. And that is 'Holding

Team Members Accountable.' In this workshop, you will discover tools and steps for developing and sustaining accountability at every level of the congregation.

"Ha! We are cooking with gas, now," said Pastor D, his eyes twinkling. "Track number four is the community development track. This will give you a broad picture of how we make community and congregational connections. In this track, there are specific skill sets that are critical for engaging your congregation with its surrounding community and beyond. As John Wesley said, 'The world is our parish.' Unless we begin to understand that our congregation is not just the people who sit in the box on Sunday—they're also the people who we live and interact with daily—well, then we'll continue to suffer from a limited understanding of what church is. And what church can be.

"So, I hope you will pay very close attention as you attend the following workshops. The first workshop is 'Understanding Your Context for Ministry.' You'll learn that ministry can only be done effectively in your community as you spend time examining your community's context. As a part of this workshop, you will take a mini-tour of our neighborhood in Columbia and learn skills for understanding community context. Workshop two is 'Engaging With Your Community.' You will learn how to do broad-based community organizing and discover how to master the skills for making your community the best! And closing this track is workshop three: 'Becoming a Change Agent.' You will discover how a 501c3 community development corporation can expand your ministry as it offers your neighbors a wide range of economic and social services.

"Last, but not least, there is the 'Ministry with the Disenfranchised' track. We hope that each of you has good team representation within this powerful track. I believe Vanessa Williams sang it best: 'you go and save the best for last.' Well, yes I did! Workshop number one, is 'Having a Heart for the Disenfranchised.' You will learn what it takes to do transformative ministry with those who are marginalized and disenfranchised. As we know, heart is not enough. The old adage goes like this: if you fail to plan, you plan to fail. So, naturally, workshop two is 'Having a Plan for the Disenfranchised.' That's where you'll learn how to develop a holistic process for helping people who are disenfranchised get up on their feet again and function as productive citizens in society. The final workshop focuses on

'Developing a Team to Minister to the Disenfranchised.' Serving marginalized and disenfranchised people is one of the main things we do here at the Fellowship—and it takes work! Trust me when I tell you, you can't do it by yourself. Discover how to build a strong team for doing ministry in this much-needed area.

"So, that's it for the different tracks. All of the pastors will come with me, and we will cover the gamut. In your packet of material and on the screen behind me, you will see where each track is meeting. To make it easier, each track leader will be standing in the room with a sign that has the track name on it. Find your track and join that leader."

Pastor D looked around the room, sensing the air of joyful anticipation that had filled the space.

"Before we move, are there any questions?" he asked. Seeing that there were none—not even from Kate—Pastor D said, "Pastor Joe, would you come forward and lead us in prayer?"

"Sure," said Joe. He came forward, faced the group, and began.

"Let's bow our heads . . . Lord, you have brought us here for such a time as this. We thank you for what we've experienced so far and for what we are getting ready to experience. May our hearts and minds be clear now to receive all that you want us to learn. And may our congregations and communities find transformation through what *You* are teaching us today. In the name of Jesus, we pray. AMEN!"

Chapter 16
Constructing the Core Four in Worship

Praise. Prayer. Proclamation. Practical Response.

As Kate, David, and Mr. Wilson, the minister of music at Last Chance, got up from their table, they looked for the "Worship" sign. Kate was the first to see it and led the way forward, saying, "I can't wait to get all my questions answered. What in the world do you think a HUGS Ambassador is anyway?" David just shook his head and smiled.

Mr. Wilson said, "I'm not sure this is for us. The music last night was very different from what we do, and I don't think our people will accept it. I'm afraid we are just wasting our time."

David wondered how to address Mr. Wilson's concerns without being disrespectful, but Kate broke into his train of thought. She said, "Mr. Wilson, I realize it must be really difficult for you. Let me encourage you to be as open as you can, and let's see where God takes us."

As he heard Kate's words, David began to ponder in his heart whether Mr. Wilson might have to be the first change in worship to be made upon their return.

~

"Hi, I'm Carol! I'm the Worship Coordinator here at the Fellowship, and I'm so glad you are here! I'd like to start by having you all introduce yourselves. Please tell us your name, your church, and your title if you have one. And then mention one question or issue you want addressed during this track that will help you improve worship. I'll give you a minute to think about your question or issue so that we can do these intros effectively and efficiently. Each of you will have only sixty seconds, and, yes, I have a stopwatch. With worship you always need to be mindful of time!"

The group smiled at that and then sat in silence, reflecting on the one issue they would each like to rise. As introductions were made, David was surprised by all the different churches in the room. Even so, almost every issue raised was one he could relate to. Looking at the group's combined issues was like looking at his own to-do list.

* Worship Issues
* Bulletin: to have or not to have
* Song Selection: how much diversity
* Sermon Length: how do we get our pastor to make it shorter
* Musicians: Paid or unpaid? How much? How to find?
* Role: which are essential & how do you coordinate?
* Change: how to make changes without making people mad
* Worship Planning
* Ushers/Greeters: personality
* Time: how to make the most of it and how much should be used
* Reaching: getting people to come to worship
* Visitors: what to do with them

"These are great, and all of these issues will be addressed by the time we are finished with all three workshops. Right now, Steve, William, and Glen are going to walk you through 'Creating a REAL Worship Culture.'"

As David listened to the presenters, he watched Mr. Wilson closely to see if there was any sign of openness or acceptance. Seeing none, David said a prayer. Then he turned to look around the room and watched as other leaders began to get as excited as he and Kate had been the first time they went through Pastor D's concepts. He was convicted that if music directors didn't have the heart for REAL worship, there was no need for them to continue.

During the fifteen-minute break between workshops, David pulled Kate aside and shared with her what he was thinking. When she agreed with his assessment, he asked her to join with him in praying for God to make a way for Mr. Wilson to step out of his role or have a change of heart.

Carol opened up the next workshop by introducing her co-leader Mary and then sharing a bit of the Fellowship's story.

"The more we began to incorporate relevance, enthusiasm, authenticity, and love into our worship experience at the Fellowship, the more the need for discipline arose. Worship went from one hour to sometimes over two and a half hours. It was at that point that Pastor D put a team together to help design and implement worship.

"REAL worship implementation requires three things: purposeful design, meaningful flow, and planning and implementing with a team. But before we can get at any of that, we need to understand the Core Four that make up powerful worship.

"Core Four?" Kate blurted out. Sometimes she simply couldn't help it.

"The Core Four are praise, presence of God, proclamation, and practical response," Mary began. "You have to understand each of these components before designing them in a meaningful worship flow."

1. Praise

"At the Fellowship, we believe that praise is the glory and honor we give to God through prayer, song, instruments, and thanksgiving. It is what we do to line up the totality of our beings to God. Praise is the act of inviting, desiring, and even demanding God to come and visit with us. When our praise is potent, our worship can change lives for the better. In the words of the writer J. Wendell Mapson, 'Worship happens when God comes and sits down with us.' In that moment, healing occurs, transformation takes place, questions are answered, worries disappear, burdens are laid down, barriers are broken, sins are forgiven, direction is provided, and confidence is instilled. In that moment, however long it is, God meets the needs of His people. And so, when we worship, we want God to sit down with us. Because if God sits down with us—with you and with me—the things in our lives that need to be changed will be changed, and the circumstances around us that need to be altered will be altered.

"Praise is critical to this. A lot of churches have a period at the beginning of their services that they call 'praise and worship'. And some have a hymn of praise that serves as their time of praise. If they are done worshipping after that segment, we have problems!"

With that, the room affirmed that they indeed had problems.

"Praise is a crucial part of worship. When the praise is potent, the totality of worship can transform lives. Instead of talking more about praise, let's study it through Scripture and our personal experience. Let's first take a look at Second Chronicles 5:11-14, and then have a period of praise and together define it."

She began to read aloud:

> *[11] The priests then withdrew from the Holy Place. All the priests who were there had consecrated themselves, regardless of their divisions. [12] All the Levites who were musicians—Asaph, Heman, Jeduthun and their sons and relatives—stood on the east side of the altar, dressed in fine linen and playing cymbals, harps and*

lyres. They were accompanied by 120 priests sounding trumpets.
[13] *The trumpeters and musicians joined in unison to give praise*
and thanks to the LORD. Accompanied by trumpets, cymbals and
other instruments, the singers raised their voices in praise to the
LORD and sang:

"He is good; his love endures forever."
Then the temple of the LORD was filled with the cloud, [14]*and the*
priests could not perform their service because of the cloud, for the
glory of the LORD filled the temple of God.

As the participants were reading the scripture, the band began to play, and by the time the last word in Second Chronicles 5:14 was uttered, the worship leader cued all to join her in singing:

When you come into His presence
Lifting up the name of Jesus
And you hear the music playin'
And you see the people praisin'
Just forget about your worries
Let your troubles fall behind you
Don't you wait another minute
Just get up and on your feet and

Chorus:
Get to dancing
Singing, jumping, leaping
Get to shouting
Make it loud and make it glorious
Start rejoicing, praising, lifting, raising
Get to shouting
Make it loud and make His praise
Glorious glorious

(VAMP)
I was created
To make Your praise glorious

I was created
To make Your praise glorious, glorious
Yes I was, yes I was

"So, how did you experience the scripture come to life just now? And what does that say to you about what's essential to praise?" Carol asked. Soon the flip chart was filled:

* You need to have the right people leading praise
* A wide variety of instruments
* Unity—common voice
* Loud, joyful, moving experience
* Singular focus on God
* Experiencing God's presence

"Wow, you did a great job!" Carol encouraged. "You are right that we have to have the right people leading praise. Those people—singers and instrumentalists—have to be sold out to God and this ministry. In verse 11, we see that the priests are sanctified. Praise can happen when the people who lead music in a congregation recognize that they have been called by God and set apart by God to prepare people for worshipping Him. These praise leaders must be actively participating in daily worship and other spiritual disciplines so that they might lead others into worship; if not, our worship experiences will lack spiritual vitality. Too many of the people entrusted with leading the praise that ushers in worship have not been called or appointed to lead people in worship. These are individuals who often sing because they like to sing and they like the music. Or they sing because singing makes them feel good. These individuals must understand that every word uttered, every note sung, every intonation offered may be the difference between someone encountering Jesus or completely missing Him in their time of need. And so we need to be mindful of who is leading our time of praise, and ensure they have been consecrated or set apart to perform this essential function."

Mary continued down the list, "And we saw and we experienced a variety of instruments."

A woman seated at the front of the room raised her hand and began speaking.

"In the Presbyterian church where I grew up, I remember the fight that young people had with some of the older saints over what instruments should be allowed or not allowed in church. Specifically, I remember that they wanted to sing other types of music besides Anglican, high-church anthems. And the type of music we wanted to sing in praise and honor to God required drums and a bass guitar in the sanctuary. However, these desires were shot down by the powers that be. And many of the very people who could have helped our church become alive left for other congregations. To this day, I don't know why they refused to allow the youth to bring in nonclassical music. And we are having a similar debate in my church now. What are your thoughts about that?"

Several people in the room called out, "Us, too!" It was clear that this was a topic of great interest.

Mary responded, "No matter their rationale biblically, they were missing the point. Divine instrumentation is critical to divine praise. In this Second Chronicles picture of praise, the Levitical priests not only looked good in their fine linens, but they were playing cymbals, harps, lyres and trumpets.

"In verse 5 of Second Chronicles," Mary continued, "we hear unity in the praise. It clearly articulates that the instrumentalists, particularly the trumpeters and the singers, made themselves heard in unison in praise and thanksgiving to the Lord. *They made themselves heard.* They didn't mumble their songs. They made themselves heard. They didn't compete over who could sing louder or who had the better voice. They made themselves heard in unison, in praise and thanksgiving to the Lord."

Just then Carol pointed to the fifth item on the list and added, "The people are clearly focused on the object of our praise—God. If a worship team isn't focused on God, they will spend more time trying to ensure that the so-called performance is excellent than on making sure the time of praise leads people toward a faith decision. We all want excellent music, multimedia, dancing, and preaching. But we must do this in a way that makes God the focus, positions us to have our minds stayed on God, and opens us to the healing power of the Holy Spirit so that no one misses God in the worship experience.

"Congregations that are growing and are experiencing transformation, *pant* for God. They do so much like the psalmist in Psalm 84 through praise that yearns for worship. They have developed an expectation that when they gather for worship with strong and compelling praise, God can't help but come to sit among them."

"Which leads us to the last point," Mary continued. "As we mentioned earlier, the cloud represents the presence of God. The presence of God comes among the people when the people praise God passionately. When we are in the presence of God, powerful things can happen. We should expect God to respond to our praise in worship.

"Second Chronicles tells us that when the five things came together— sanctified priests, Levitical singers, variety of instruments, unity, focus on God—the house of the Lord was filled with a cloud, and the priests were unable to minister. As we say in the church, 'When praises go up, blessings come down.' For the glory of the Lord filled the house of God. God did not just show up—God showed up *powerfully*. So powerfully that the entire worship service halted to dwell in His presence."

"I've never seen a cloud in our church," someone commented. "I've always thought that was just a metaphor."

"I've seen one," Carol testified, "but let's not miss the point here. Our praise offered to God should be so compelling that God has to respond; that God has to sit down in His Glory, in the midst of His people, move the priests out of the way, and minister to us. And God will do everything with us that He needs to do to heal and forgive. We know that real worship has happened when God comes and sits among his people."

"Now, are there any questions about the nature of praise?" Carol asked.

Mr. Wilson sat up a bit. "Well, does it always have to be so loud?" he asked.

"Not always, but if we have more passion at sporting events or parties than we do in worship, what does that say about what we feel about God? Some people, in their desire to be reverent, have missed the main thing: the passionate relationship God wishes to have with us."

"Are praise songs different from hymns?" Kate asked.

"Yes, Kate. There are different types of songs: psalms, hymns, and spiritual songs. All of them can be rendered in praise to God, which is why we ought not argue over types of musical genres because all of them are created to glorify God."

"So, are you saying the only thing that determines whether or not something is praise is the way in which it is performed?"

"We are saying that praise is about an attitude that gives honor and glory to God. But the words are also very important. All gospel music is not gospel. The word *gospel* literally means 'good news,' so gospel music should communicate the good news of life change and transformation."

"Well, we have pretty much exhausted praise, haven't we?" said Mary.

"We sure have!" Kate blurted out. "Even I don't have any more questions about praise!" The room erupted in laughter, and Mary readied herself to transition the conversation.

2. Prayer

"Good, well, let's talk now about prayer. Being surrendered to God in prayer is essential in worship. Whether you do that standing, kneeling, with outstretched hands, or in some other posture, our response is to surrender ourselves in prayer and talk with Him. Let's look at King Solomon's prayer in Second Chronicles 6.

As the group shared their reflections and insights, David took notes:

From Scripture we learn that surrender looks like this:
1. Solomon acknowledges God's power (6:14)
2. Asks God to keep His promises (6:15-17)

3. Petitions God for healing and forgiveness in the following situations (6:18-21)
   a. When we sin against another (v. 22-23)
   b. When we sin against God and that leads to defeat (v. 24-25)
   c. When we sin against God and that leads to drought (v. 26-27)
   d. When we are in times of suffering and sorrow (v. 28-31)
   e. When others get lost, so that they would find God (v. 32-33)
   f. When we need victory in spiritual warfare (v. 34-35)
   g. When we sin against God and find ourselves in captivity (v. 36-39)

"Petitioning prayer is only one form of this powerful spiritual discipline. We sprinkle various types of prayer throughout the worship experience. And it's important to have a variety of prayer to not only reach people where they happen to be, but to teach people about the many forms that prayer might take. For example, we have a centering time of prayer where sometimes we are quiet; at other times we pray different scriptures, and still other times, the worship leader or pastor leads us in congregational prayer. We may pray either sitting or standing. Eyes opened or closed. Sometimes we get into groups of two and invite each person to pray for the needs of the person they are praying with. Your congregation might connect with God by saying a printed prayer together. Or it might connect through types of prayer that are more spontaneous.

"We also pray for the giver at offering time. We pray for the gifts after they are given. We pray for the word to come before it is to be given. After the altar call we give God thanks in prayer for the blessings He has bestowed during the service. And we ask his final blessing upon us before we leave the sanctuary. We also have prayer ministers available to pray with people during the centering and closing times of prayer.

"Our prayer team prays with the preacher of the hour before every worship service. Our ministry of music prays for the worship experience before they enter the sanctuary. Even our ushers are beginning to pray before they usher at every worship service.

"We're committed to developing the discipline of praying to God before, during, and after every worship experience because prayer is that important," Mary explained.

"So, what are some ideas you have to make prayer more present and powerful in your worship experience?" Mary asked the group.

"I feel like we pray a lot, but I don't feel it's powerful. What do you think is preventing our praying from being more powerful?" Kate asked.

"Are your prayers rote and routine, or interactive and personal?" Carol asked. "Because when prayers are interactive and personal, you are engaging in prayer for somebody's life, and when positive results come from that prayer, it is a very powerful experience," she explained.

"We have a different situation. We only pray the Lord's Prayer and the benediction. I'm not sure how to introduce more prayer—let alone different kinds of prayer—to the congregation," someone from the back of the room offered.

"That's actually not an uncommon issue," Carol replied. "When we start doing work on your worship flow and design, I would challenge you to look for where in worship you can introduce more prayer."

"You know," said David, "I think if we could have more people actually leading the prayers, it would be more powerful and more present. Right now, there are only about two people who lead us in prayer."

"That's a great idea—*but* you need to be sure that you have the right people leading prayer. We already talked about the right praise leaders. Prayer is another place where anointed spiritual leadership is critical. Mary, could you take us to the third element?"

3. Proclamation

"No problem," Mary answered. "So, we've talked about two of the four core elements in a worship service: praise and prayer. The third thing we want to explore with you is proclamation. To proclaim means to announce publicly; to show or indicate plainly; to praise or extol. While many people recognize preaching as proclamation, there are other times in the worship experience where worshippers announce publicly or indicate plainly their faith in Jesus Christ. Reciting the creeds, giving our tithes and offerings, communion, singing fervently the Word proclaimed through song—all of these represent a response on the part of the worshipper to an invitation or call.

"But let's be clear. The proclamation of the Word is central to the worship experience because people need to hear a word from the Lord. The sermon is the central place where that happens. The Word of God is that which is revealed to us in Scripture. Our pastor likes to say that proclamation accomplishes two main things: speaking to the human condition of those gathered and revealing how God resolves the negative consequences produced by that very human condition.

"It is imperative that congregations work with their preachers to give them the support they need to prepare a weekly sermon that is relevant, enthusiastic, authentic, and loving. This means that the preaching moment is a *congregational* responsibility. So here's what that means:

"First, the preacher needs time to study. Pastor D doesn't believe in "Saturday night specials." Nor does he feel the congregation should tolerate them. A sermon shouldn't be prepared the night before it is to be delivered. Preparing a sermon requires that a preacher pray over the scripture, study that scripture, and then give enough time for that scripture to marinate in his or her soul. And the congregation should be praying for whoever is delivering the word from week to week. The best steaks that my dad used to put on the grill in our backyard were the ones that sat for a while in the pan of spices and sauces that he prepared for seasoning. People need a marinated word on Sunday morning—not one that has been microwaved.

"The second point is this: sermon and teaching preparation need to be your pastor's number-one priority in the scheduling of his or her week. You need to help your pastors protect that time and priority. The reason it should be their number-one priority is that preaching and teaching moments are points of maximum impact for the congregation as a whole from week to week. Leadership development is a close second. If preaching and teaching moments are taken lightly, people miss out on the substance that makes for strong disciples of Jesus. Somebody's salvation, well-being, deepening faith, or mental and emotional condition could hang in the balance."

"That reminds me of what one of my professors once said: 'Sermonettes make Christianettes!'" someone called out.

"Exactly! And we definitely don't need any more Christianettes!" Mary agreed.

"Okay, well, let's move on to the third point about congregational responsibility," she continued. "Preachers and worshippers need to pray that the anointing of the Holy Ghost be upon the preacher at the time of sermon delivery. If the preacher has studied and has surrendered his or her sermon work to God, and if the congregation has come prayerfully expecting to hear a word from the Lord, God will take the preaching moment and use it as a vehicle for transformation. God will cause the preacher to speak words people need to hear and will position the proclamation to move people further in their walk with Jesus.

"Always remember that powerful proclamation of the Word leads to transformed lives. Therefore, we should yearn to hear God's proclamations and to give God's proclamations. As we develop this expectation of hearing from God within our congregations and communities, our lives and the lives of others will grow, mature, and fulfill the plans and purposes that God has for our lives."

4. Practical Response

Carol wrapped up the core elements by introducing the fourth and last one.

"The last of the Core Four is practical response. As you all know, worship is not a spectator sport. It is a conversation that requires active replies to God's call. We gather not only to give God honor and praise but also to lead people into a deep and abiding relationship with Jesus. Our hope is that with every worship experience, people will move closer to God and further into His plans and purposes for their lives.

"We know we have done great work for the Lord when people have some sort of practical response because of worship—usually some type of faith decision. There are a number of faith decisions people make in worship. One is to begin a relationship with Jesus Christ. Another is to unite with a fellowship of believers so that they can grow and develop as followers and learners of Jesus Christ. Yet another practical response is rededicating oneself to Jesus Christ—while some have already started a relationship with Jesus, life's challenges sometimes cause people to backslide, so the chance to return is a major decision that people make.

"Those seem like some pretty basic faith decisions. Are there any others that can happen in worship?" David asked.

"Good question. Other decisions may not be so obvious but are just as important in the overall process of salvation in our lives. For example, someone who needs to forgive a family member for a wrong deed may be moved in worship to do so. Someone else may decide that a career change is necessary in order to please God. Or a spouse may renew a commitment to his or her partner. Another response might be answering a call. The overall point is that when God has taken over, people respond. Worship should be constructed in such way that responses are plentiful."

Mary looked around the room and smiled, ready to wrap up what had been a very productive session.

"I know we have covered a lot of detail," she said, "but laying a solid foundation is necessary before constructing anything of value and beauty. Does anyone have any questions?"

"I'm ready to respond right now by taking these ideas back to the church and making it happen!" David said. "But . . . I'm not sure exactly how to implement this."

"You must be reading our minds," Mary said. "That's precisely what we are going to work with you on next."

Core Four: Building Blocks for Worship
   1. Praise (2 Chronicles 5:11-14)
      a. You need to have the right people leading praise
      b. A wide variety of instruments
      c. Unity—common voice
      d. Loud, joyful, moving experience
      e. Singular focus on God
      f. Experiencing God's presence
   2. Prayer (2 Chronicles 6)
      a. Depth and breadth of prayer
      b. Throughout the worship experience
   3. Proclamation
      a. Congregation's responsibility to protect preacher's preparation time
      b. Preacher must prioritize the teaching/preaching moments
      c. Pray for an anointed word
   4. Practical Response
      a. Response to God's Prompting
      b. Faith decisions

Chapter 17
Designing and Planning Worship

Design. Flow. Plan. Team.

"**O**kay, now that we've talked about the core aspects of worship—prayer, praise, proclamation, and practical response—let's talk about how to use all four to design a worship experience that allows God to move," Mary continued.

"As you are putting these pieces together, consider how you are creating a rhythm of call and response. Call and response offers a unique, intimate view of how a worshipper interacts with God and how God interacts with the worshipper. In one regard, we do the calling, and God responds. In another, God calls, and we respond. In designing flow, it is critical that you build in the rhythm of call and response so that an intimate relationship between God and the worshipper in the corporate experience can be created and sustained for a lifetime.

"In most lively churches, there is lots of call and response going on. In most dead churches, there is little if any call, let alone any response. What we find there instead is an empty ritual—but what God wants is a thriving relationship with His people. If there is not a strong call in the rituals you engage in, you will not elicit a response, and you will not bring people into relationship with the Divine."

"So, how do you create a flow or a rhythm that brings about this relationship?" Kate asked.

Carol, by now anticipating Kate's rhythm of asking questions, responded quickly: "We recommend seven fairly simple steps. Seven is the number of completion, right?"

"Yes, it is," David chimed in.

"As you are designing flow, start with an *invitation* for the Holy Spirit to dwell in your midst as you worship. We do this by praying for the worship service during the week, and by an invocation or call to worship at the beginning of each service that formally lets God know of our collective intent to worship him.

Time of Praise

"After that, move immediately into a time of praise. In the invitation, you have alerted God that you desire to worship Him. God sees and hears that intention through our praise. Acknowledging God's power and the honor we give him first and foremost through praise, we believe, stirs God to want to pay attention to our worship and respond to our collective need. Right, Mary?"

"Right!" Mary affirmed as she picked up the train of thought. "I know we've talked a lot about praise already, but when it comes to flow, it's important to emphasize that an assortment of praise songs can and should be used. There should be a variety of songs because our praise to God moves in different rhythms. You need praise music that celebrates who God is in an upbeat way—but you also need contemplative music because in praise, it is also important that people begin to feel, sense, and hear God's nature. You need to reconnect with God's very nature—love, grace, forgiveness—at the very beginning of worship. If we do that at the start, then the tone of worship is set. We are able to block out and destroy any demonic activity or distractions that would keep us from being able to worship God through praise. We can confess our sins, request forgiveness, find strength to forgive others, fall in love with God, remember God, and be restored with God through praise. We can laugh, cry, and rejoice with God through praise. That's why the early presence of praise in your worship service is critical. If a worship experience gets off to a bad start, it can be very difficult to create an environment for people to encounter God in the remainder of the service."

"Everybody got it?" Carol asked. Seeing heads nodding, she moved on.

Prayer Follows Praise

"Thirdly, prayer *follows* praise. In our experience, when the praise is God-centered, people are moved to have a conversation with God. That's what prayer is. Think about it—if someone is sensing, hearing, and feeling God in their thanksgiving to Him, there is a natural movement to want to keep the conversation going. We've already talked about different types of prayer in worship, and it's important in designing flow that this prayer time is authentic, transparent, and real."

Passing the Peace

"We have discovered that passing the peace is a practical response to prayer. So, in our design and flow of worship, after talking with God, we take time to reach out to others in affirmation, encouragement, and with signs of love. For us, that includes hugging. Many folks don't get a hug all week long until they get to church, so affirmation through a hug is critical for them—and for all of us—because encouragement through a positive touch goes a long way. It helps to build relationship between individuals. And that is what God wants from us—relationship! For us, the passing of the peace serves as a foundational moment in worship because it connects people with God and with one another and then positions people to go deeper. The deeper I'm willing to go with God, the more willing I am to share all that I have and all that I am and all that I wish to be with God."

Offering and Communion

"Offering and communion are almost simultaneously proclamation and practical response. We encourage clapping at the announcement that it's time to give because the Bible says that God loves a cheerful giver. The Greek word for cheerful is *hilarious*; the opportunity to give in worship should be a moment of great joy. We are called to give, and so in one way our giving is a response to that call. But it is also more than that. Our offering proclaims our willingness to give and share our all with God and with the fellowship of believers. Likewise, in communion—the sacrament of the Lord's Supper—we proclaim His life, death, and resurrection, while at same time remembering our *response-ability* to embody Christ in the world to those who are hurting and in need of healing. You and I become the reflection of who He is, a living sacrifice for the well-being of others and an example of how one can overcome all things. Our communion is proclaiming our willingness to sacrifice our all to God and one another as the Lord has done for us, proclaiming my willingness to forgive even as I am being forgiven. I am being restored as I am also proclaiming my willingness to restore others."

Mary paused to let her words sink in.

"Are you all seeing the flow, feeling how the design is put together?" Mary asked.

"I'm getting it," David said. "I like it, too."

Preached Word

"Great! Hopefully you see how offering and communion prepare us for the preached word. When we approach God authentically through praise, prayer, and our acts of proclamation, we are positioned for God to enter into the brokenness of our lives and to make us whole. The power of His proclamation on our lives often hinges upon our expectation to receive it. When designing worship, it is helpful to view these three types of proclamation as connected. Offering and communion are outward and visible signs of our proclamation and better prepare us for joining in the proclamation of the preached word.

"So, when there is proper flow into the preached word, the proclamation can become a more powerful experience because we are better able to hear what God wants to tell us. When those elements are not present, it becomes much harder for us to focus on what God has to say to us."

She turned to Carol with a smile and asked, "Is there anything you would like to add to that?"

"Well, when I was growing up," Carol said, "there was a man I admired who was a regular worshipper at the church. His name was Mr. Anderson. Mr. Anderson loved the kids, and the feeling was mutual. However, worship at that time in this church was so boring and the presence of God so ignored that as soon as the preacher would stand, Mr. Anderson would go to sleep. Then, when the preacher said, 'Amen,' Mr. Anderson would wake up, wipe the drool running down the side of his mouth, and say "Amen!" He never heard one word of any of the sermons, and as a result, he often missed his blessing. Anybody got any Mr. Andersons in your congregation?"

Laughter filled the air, and hands rose all over the room. "I'm willing to bet one of y'all *is* the Mr. Anderson in your congregation. It's okay—you can admit it!" Mary teased.

After folks settled down, Mary continued.

"So, the flow begins with the invitation, the time of praise, prayer, passing of the peace, offering, and communion, followed by the preached word. Can anybody tell me what the logical conclusion should be to this flow?"

The room was silent.

Practical Response

Mary tried again. "Okay, well let's back it up a bit. What is the purpose of our worship? We gather to give honor and glory to God. We also gather with the hopes that our worship will lead God to call people into relationship with Him and that people will respond to that call. Andy Stanley challenges us to consider that during the preached word, our goal should be life change.[15] He talks about how he feels he's failed unless he sees people living a life that reflects the values, principles, and instructions laid out in Scripture. So if this is true, what should follow the preached word? What is the final step in the worship flow?"

"I'm guessing it's some type of practical response," someone offered.

"You got it!" said Mary. "*Practical response.* Stanley says that a preacher's preparation is not complete until the preacher has answered two very important questions: 'So what?' and 'Now what?' We believe that designing worship is not complete until we join with the preacher to see that those questions are answered in the greatest detail. Here at the Fellowship, we finish the flow with an altar call. An altar call that supports the challenge issued during the preached word.

"Altar calls are special by their very name. Altars are referenced all throughout the Old Testament. The word *altar* literally means 'place of slaughter.' Considering that the altar was the place where animals were offered as sin offerings to God, the altar is the place where our sins can be slaughtered and where God can renew and restore us. So often, people who are learners and followers of Jesus, simply need to release sin and be renewed. The altar historically is the place in the sanctuary where this can be done. It is a place of practical response. Do any of you invite people to the altar in worship?" Mary asked the group.

"We used to do altar calls, but it got discouraging because we would go months before someone would come forward," a woman from a struggling church in the country offered.

"Well, what if the altar call was for more than just the new believer?" Carol asked. "What if going to the altar became a common trip for any worshippers actively engaged in their spiritual journey? We almost always include a three-part invitation: first, to those who have made a decision to follow Jesus; second, to those who want to become a part of the fellowship; and third, to those who want to pray or make a commitment based on what they heard in the sermon. In this way, we often have more people at the altar than we do in the pews at the end of the service."

"I don't know about anyone else, but to me, it feels a little too pushy and uncomfortable," a man from the suburbs confessed.

"Thanks for being honest," Carol said. "If we as worship leaders aren't comfortable extending and modeling an invitation to discipleship, how are we helping our worshippers do it? It creates quite a dilemma. It is true that some people say yes to Jesus without ever walking the aisle. And, more and more people are not familiar with the concept of altar calls. For all of these reasons, it is important that the altar call be naturally transitioned from the preached word. And that enough explanation is given so that people are clear about what is happening. Even if you are not doing an altar call, you need to think about how people might demonstrate their faith decision or respond to the nudging from the Holy Spirit after the preached word."

"Now," Mary instructed, "it is your turn to see how applying this simple flow to your existing worship service might look. First, lay out your current worship service. Then eliminate those things that do not center around the core four of worship (praise, prayer, proclamation, and practical response). Finally, construct your new worship flow. You have twenty minutes to do this. Any questions?"

Kate was the first person with her hand in the air. "What about announcements or ministry reports or presentations? I don't see how those fit within the core four you laid out."

"If you must do announcements, insert them before the call to worship—before the official beginning of worship. We recommend refraining from doing them at the end of the service because you want people to leave with the Word resonating in their being. Along those same lines, some of you may be wondering what to do with special occasions like recognition of graduates or Mother's Day."

Many hands went down as it became clear those issues were going to be addressed.

"We like to put brief presentations immediately before the passing of the peace. You can do this effectively by ensuring that the recognition or presentation is brief and that the topic is then tied into the passing of the peace. For example, you could announce graduates and have them stand with you. Then you would ask the congregation to join you in recognizing the graduates during the passing of the peace. In this way, you keep the service flowing and connected."

As Kate listened to the answers being given, David started writing down their current order of worship:

Prelude
Choral Introit
Call to Worship
Hymn of Praise
Affirmation of Faith
Gloria Patri
Words of Welcome
Minute for Mission
Announcements
Pastoral Prayer
Lord's Prayer
Presentation of Tithes and Offerings
Offertory
Doxology
Hymn of Preparation
Scripture

Sermon
Communion
Congregational Response
Hymn of Faith and Dedication
Benediction and Response
Postlude

"Well, I don't see anything here that we can do without," Mr. Wilson began, as he looked over David's shoulder at the list he had prepared. "And I don't see what is actually wrong with what we are doing now. Furthermore, I'm not sure we can veer away from our denomination's order of worship."

David took a deep breath and dove in. "Maybe it is better to think about this as an opportunity for improving what worship is rather than debating what is right and wrong."

Kate couldn't resist asking a question, "Mr. Wilson, are you willing to try something new?"

"I don't think we should be changing worship just to do something new. We shouldn't throw out our heritage just to follow some new fad—or worse, to pander to the lowest common denominator. Pastor Joe and I have had many debates about this, and I am still not convinced."

"What would it take to convince you?" Kate asked.

"I don't know," Mr. Wilson answered honestly.

"Well, I am convinced if we don't at least try to apply the concepts we are learning here that we'll have wasted an opportunity to breathe new life into Last Chance!" David said boldly. "What have we got to lose?"

For the next five minutes, Kate and David worked at assigning one of the four elements to each of the parts of the service David had listed. They tried to reflect Mr. Wilson's input while putting question marks beside points they didn't agree on or weren't sure about. Their list looked like this:

Current Order of Worship	Core Four
Prelude	praise?
Choral Introit	praise?
Call to Worship	
Hymn of Praise	praise?
Affirmation of Faith	praise?
Gloria Patri	praise?
Words of Welcome	
Minute for Mission	
Announcements	
Pastoral Prayer	prayer
Lord's Prayer	prayer
Presentation of Tithes and Offerings	proclamation
Offertory	proclamation
Doxology	
Hymn of Preparation	
Scripture	proclamation
Sermon	proclamation
Communion	proclamation
Congregational Response	practical response?
Hymn of Faith and Dedication	
Benediction and Response	practical response?
Postlude	

"Wow. Look at all the things we are doing in worship that don't seem to relate to the Core Four. Do you think we did something wrong?" Kate put her hand up to get some help from one of the leaders at the Fellowship.

"How's the Last Chance team doing?" Carol asked as she looked over their two columns. "Hmmm . . . I see you have a lot of blanks and question marks—but that's good. As you move to the next part of the exercise—designing your flow—treat each question mark as an improvement opportunity."

"Well, we did notice that there are some things that you mentioned in your flow that weren't a part of the Core Four," Kate began. "Does that mean that something like the call to worship is there simply as a needed transition?"

"I guess you could say that. As you are planning your flow, try to minimize the number of transitions. This will help you stay focused on the proper sequencing of the Core Four," Carol added.

"What if we are in disagreement about whether or not something meets your definition of praise, for example," Mr. Wilson asked.

"The overarching question is: In your worship design, how are you intentionally creating a space for God to take over?" said Carol thoughtfully. "It is not about all the little pieces and what they are called—it *is* about getting out of the way and letting God move."

"Is it even reasonable to expect God to move during worship?" said Mr. Wilson, determined to get in one more question.

"You are not alone in wondering that, sir. Some research[16] has shown that roughly 73 percent of the people who come to worship every Sunday do not come expecting to have an encounter with God. Furthermore, the same research reveals that roughly 97 percent of pastors show up for worship not expecting God to move either. If the expectations of our leaders are so low, it is no wonder that we struggle in designing meaningful worship!" Carol answered.

"You all have five minutes left," Mary called out to the group. "See if you can get a sketch of what your new flow might look like," she encouraged.

So the team from the Last Chance huddled once more, this time with the notion of creating a space for God to show up and for people to expect it. Kate and David were less tentative about questioning the impact of some of the elements that Mr. Wilson had been advocating for. Their energy surged as they crossed out some elements and repositioned others. David even added times to the various parts in their new flow.

Current Order of Worship	Core Four	New Flow
Prelude	<praise?	Prelude
~~Choral Introit~~	<praise?	Announcements (:03)
		Monthly Minute for Mission
Call to Worship		Call to Worship (:01)
~~Hymn of Praise~~	<praise?	Time of Praise (:08)
Affirmation of Faith	<praise?	Centering Prayer (:05)
~~Gloria Patri~~	<praise?	Welcome & Greeting New Guests (:02)
Words of Welcome	practical response>	Passing of the Peace (:05)
~~Minute for Mission~~		
Announcements		
Pastoral Prayer	<prayer	
Lord's Prayer	<prayer	
Presentation of Tithes & Offerings	<proclamation>	Tithes & Offerings (:05)
	& practical response>	With Offertory

Current Order of Worship	Core Four	New Flow
Offertory	<proclamation	
Doxology	praise>	Doxology
Hymn of Preparation		
Scripture	<proclamation	Communion with
		music underneath
	proclamation &	and Lord's Prayer
	practical response>	
Sermon	<proclamation>	Taught/Preached Word
Communion	<proclamation	
Congregational Response	<practical response?	Invitation (with music underneath)
	Practical response>	
~~Hymn of Faith and Dedication~~		
Benediction and Response	<practical response?	Benediction
	Practical response>	
Postlude		

When time was up, Carol affirmed their work. "As Mary and I walked around the room we saw lots of creative ideas and ways you incorporated the Core Four. We celebrate your efforts at creating spaces for the Holy Spirit to move. Some of you seemed to need to adjust only a few things, others did a complete overhaul. It is all good. How's everyone feeling about their new flow? Any questions?"

"I think we fall in the overhaul category," Kate said as Mr. Wilson clenched his jaw and crossed his arms in clear disapproval. "How do you recommend we implement this? How long do you anticipate that it will take us?"

"The simple answer to your question is 'it depends,'" Mary answered. "Your timing is great, though. I was just going to shift us into a discussion about planning and implementing worship. So, what do you think it takes to plan worship?"

"Lots of prayer and some good food," David called out.

1. You have to have a good planning team.

"Prayer is essential, and food is helpful!" Mary agreed. "If you want to implement a relevant, enthusiastic, authentic, and loving worship experience, then you've got to construct a diverse, creative team of real worshippers. These worshippers should reflect the demographic that you seek to reach. Additionally they should be people with a passion for honoring God in worship. Furthermore, they need to be people committed to the process of purposeful design and planning. So, first, let's talk about who needs to be on your team.

"The pastor, music ministry lead, and a group of passionate worshippers with a diverse set of gifts. Pastors need to be on the team because they are the chief worship leaders. They are ultimately responsible for ensuring that worship takes on the character of God.

"The person leading your music ministry needs to be present in the planning of worship because music can make or break a worship experience. If you do not have the right music for the right occasion, and if you do not have the right songs in the right places, you can block people's openness to the movement of the Holy Spirit with the snap of a finger. It is vitally important that the pastor and the music director be on the same page about the role of worship, the role of music in the worship experience, the role of music as it relates to the word of God being preached, and the role of music as it ministers to the congregation at different places and spaces in the worship service. Whoever is leading your music must be disciplined, just like the pastor, in the movement and rhythm of the Holy Spirit. Both need to be able to feel the flow, discern the moment, be sensitive to the spirit, and know how to be led by God at any moment and at any time. This is a gift, and it is a gift that is cultivated as one grows in daily worship.

"A strong group of passionate, gifted worshippers from the congregation is required to ensure excellent implementation. These people aren't just church attenders; they are people who love to worship God and who make worship their daily and weekly priority. They need to understand worship, be serious about worship and its proper execution, and be people who are faithful, available, and teachable, and willing to learn the skills they need to plan and execute worship. These individuals also need to have abilities that cover the vast responsibilities of worship, from ushering to communion stewarding to worship leading. You need people who view the planning of worship as a calling because the planning of worship requires great energy, discipline, and attention to detail. This is not a popularity contest. We are contending against Satan for people's lives. And so, in this representative group of the congregation, you need to have people who are anointed by God, grounded in a relationship with Jesus Christ, and filled with the power of the Holy Spirit. They do not need to be 'yes' people, but people who will work effectively with others to see that God's worth is revealed in its highest order."

Mary paused to get a pulse on the room. "Any questions before we go to the next point?"

"How many people should be on this planning team?" Kate asked.

Carol stepped in to field the question, answering, "We have found that if there are more than six to eight people, managing the team is more difficult. In addition to being gifted, it is important that each of the people on the team has a clear role and responsibilities so that the coordination of worship implementation and planning is seamless."

"Okay, I understand," said Kate. "You also said that it was really important that the pastor and director of music are on the same page . . . but talking with some of my colleagues, even in this session, it seems fairly typical for tension to exist in this relationship. Do you think it is realistic to expect that they can get on the same page?"

"Not only is it realistic, it is critical," Carol emphasized. "If there is a tug-of-war between the pastor and the music ministry, the requirement of unity is not met. Alignment needs to begin around the purpose of worship. Too often, different parts of the worship team forget that they are part of a common goal. If we know we are in the business of creating an environment where God can make life change happen, we might make different decisions than if we see ourselves in the business of spiritual entertainment, yes? You need to have honest conversation about what the purpose of worship is, followed by conversation about what role music has to play in making that happen. There also must be a clear decision maker and the expectation that once debates have taken place, that they don't get re-lived outside the confidence of the honest conversations.

"The most successful music ministry leaders have great teaming ability," Carol continued. "They are able to support the vision of the pastor without sacrificing the quality of the music."

She looked around the room and saw a few heads nod in agreement.

"Well, are we ready to move on?" she asked.

Carol was always amazed by how consistently this category of question was asked. She understood that both music ministers and pastors had to have strong creative leadership gifts and that disagreements were inevitable. It was for exactly that reason that vision alignment and the spiritual maturity of each leader were so important.

Moving on the to the next point, Carol said, "Alignment and right people are incredibly, but they aren't enough. Team members have to have discipline." She continued to the next point on her flip chart.

2. Team members have to have discipline.

"If worship is the work of the people giving honor to Jesus Christ, then the people on your team have to be willing to work. Worship is work. It takes time, much prayer, persistence, and patience to plan a worship service. It also takes flexibility because things can change at any moment and you need to be able to go with the flow. People who are not willing to work, don't need to be on the team. Team members who slack off in carrying out their responsibilities need to be invited to pursue ministry in another area. An unwillingness to work in this area and a perpetual attitude of ambivalence hinders and disrupts the movement of the spirit in the planning and execution process. Members of the worship team must commit themselves to being accountable and being willing to hold each other accountable so that God and God alone can be honored.

3. Have a planning process that incorporates cycles of strategic, creative, and tactical work.

"The third key point is that you've got to have an effective planning process that allows time for each season in the worship planning process: creative concepts, tangible actions, as well as implementation and evaluation on conceptual and detailed levels.

"At the Fellowship we have quarterly meetings, monthly meetings, and weekly meetings, each with a different purpose and with slightly different people to ensure that worship is consistently planned and implemented with unity and harmony. In *Death by Meeting*, Patrick Lencioni talks about the importance of separating out strategic issues from tactical issues in order to make meetings most effective. On Resource D in your resource packet, you will find a picture of this model.

"Here's how these ideas play out in the worship planning process at the Fellowship," said Carol, pointing toward her flip chart again.

Quarterly Creative Retreat

"First is the quarterly creative meeting, which takes sermon themes six to nine months ahead of where we currently are and sketches out how we are going to express those themes creatively in worship and beyond. Your pastor or preaching team should bring those themes to the table and then allow the team to bring the themes to life. This group should include key members of the preaching team, creative folks (visual arts, music, dance, etc.), and others from the worship team who would be good at bringing a theme to life. One of these meetings per year is a larger meeting for all leaders in worship to evaluate the year and discuss issues of overall strategy as well.

Monthly Series Action Meeting

"In addition to the quarterly creative meetings, we have monthly meetings to convert ideas from the quarterly meetings into action. They address details for the upcoming sermon series. For example if we are preaching a seven-week series on 'Navigating Your Way through Life's Challenges' and the following series is 'Financial Freedom,' the monthly meeting begins to hash out details for the 'Financial Freedom' series at least four weeks prior to its occurring. This enables the team to purchase books, get multimedia together, conduct street interviews, plan skits, etcetera. The people at the monthly and weekly meetings should be leaders in key areas of worship like multimedia, creative, greeters, and so on.

Weekly Coordination Meeting

"The weekly meeting can usually be done by phone or online. This ensures that details and people are in place for the upcoming Sunday worship experience. The details of weekly worship, including worship volunteers, should be in place no later than four days before the day of worship. This is also the time to evaluate the effectiveness and efficiency of the previous service and to make minor changes if necessary. If a major change needs to be discussed, it gets held until the next quarterly meeting. We are all human, and last-minute changes, additions, cancellations, and the like do arise. Additionally, sometimes God speaks another plan late in the game. Those who participate in this weekly meeting have to be mindful of these things and have the flexibility to make the necessary adjustments. Let's say a scheduled worship leader is out of town and plans to return on Saturday night, but his plane gets canceled and he can't get in until Sunday afternoon. Having a back up plan is essential."

Carol looked around the room and smiled brightly. "Are there any questions about the planning cycle?"

A young minister of music from a church in transition in the city raised his hand hesitantly. He was having a hard time seeing how a church like his would ever be able to plan consistently for the short term—let alone months in advance.

"Yes?" asked Carol kindly.

"Well, uh . . . I can't really imagine us ever getting to the point where we know what sermon will be preached two weeks from now. How do you get this type of longer-range planning in place?" he asked.

"Very carefully!" kidded Mary. "Actually, it is helpful if you can get two to three of the right leaders locked in a room until they sketch out a year of sermon ideas. Soon after that's been pulled together, start your quarterly reviews. With each quarterly review, add four months of sermons and series until you've caught up to your desired length of time. We found that in the first year of implementing the system, three months out was all we could handle. The big idea here is to plan ahead and focus your energies on the appropriate task at the appropriate time with the appropriate people."

"Which sort of brings us to our last requirement for successful worship planning and implementation," Carol continued, "trust in the teams responsible for performing and implementing the plan."

4. Trust in the teams responsible for performing and implementing the plan.

"Planning is nothing, if it is not executed well," she went on. "Everyone in worship has an important role to play. Each individual responsible for an area needs to understand the overall plan for worship and needs to be flexible in the event that a change is required during worship. For example, the minister of music needs to be able to cut a song or add a song, if necessary. Ushers need to know the most effective way of seating people, particularly when worshippers are late and want to sit where they want to sit. The worship leader must have the freedom to improvise when improvisation is called for. The pastor needs to be able to preach and singers need to be able to sing in the event that there is a power failure and the sound system shuts down.

"Pastor D likes to tell the story about the 'power' worship service," Carol said with a chuckle. "It was winter time, and we had just come off of a blizzard. It was 20 degrees outside, and the power failed. But cancelling worship was not an option—we had to go forward. In order to stay warm, we had to make use of our own body heat. One way we did that was by making sure that the songs we sang were upbeat and enticed people to get up and move around, thereby creating more personal heat. We also shortened the service to the bare necessities and prayed that somehow God would intercede through the utility company wires and send power at the right time. I'll never forget calling our utility company and them telling us that the power would be back on at 11:52 a.m. Well, wouldn't you know, it was while Pastor D was closing out his sermon and referring to the power of God through the prophet Elijah, that somewhere around twelve thirty in the afternoon the power came back on! It was so profound that people started running and dancing in the aisles. And no one had any concern that there was no heat."

After Carol had conveyed her final thoughts, Mary prepared the group to transition to lunch.

"The things discussed during this workshop should give you the foundation you need to create a REAL worship experience in your congregation. When an effective worship team ensures that the Core Four are present and placed in a flow that creates an environment for God to move, life change will happen!

"At our church, we simply seek to create a space for God to do what God wants to do in worship, but this must be planned with the full expectation that God *can and will change the plan.*

"But remember, leave space for the Holy Spirit to move. The best illustration of this is a poem I keep before our worship team at all times. Let me read it to you as we prepare to go to lunch:

What makes a fire burn
is space between the logs,
a breathing space.
Too much of a good thing,
too many logs
packed in too tight
can douse the flames
almost as surely
as a pail of water would.

So building fires
requires attention
to the spaces in between,
as much as to the wood.

When we are able to build
open spaces
in the same way

we have learned
to pile on the logs,
then we can come to see how
it is fuel, and absence of the fuel
together, that make fire possible.

We only need to lay a log
lightly from time to time.
A fire
grows
simply because the space is there,
with openings
in which the flame
that knows just how it wants to burn
can find its way.[17]

"I love that," Kate exclaimed. "Can we get a copy?"

Carol laughed at the enthusiastic response from the entire group, "No problem. It is in your packets. Well, it's time for lunch. When we resume at one thirty, you will learn everything you ever wanted to know about HUGS ambassadors. I know that will make Kate happy!"

Worship Flow:
* Invitation
* Time of praise
* Prayer
* Passing of the peace
* Offering and communion
* Preached word
* Practical response

Implementing Your Flow:
1. You have to have a good planning team.

2. Team members have to have discipline.

3. Have a planning process that incorporates cycles of strategic, creative, and tactical work.

   a. Quarterly creative retreat

   b. Monthly series action meeting

   c. Weekly coordination meeting

4. Trust in the teams responsible for performing and implementing the plan.

Chapter 18
Keeping the Main Thing the Main Thing

God's Mission. Discipleship. Focus.

Crystal and Monica were sitting together during the orientation, yet they seemed to be in different worlds. Crystal was wondering if this discipleship track would actually help her figure out how to kick-start Sunday school. Currently it was just an adult Bible study with about four regulars. There were a handful of children in the church who did some arts and crafts and played games that were related to the curriculum published by Last Chance's denomination.

Monica was excited about the notion of actually starting to get young adults reengaged in the church. She wasn't sure that the Sunday school was a good strategy anymore. She imagined that at one point it had been a thriving ministry that had helped the church make disciples. But she wasn't sure. Right now, it seemed a little like a social club for older people.

As Monica and Crystal got up from the table to find the discipleship track, they smiled politely, but both seemed a bit apprehensive about what they would find.

"Welcome to the discipleship track! My name is Bill, and this is Aida.

We are leaders of the Connect and Experience teams, respectively, and we are so glad to have you with us. At your seat, each of you will find a penny that we're going to use for our introductions. Take a look at the date on your penny, and then take a couple of minutes to think about what was going on in your discipleship journey during that year. You will have a minute—that's sixty seconds—to share your name, the church you are from, and the discipleship step you took during the year that is on your penny. So, for example, my name is Bill, and I'm from the Fellowship of the Used-Tos in Columbia. The year on my penny is 1980. During that summer, I accepted Jesus as my Lord and Savior during a youth witness tour. We sang and witnessed across the state, saw young people from all walks of life give their lives to Christ, and experienced miracles of healing."

As the opening activity unfolded, tragedies, triumphs, and trials were shared. No matter the year, there was always something to be said about discipleship. Even if someone wasn't a disciple yet, they were able to talk about their relationship with or questions about God.

"Thank you for sharing a piece of your journey with us," said Aida warmly when the last person had made her introduction. "As we heard, the discipleship journey is a thread that weaves through our lives. It is not always predictable, nor do two people experience or describe it in the same way. Some of you described an inward experience while others talked of an external expression. Some of you talked about your relationship with God; others talked about your relationship with others. That is the richness of the journey."

As Aida talked, she drew a cross. "Pastor D often describes it in terms of the cross," she explained.

"The vertical line represents our relationship with God. The horizontal represents our relationship with others. To reach and love more people without junk getting in the way, our relationship with God—the vertical—needs to be strong. When our vertical is strong, then we can extend God's love to others. When our horizontal relationships get rocky, often times it is because our vertical relationship with God is out of whack. We need strong vertical and horizontal relationships in order to live as disciples of Jesus Christ."

Bill added, "We spend a lot of time teaching what it takes to grow a strong disciple in the leadership development track. Because ultimately, if you are a disciple, you are a leader—leading people to learn about and follow Christ so that the world might be transformed. So, in this track, we are going deal with how congregations can help more people go deeper and further along in their walks with Jesus."

"But before we launch into the nuts and bolts of that," Aida interjected, "I'd like to explore an analogy. And bear with me—there is a point to this!"

Bill and Aida exchanged looks and laughed.

"So," continued Aida, "let me ask you this: what is the purpose of a garage?"

"Well, if you asked my husband, he would say it's to store stuff that won't fit in my house or that I don't want in my house," Crystal said.

Many in the room murmured in agreement.

"But is that the original purpose of a garage?" Aida pressed. "The reason the garage was originally invented?"

"Well, no . . . I would imagine the original purpose of a garage was to house and protect a vehicle," Crystal said.

"I think that is a safe assumption. Yet if your garage is like my garage, there is too much stuff in it to fulfill its original purpose. In order for us to get the garage to serve its main purpose, what do we have to do?"

"HAVE A GARAGE SALE!" Monica yelled out.

"Build shelves and organize the stuff that's left," another participant offered.

"Exactly," Aida affirmed. "We have to do what we see the professional organizers do: sort, throw out, sell, give away, and organize what's left based upon what is useful and sustainable."

"Yeah, but what if you don't have a garage?" someone asked. Others nodded in agreement.

"Yes, well, the same thing might go for a drawer or a closet—or even a room in your home. Has anyone ever had to reclaim a garage or a drawer or a closet or a room?"

All hands went up.

"Great!" Aida replied enthusiastically. "So you all have an experience that can be used to improve your church's ability to equip followers and learners of Jesus."

At that statement, about half the room looked puzzled.

"Okay, okay, let's break it down," Bill continued, smiling. "What is the purpose of your church?" He wrote down answers as they were called out:

* To save souls
* To help people understand that God loves them
* To make disciples of Jesus Christ
* To help the least, the last, the lost
* To support each other in being better Christians
* To fill up our spiritual tanks so that we are more effective in our lives
* To worship God
* To teach people the Bible

"What if, just like our garages and closets, we have lost sight of our main purpose? If we go back to the birth of the church at Pentecost, we find the original purpose of the church: to continue the mission of Jesus Christ in the world. This mission is about connecting all people to God and leading them into a life of physical, spiritual, relational, mental, and financial wholeness."

"David Jacobus Bosch explained it this way: 'Mission is thereby seen as a movement from God to the world: the church is viewed as an instrument for that mission. . . . There is church because there is mission, not vice versa.'[18]

"But sometimes we are so busy *doing* church, that we forget to be the church," Aida continued. "Most places in need of new life must undergo a spiritual yard sale of sorts: sorting, shedding, and reorganizing to get back to the main thing. We are going to walk through a reorganization process with you now. Are you ready?"

"Yes . . . ," said one voice hesitantly. "I hope so," another said quietly. Eventually the collective response seemed to be a cautiously optimistic yes.

"Okay, well, now that we've identified the purpose of the church, it's time to lay out a simple means of accomplishing this purpose. Thom Rainer and Eric Geiger wrote a groundbreaking book called *Simple Church* that shows us two different models of church. One kind of church is complex, has a packed calendar, and is constantly meeting just to coordinate its ministries."

"That sounds like our church!" one participant shouted out from the back.

"We don't have anything on the calendar except Sunday school, worship, and choir rehearsal," another person offered.

"Well, one of you understands complex, and the other understands *ineffective* simple. But the kind of simple church that Rainer and Geiger lift up has just a few highly effective things on the calendar, and most of the meetings are to evaluate and improve the impact of the few ministries they engage in. You can almost always identify a leader that has read *Simple Church* because he or she tends to publicize the church's uniquely articulated three-part disciple process like many other churches publicize their vision or mission," explained Aida.

"So, many people have sought to implement 'simple,'" Bill said, "and have discovered that simple is not easy. Often, we use it as a new structure that we place our existing ministries into rather than as a process where we select or create only one focus per discipleship area. Let me use our situation as an example.

"At the Fellowship, we seek to be a REAL church by leading people from all walks of life to be followers and learners of Jesus Christ—you can take a look at Matthew 28:19 for the scriptural basis for that. And this happens through experiencing the love of God, connecting with Jesus and one another, and serving—so that the world might be WHOLE.

"So our three discipleship areas are experience, connect, and serve. And our primary vehicles for each are worship, REAL groups, and ministry teams.

"You'll notice," Bill pointed out, "that the arrows in this diagram point in both directions. We draw it that way because discipleship is not a linear process. People enter at various points. Many are entering our churches through the doors of mission projects and small groups. And they may go from there to worship or to something else."

"Can you give me a simple breakdown of what you've laid out?" Monica asked.

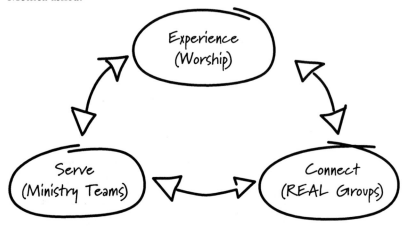

"Sure," Aida said. "Our primary vehicle for experiencing the love of God is worship. We help people connect deeply to God by offering REAL worship opportunities that include strong biblical teaching. Every ministry that serves worship is focused on helping people experience the love of God whether they are musicians, ushers, readers, greeters, or part of our multimedia team. People may come to experience the love of God in a variety of ways, and all of those ways eventually lead to worship. And our worship compels people to serve and connect with Jesus and one another."

"Our primary vehicle that helps people connect with Jesus and one another are REAL groups," Bill continued, picking up where Aida had left off. "This is what we call our small groups. To place people in the context of biblical community, we offer REAL groups for study, prayer, care, and service."

"Would Sunday school fit under REAL groups?" Crystal asked.

"If Sunday school classes meet the definition of REAL groups, this is exactly where they would go," Bill answered.

"Okay, well then, can you describe REAL groups for me?" Crystal pressed, seeking clarification.

"Here's how we describe what a REAL group is. Christian faith has always been communal, lived out within a community of other followers of Jesus. In Acts 2:42-47, we see the first Christians live out this communal life in profound ways. From that, we identify four devotional practices in their community that we expect of our REAL groups

Practice #1: Study

"**We take our first cue from Acts 2:42:** 'They devoted themselves to the apostle's teaching and fellowship.' Without God's Word, our community is weak. We offer our groups a variety of material that is consistent with the Word and often aligned to our weekend messages. This reinforces teaching for maximum learning, ensures the doctrine is consistent, and allows REAL group facilitators to focus on shepherding the people in the group.

Practice #2: Prayer

"The second practice emerges out of verse 42 as well, which makes reference to 'the breaking of bread and prayer.' We ask our REAL groups to pray together and to pray for each other. We also ask people to intercede in prayer for special matters, for specific situations and people, and for various leaders and conditions. We pray for God's healing, deliverance, and wholeness for all.

Practice #3: Care

"Verses 44 and 45 inform our third practice: 'All the believers were together and had everything in common. Selling their possessions and goods, they gave to anyone as he had need'. We ask our REAL groups to practice the 'one another's' of the Bible: to care for one another, love one another, be accountable to one another, and serve one another. We ask each person in a group to make a commitment to the well-being of their fellow group members.

Practice #4: Reach and Multiply

"And finally there are verses 46 and 47—'and enjoying the favor of all the people. And the Lord added to their number daily those who were being saved.' Those verses inform our fourth practice. We ask our REAL groups to reach beyond the walls of our church and groups, to serve their immediate community, share the Gospel in their respective surroundings, and do ministry with the marginalized and disenfranchised in their area. Additionally, we expect our groups to divide and multiply as leaders emerge," concluded Bill.

"We've tried to start small groups, but it hasn't really worked," a gentleman commented from the back of the room. "We were sort of trying to start book study groups, but it never really took off. What tips can you give us about how to get started? And how big should the groups be?"

"At the Fellowship, REAL groups come in many shapes, sizes, and formats, and they even include members *and* nonmembers. Some meet weekly, others meet monthly, and still others somewhere in between. Some meet in homes, some meet in restaurants, others meet in bookstores . . . The important thing is to give simple parameters—like the four we've given you—and provide adequate support for the facilitators.

"So, moving on to the subject of facilitators, there are two differing thoughts about the role of the small group facilitator. One thought is to make it easy for anyone to be a small group facilitator so that anyone in the group feels like they could lead. A facilitator like this tends to function more like an organizer or host than a leader. A second approach is to use gifted facilitators. This second model requires a potential facilitator to enter a group as an apprentice of an exceptional small group leader—often the pastor or another strong spiritual leader. Apprenticeship looks like this."

Bill pointed to the list and walked through the steps with the group.

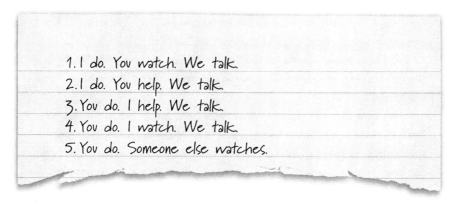

1. I do. You watch. We talk.
2. I do. You help. We talk.
3. You do. I help. We talk.
4. You do. I watch. We talk.
5. You do. Someone else watches.

"In the case of small groups, the fifth stage is where the apprentice becomes the leader of a new group."

Crystal raised her hand to speak. "I love the apprentice model and can see how it would enhance the development of leaders in our congregation," she remarked. "I also see how adopting that approach would help increase the number of groups over time, so thanks for sharing that. I think it's really going to help us."

"And," Monica added. "I love the first model because it allows people to sign up who may not consider themselves leaders, and that way you get more people involved right away."

"Yes, both models are useful," Bill responded. "The Lord will make it clear which model you should pursue.

"Okay, well, now let's talk about the third area in the discipleship process," he continued. "Our *primary* vehicle for serving so that the world might be WHOLE—Well physically, Healed emotionally, Obedient spiritually, Loved unconditionally, Empowered financially-- is ministry teams. These teams serve in the congregation and in the community. In serving the congregation, the teams help people to use their spiritual gifs and develop as leaders. Serving the community sends us into the streets where we walk with God and one another in creative ways to lead people to WHOLEness. A congregation has to be careful not to have more people investing time into serving the congregation than serving the community. Some leaders in the church are even suggesting an 80/20 split: 80 percent of the volunteers serving in the wider community, and 20 percent of volunteers serving ministries of the congregation. We also need to continue to use this part of the disciple-making process to emphasize the fact that if we are disciples of Jesus, we are called to be servant leaders. This element of serving others is a *critical* spiritual discipline."

As Crystal and Monica looked on, they could both see very clearly that the Fellowship was dedicated to embodying servanthood in meaningful and effective ways.

"So, now that we've laid out these three basic areas," Bill continued, "we'd like you to take about fifteen minutes to do the following: First, put your current ministries, committees, recurring activities, and other teams on the index cards at your tables. Use just one card per group. Second, you're going to sort them into four piles: worship, small group, serve, and other. Third, on each card, write a *T* for "thriving" or an *N* for "nonthriving."

"What do you mean by 'thriving'?" Monica asked immediately.

"I mean something that is growing in size or impact," Aida answered.

"Okay, got it," said Monica, her wheels turning.

The exercise began, and as Aida and Bill walked around, they could see that some churches were struggling under the burden of cluttered closets while others were starving due to the lack of ministry happening in and through their churches.

Aida stopped by the table where Crystal and Monica were seated to check on their progress as they worked. One of the first things she noticed was that there were only three piles of index cards, and one was much larger than the others.

"Ladies of the Last Chance, how's it going?" she asked.

"Well, worship was the easiest for us. We were in agreement on that, and it's clear who belongs there. We have a worship planning team, ushers, choirs, communion stewards, and readers in that category. As a church, we have just begun to talk about small groups, but we don't have anything in place yet," Monica explained.

"But," said Crystal, a bit defensively, "I believe that our Sunday school is something we actually do have going in that area. Monica disagreed, however. She said it didn't meet the criteria of small groups that you laid out. But we do have a Bible lesson, and we do care for those kids!"

"Are the kids and teachers checking in with one another as accountability partners?" Aida asked.

"No—but I'm not sure that would be appropriate. Can the children handle that?" Crystal asked.

"Well, let's talk off line about possible models," Aida responded gently. "We are finding that there is a lot of power in having children in accountability groups. It is even being done in school systems that are seeking to transform test scores. For now, why don't you explain your other piles."

"Okay, so in the serve category, we have the trustees, finance team, staff-parish relations committee, administrative council, and Meals On Wheels," Monica explained. "Everything else—like Sunday school—falls into the 'other' category."

"That isn't unusual," said Aida. "Did you identify your thriving and nonthriving ministries as well?"

"We did, and we realize that some are on the way to thriving, but aren't quite there. Others are basically ministries in name only. We also talked about some ministries that we are looking to start, like a young adult ministry, so we put those in the 'other' pile, too."

"Okay, well I guess that explains why your 'other' pile is so big! It is really important that age-group and gender-based ministries see themselves calling and shepherding their constituencies through all three areas of the process. It is great to be starting one of those from scratch so that you can be very intentional about leading young adults to and through the process."

A few moments later Bill called the group back to learn a little more.

"It looks like all of you got some clarity on where your existing ministries fell in terms of the three core areas," he said. "Now we want to help you process your 'other' pile.

"First, let's take a look at the things that are there. You want to think about whether any of these things help bring people **to** the process—worship or small groups or serving—or through the process? At Christ Fellowship in Florida—which is where Eric Geiger serves as executive pastor—they refer to these as on-ramps, which bring people to the process, and off-ramps, which bring people through the process. You need to be really clear on the simple steps people can take to get immersed in all three parts of the discipleship journey. And you also want to be sure that you are encouraging people to go deeper in their journey."

Bill opened up his binder and flipped through the pages until he found the worksheet he was looking for.

He looked up and instructed, "Pull out the 'Connecting the Journey' worksheet from Resource E in your resource packet. We are going to use this to help you understand what you have—or could have—that would help to lead someone to or through an aspect of the discipling journey."

"So, can we invent new things that will help us do a better job of transitioning people into the three core areas or from one to the next?" an older man seated toward the front asked.

"Yes, but try to keep it really simple and obvious—and only add something as needed. We can't encourage you enough to think *steps*, not programs. Andy Stanley and his team articulate and live out this concept beautifully, which I'd encourage you to read more about in *7 Practices of Effective Ministry* if you are interested. In your resource packet, you'll find a chart of all seven practices on Resource E. 'Think Steps, Not Programs' is the second practice. We have all seen firsthand how competing programs can fight for budgets, dates, and volunteers. When you think in terms of steps, there is a fundamental difference in your perspective. The primary goal is not to meet someone's need, but rather to help someone get where they need to go. A step is a part of a series of actions that systematically take a person somewhere.

When You Think "Programs"...	When You Think "Steps"...
You start by asking the question: What is the need?	You start by asking the question: Where do we want people to be?
Second question becomes: How are we going to meet that need?	Second question becomes: How are we going to get them there?
The result is: A program-oriented ministry	The result is: A ministry that works as a step in a strategic process[19]

"Every step should be easy, obvious, and strategic.

1. Should Be EASY.

"So, in order for someone to be able to take the next step, it can't be too much of a jump. You will know you need a step when people are stuck in one place. For example if you have sixty people in worship, and only five people in a small group, you need a step.

2. Has to Be OBVIOUS.

"Next, people need to understand where they are now and where they need to go next. In order to make the next step obvious, leaders need to consistently explain what's important and what's next.

3. Must Be STRATEGIC.

"And as long as we want to lead people to a specific destination, then it is important that each step continues to move them in a clear direction toward where we want them to go. Be careful of a popular ministry that takes energy away from a strategic next step."

Bill looked around the room to make sure the group was following his explanation, and then dove in again.

"An example of what happened at the Fellowship when we decided to think steps, not programs, was the creation of stops along what we call our Journey to WHOLEness. Like a bus or a train, people get on and off the journey at different places. Here are the stops we've identified as essential for the journey. You can read more details about our journey to WHOLEness on Resource G in your resource packet.

Monica flipped to the appropriate section and read quickly through the list.

- Christian Basics Stop: Engage in FOLLOW ME with Pastor D
- Gifts and Expectations Stop: "First Step"
- Worship Stop: Sundays at 8, 10, and noon
- Small Group Stop: Participate in a REAL group
- Deep Water Wednesday Stop: Large study and prayer group
- Intensive Study Stop: Join in a DISCIPLE group study
- Action Stop: Test drive a ministry
- God's Call Stop: "Living on Purpose"

Once she'd reviewed the list, Monica looked up and tuned back into Bill.

"Obviously, once a person has experienced each stop, the journey isn't over. In fact it has just begun. Continued practice of spiritual disciplines (worship, prayer, fasting, tithing, small groups, study, etc.) and growth as a spiritual leader are encouraged and expected.

"Now, somewhere in front of you, find your 'Connecting the Journey' map again. Using cards from your 'other' pile, please identify: First, which of these either leads people to or through the process? Put those cards in the appropriate on-ramp or off-ramp areas. Next, which of these should you stop doing? This might be something that is not working as an on-ramp or off-ramp, or it might be something that is simply disconnected from the journey. And last, what must you start doing? Write down a simple step that is missing and put an exclamation point next to it so that we know it is new."

The group got busy sorting, flipping, and writing on cards. Fifteen minutes and a couple of heated discussions later, the group had completed the task.

"Before we wrap up, do you have any questions?" Aida asked.

"What would you recommend we do about our nonthriving ministries that serve as main vehicles for your discipleship system?" Monica asked.

"Begin praying for God to transform those ministries. Discern whether or not each one has a called and gifted leader who is a good fit. Then work through improving the ministry by clarifying its purpose, evaluating its strengths, and putting a plan in place that builds on the strengths while addressing any leadership issues. We highly recommend not attempting to improve a ministry without the right leader in place."

"Thanks, that makes sense to me," Monica replied. "I think I remember Jim Collins talk about first getting the right leaders in the right seats before determining where the bus is headed in his book, *Good to Great.*"

"You remember correctly!" Aida answered, with a laugh. "Any other questions?"

Monica looked over her notes and felt like she had a clear idea of what to do next in order to start a young adult ministry that would actually help fulfill the purpose of the church. She could hardly wait to tell her dad.

1. Get clear about the core areas of your congregation's disciple-making process and identify one primary vehicle per area.

2. Age-Group or gender-based ministries need to connect their people to each aspect of the journey.

3. If an activity doesn't make learners or followers of Jesus Christ or clearly and directly lead people to or through the disciple-making process, cut it.

4. If a ministry doesn't have a leader and isn't essential in the disciple-making process, put it on hold.

5. If a ministry isn't multiplying, put it on hold and decide whether it is better to start something new or restart the ministry with multiplication DNA.

6. Before starting a new ministry:

   a. Clarify the step it provides to lead people to or through the disciple-making journey

   b. Ensure that it will be more effective than something else currently being done (even if the thing you are currently doing is working)

7. Do an annual discipleship check like the exercise we did today.

Chapter 19
Increasing Leadership Capacity

Called. Experienced.
Accountable. Pipeline.

During the orientation, as Janelle had listened to the review of workshops, she had also thought about how helpful this weekend would
be to her husband if his new leaders would actually pick up these various
ministry areas and run with them. She was a little worried about how long
Joe could continue pouring almost all of his energy into the Church of
the Last Chance without his health, their young family, or something else
falling apart.

When Pastor D had begun talking about the leadership development
track, Janelle had tuned in. She worked in a nonprofit as a manager and
was curious about how leadership development looked different in the
church than in her work. She couldn't imagine her husband creating the
mind-numbing evaluation forms that her HR department put out. Nor
could she imagine everyone on the new lead team at Last Chance helping
to model and drive the development of leaders. As a pastor's wife, she had
learned to be careful about what she said, the questions she asked, and the

people she got close to. It seemed that people assumed anything she did or said was directly related her husband's viewpoint. Even though she really liked Daryl, the other Last Chance member in the leadership development track, she was planning to keep a low profile at this event.

As Daryl and Janelle made their way to the leadership development session, Daryl filled her in on the conversation from the van.

"Your husband asked us to share what we wanted to learn at this event. And I mentioned that we needed to learn how to increase the number of volunteers, how to prevent burnout, and how to develop people who do too much, those who do too little, and those that don't even know they are leaders. Kate added that she would like to know what the Fellowship's definition of a leader is and how can we recognize a potential one."

"Sounds like a plan to me," Janelle replied. "I'm also really looking forward to hearing what the leaders from the Fellowship think is important to know about leadership development in the church."

"Welcome to the leadership development track! I'm Rachel, and this is Elvin. We are members of the leadership development team here at the Fellowship, and we are excited to share with you how we are approaching this important ministry and mission.

"Before we start introductions, I'd just like to say a bit about leadership development. Helping people learn about and follow Jesus is at the heart of leadership development in the church. An ongoing discipline of spiritual growth enables people to sense God's calling. Growing saints automatically find themselves being summoned to leadership—spiritual leadership. We must guide people to be grounded in a relationship with Jesus Christ and help position them to influence congregations and communities to be all that God has created them to be. If you don't already, your church needs to have a leadership development process where people can be equipped to go to the next steps of their ministry.

The world *needs* spiritual leaders.

"And," she continued brightly, "the church needs to let go of the notion that leadership is about position! At the Fellowship we say often, 'If you are a disciple, you are a leader.' Spiritual leadership is about influencing someone else to make a life change—or a ministry change—based on the direction of God, Jesus, and/or the Holy Spirit. Now, let's get to know one another a little better before we begin to further explore this topic of leader development."

Elvin stepped forward and began to talk and point at the same time.

"As you look around, you'll see pictures spread throughout the room. Please take about five minutes to locate a picture that you feel represents good leadership development and one that represents bad leadership development. You will each have one minute to introduce yourselves with your name, your church, and why you chose your pictures. This doesn't need to be a lengthy explanation—it should just give us an idea about what your hopes are and what your bad experiences have been. If you are having difficulty choosing a picture, let one choose you, and then figure out what the Holy Spirit might be telling you."

With that, a flurry of activity began. Some pictures were of beautiful natural landscapes; others were fine art; still others were action shots—and some seemed just plain morbid. As people got up to share their pictures, it was interesting to see the overlaps.

When Daryl's turn came, he introduced himself and said, "The picture that represents good leadership development to me is this one of a group of parachutists getting ready to jump out of a plane. A good leadership development process should equip people to do something risky for God."

Gasps and laughs rang out around the room as Daryl held up his second image.

"Sorry if I startled anyone," he said, "but this roadkill is actually how it feels in the church sometimes—like our lack of a healthy development process ends up burning out or killing those in leadership positions."

Heads around the room nodded as Daryl's words resonated with many in the group.

"My name is Michael," the next participant said. "This picture of the three people playing guitar and singing in the fresh air is what I want our leadership development process to feel like. People doing what they love to do and what they are gifted to do, together, in harmony—and all to the glory of God. Bad leadership development feels like this dart that has hit the bull's eye: cold, exact, calculated. I don't think leadership development should be so exact that it makes people feel discouraged about ever being good enough as leaders."

When Janelle's turn came, she introduced herself and launched into her explanation. "I chose this picture of two people holding hands and walking as my image of good leadership development. I think it is only when we walk with someone that we know what they are capable of. And it also represents this notion of mentoring or 'each one, teach one' that I think would be great to make happen in our church. I chose this image of sheep as my example of a bad leadership development process. It struck me because so often we seem to expect the sheep to become shepherds . . . Maybe we need to change our paradigm."

After each participant shared his or her images, Elvin sought to illustrate the scope of what had been shared through an image of his own.

"You all have brilliantly shared the dos and don'ts of leadership development. You have even begun to explore some of its nuances. I was struck by some common themes in your selections. First, almost all of you had leadership development as an active, engaged process—not some cold training, but some *intentional activity* with people. That's great. Secondly, I noticed that some people focused on the 'what' of leadership development, and others focused on the 'how.' That seemed to be a pretty even split. In reality, we have to address both dimensions in order to have a complete process. Third and last, most of you have clearly experienced what happens when there is a lack of leadership development or when the expectations were unrealistic. How many of you have ever felt unsupported in your development as a spiritual leader?"

As three-fourths of the hands went up in the room, Rachel took her cue.

She began, "Very few churches really make the time necessary to develop leaders, so those of you who raised your hands aren't unusual. The common scenario goes something like this: We have already established positions in our administrative structure, which means we have slots to fill. We place people in these positions without regard to their giftedness and passion because there are empty slots to fill. And then, we explain to the newly recruited leader what they've signed up for—at least most of the time we do! But if we are going to be a REAL church—a church that creates followers and learners of Jesus Christ for the transformation of the world— then we must become intentional about developing spiritual leaders.

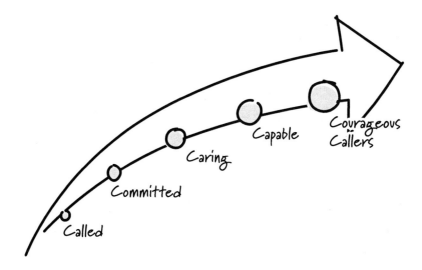

"This begins by helping people hear their call and assisting them in understanding their call. It continues by equipping people to lead out of their call and evolves into these individuals helping other people hear their calls and equipping them to lead. Rev. Vance Ross, a great leader in the United Methodist Church, describes spiritual leaders as being 'called, committed, caring, capable, and courageous callers of other leaders.'

"Scripture gives us a clear image of this," Rachel continued. "Think of Jesus calling his initial disciples in Luke 5. Jesus had his eye on Peter and his fishing comrades. While they were fishermen by trade when Jesus encountered them, by the end of the encounter, Jesus had called them to be fishers of men. He then spent three years equipping them to live and lead as he himself lived and led. Then at Pentecost, described in Acts 2, he empowered them to carry out the very lessons he had taught them. Even Jesus had a leadership strategy. If He had one, you and I better have one, too."

"Amen!" several in the workshop affirmed, and Elvin stepped back in to wrap up the picture exercise.

"As we move through today," he said, "I want you to be listening for how all the hopes lifted up in your positive images might come to fruition in your congregation's leadership development process. But before we start laying out the details, I want to direct your attention to the image on the screen.

"These little fish are Japanese koi. The incredible thing about koi and other fish like them is their strength and adaptability. They can outsurvive most other species of fish because they are able to adapt to many changes in their environment. Pastor D once had one of these in a large tank with a bunch of other fish, and it was the only one that survived his kids pouring grape juice in the tank. Apparently his young daughter thought the fish looked thirsty and shared her juice with them!"

Elvin continued amidst laughter. "A koi's growth is limited by the size of its environment and the amount of nourishment it receives. If you took one of these little fish and put it in a pond, it would grow to be more than ten times its current size, given appropriate food. But as long as it is swimming in this little fishbowl, it won't get any larger. Said another way, a koi's internal capacity for growth often exceeds its environment's ability to support that capacity. Likewise, I think our churches unknowingly limit the growth of their people.

"So, with the koi in mind, we want you to take five minutes to discuss the following questions in pairs:

"How are you ensuring that your leaders have the ability to thrive regardless of how the environment they are swimming in changes?

"What type of environment are you creating for leaders? And is it large enough?

"And how do you know when one of your leaders is ready to make the leap to the next level of leadership?"

"Wow," Daryl said as he turned to Janelle. "I thought we were just going to be talking about what a leader does, how to train them to be better, and how to recruit more. Boy, was I wrong!"

"I know what you mean," Janelle affirmed. "How would you answer the first question they raised?"

"Well, I think, like the fish, either people are adaptable, or they aren't," Daryl said. "I'm not sure how we teach adaptability—except if our adaptability increases as we surrender to God and grow in our discipleship."

"Daryl, I think you are on to something," Janelle said, mulling his words over. "Often we as leaders have difficulty adapting to a change in the environment due to selfish reasons. If we really believe that nothing is impossible with God and we let go and let God *really* be in control of the situation, we would be able to thrive—or at least survive—in almost any situation."

"Thanks, Janelle. Okay, so we've answered the first question. How about the other two? I think we haven't even touched those yet at Last Chance. And we don't usually wait for someone to be ready to make the leap—they just get pushed, pulled, prodded, and forced!"

At the conclusion of the exercise, Janelle and Daryl discovered that most of the other pairs had had similar experiences and revelations. Rachel moved the group forward to the next stage in the workshop.

"For the next forty-five minutes we are going to lay out a leadership development process that answers all three questions. Leadership capacity determines personal and organizational capacity. This is one reason why having a simple leadership development process is so important—your church will only grow to the size allowed by its leaders.

"Like the koi in the fishbowl!" someone called out.

"You got it. But furthermore, great ministry takes place because great leadership is in place to make it happen," Rachel continued. "Poor ministry happens when there is poor or no leadership to make it happen. So, what becomes imperative for any congregation seeking to be a relevant, enthusiastic, authentic, and loving congregation within its community and the world is the presence of effective spiritual leaders."

She stopped for a moment to let the group process her words, and then continued.

"There are several leader development strategies that various churches are using across the country. Some focus on equipping people for particular roles; others focus on identifying spiritual gifts and encouraging their use. Some include clarifying roles, interviewing, and systems of accountability. All of these have value. What is missing, however, is an overarching process for identifying, placing, equipping, and providing feedback in a way that naturally develops people into being servant leaders; more than just leaders of different ministries.

"Eric Geiger, one of the authors of a book called *Simple Church*, has developed a leadership pipeline for the church where he serves as an executive pastor. It is this model that we would like to lift up, unpack, and explore as a model that can: first, help people attain the highest level of personal and spiritual effectiveness; second, clarify expectations and benchmarks for congregational leaders; and third, provide a system of leadership for your congregation that naturally nurtures and replenishes leaders for the long haul. When you think about a pipeline, what comes to mind?"

"The Trans-Alaskan Pipeline that was built to move oil from the North Slope of Alaska to the northern most ice-free port in Valdez, Alaska," Daryl shared. "I remember being fascinated watching reports of them building that thing."

"I was thinking oil pipeline too," a gentleman at the table next to Daryl offered. "But that made me think of the BP disaster in the Gulf of Mexico. Are you saying that we have to be careful or we will make a mess of things?"

"Well it is true that leadership can be messy. But we are focused here on developing a clear pathway for spiritual leaders to grow. The dictionary defines a pipeline as a 'route, channel, or process along which something passes or is provided at a steady rate; it is the means, system, or flow of supply or supplies.'[20] When we say something is 'in the pipeline,' we mean it is in process, underway, or being developed. Leadership is something that should always be in process or developed in our churches. Much of the decline in our churches reflects the minimum trickle of spiritual leaders being developed. In its simplest form, Geiger's leadership pipeline looks like this." Rachel pointed up at the screen.

"His core premise is that you can't lead others without first being able to lead yourself. And you can't effectively lead leaders if you haven't first

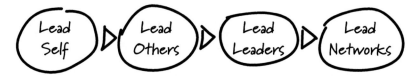

effectively led others. The ultimate goal is to develop enough leaders at each stage of the pipeline who can effectively lead in a way that reaches, serves, and influences the largest number of people who then become followers and learners of Christ for the transformation of the world.

"The Fellowship has taken this premise and adapted it to our own setting. We see this as the process that helps us develop a REAL leadership culture. In order for this to be a practical, useful tool, you must adapt the concept to meet your own context. This includes identifying the purpose, arena, experiences, evidence, and accountability relationship for each stage in the pipeline.

"On Resource H in your resource packet, you will find a chart for you to fill in. We want you to begin to fill in the 'Lead Self' and 'Lead Others' columns of this worksheet so that you can go home with some clarity about what you need to put in place.

Janelle turned to Daryl and said, "If we can even fill in the first column, I'd be thrilled!" Daryl nodded enthusiastically in agreement.

"Let's walk through ours as an example so you have a better idea of what each box represents," Elvin said. And with that, he began walking the group through the table displayed on the screen.

	LEAD SELF →	LEAD OTHERS →	LEAD LEADERS →	LEAD NETWORKS
PURPOSE of this stage in leadership development process	Instill in each person a commitment to experience the love of God, connect with Jesus and other believers, and serve so that the world might be WHOLE	Foster the growth of servant leaders. (1 Timothy 3:8-10)	Develop mature shepherds of leaders. (1 Timothy 3:1-7)	Develop staff who relevantly, enthusiastically, authentically and lovingly live out Fellowship values and effectively train people for ministry. (Ephesians 4:11-12)
ARENA of operation	Group/Team Member	Group/Team Leader	Mentor/Area Leader	Director/Pastor
EXPERIENCES to prepare leader for next stage	Journey to WHOLEness stops	**Mentoring workshop, call seminar (step 5) and leadership summits**	**Mentoring**	**Continuing education via regional and national training events. Mentoring.**
EVIDENCE that leader is ready to move to next stage	Tithes, regularly participates in worship, a member of a REAL group, serves community, and is REAL FAT	Apprentices/ mentors new leaders and demonstrates core competencies	Develops leaders of leaders and builds relationships and partnerships with those outside Fellowship	
ACCOUNTABILITY RELATIONSHIP	Leader meets with group and/or team regularly	Mentor has personal and/or ministry discussion monthly with leader	Director has personal and/or ministry discussion monthly with leader.	**Personnel Committee**

"The purpose simply defines the desired outcome for a person in that particular stage in the leadership process. So the goal for those working on leading self in the Fellowship's context, for example, is to instill in each person a commitment to be a follower and learner of Jesus Christ by experiencing the love of God, connecting with Jesus and one another, and serving so that the world might be WHOLE. We define WHOLE as being Well physically, Healed emotionally, Obedient spiritually, Loved unconditionally, and Empowered financially—W-H-O-L-E. Whole.

"The arena delineates the nature of the stage upon which a person needs to act in order to be appropriately aligned with the leadership development process. We need to be intentional about roles we assign folks and the size and/or influence of the arenas in which we place them. For example, we don't want someone working on leading self to be participating as a group leader because that person's effectiveness in leading a group will be minimized until they can lead themselves. It is critical to align people to the role where their gifts, commitment, and skills currently place them with the understanding and intention of moving them deeper and further as leaders."

"When I hear the word arena I think of the theatre or a stadium," Daryl interjected. "Places that have 50 to 50,000 spectators. Does each stage of the pipeline represent a different size group that a person leads?"

"Sort of. It is about influence and the growing number of people that one influences at each step along the way. If you can't influence one (yourself), it is cruel to expect you to successfully influence or lead a larger group."

Rachel continued where Elvin left off: "Experiences meet people where they are and prepare them for the next stage of leadership development. We must intentionally create experiences and environments that give people the opportunity to learn and practice necessary leadership skills.

"Evidence is the results that reflect that someone is ready for the next stage of leading. It is when one produces fruit that reflects s/he is ready for the next level of leadership. For example, if someone has apprenticed new leaders and demonstrated the ability to lead others to something greater than themselves, we have evidence that they are ready to lead leaders.

"And," said Elvin, pointing to the bottom of the chart, "all of this is dependent upon clear accountability relationships. Accountability relationships happen when leaders hold each other responsible for fulfilling commitments entrusted to them, while at the same time providing an environment of support and encouragement. Crucial to this is relationship building—the stronger relationships are, the more powerful the accountability will be. And unless a congregation is truly authentic, it cannot create a culture of accountability."

"So, do you have any questions before you start filling in your worksheet?" Rachel asked.

"Yeah . . . I'm looking at the evidence block under 'Lead Self.' I think I understand everything except 'REAL FAT.' I'm guessing you aren't promoting obesity," the young woman said, giggling along with the rest of the room. "Could you please explain?"

Elvin laughed. "That's Pastor D for you. He always trips people up with that one! But let me explain. It relates to the evidence we are seeking before transitioning someone into a leadership position. The first three pieces of evidence are basic expectations of walking in relationship with Jesus Christ and are foundational for leading self. Fundamentally leading self is about living a surrendered life. In Acts 2:42, immediately after people decided to follow Jesus, we are told that they devoted themselves to the apostles' teaching, which was study of the Word; fellowship, which was the active participation in the community of faith—the *koinonia*; the breaking of bread, common-union or communion; and prayer. Central to leading self is participation in these and other spiritual practices; they help us get—and stay—grounded in our relationship with the Christ. To help me lead myself, I need to be in worship regularly. To help me lead myself, I need to grow in faith and be able to trust that God has provided and will continue to provide. Tithing and offering is a demonstration of this. To help me lead myself, I need to be in an accountability group where I can pray, study, serve, and care for others."

Elvin surveyed the room to make sure the group was still with him.

"The last piece of evidence is about the alignment of a person's readiness with the culture we seek to create. Simply put, this person is: Relevant, Enthusiastic, Authentic, Loving, Faith-filled, Available, and Teachable. R-E-A-L-F-A-T. 'Real fat.'"

As Elvin spoke, Rachel wrote each word on the flipchart.

Relevant

"When Jesus came to the earth, His central mission was to rescue people from disconnection with God. And so when a person becomes relevant, that person is surrendered to be with people in their brokenness and to lead them to wholeness in the name of Jesus. Relevant people have a heart for the least, the last, and the lost, and they work for people to experience soul justice and social justice. Justice is the absence of oppression in individuals' souls and in the corporate community.

Enthusiastic

"People become enthusiastic when God takes possession. This enables people to inspire others who are down and in despair. If a person is possessed by God, you will see it in his or her eyes. The Bible says that the eye is the lamp unto the soul. Ben and Roz Zander would define this as having 'shiny eyes.' You can look in people's eyes and see from their brightness whether they are passionate about serving God and serving others. If you see it, get to know them, share vision with them, listen for the other pieces of evidence. It is through God being active in them that they influence others.

Authentic

"Authentic people are transparent, honest, down-to-earth folks; they engage with others in genuine, nonjudgmental ways. Authenticity breathes with the reality that an abiding relationship with Jesus Christ gives us the confidence that we are neither condemned nor judged, but loved for who we are and for who God wants us to become. This informs our life story and attitude toward others. You know you are with authentic people when life stories are told freely—stories of joy, pain, and struggle. Stories that point to the movement of God and His goodness in people's lives. Authentic people are people grounded in Christian tradition without being caught up in traditionalism. Dead faith tells fake stories. Living faith offers an authentic witness of what God has done in difficult situations. Dead faith tries to hide while living faith can't help but share. When people are authentic, God positions us to allow our faith to become transformative in people's lives.

Loving

"REAL FAT people have love at their core. They truly desire the well-being of others. They don't care where you've been or what you've done. Loving people are consumed with what God wants you to be. Furthermore, people with love at their core are focused on what they can do for others as opposed to themselves. We see this focus in their conversation and in their actions. They don't perpetuate the '-isms' of life, they don't gossip or tear others down. Instead, we find loving people talking about the good in others, lifting up the positive qualities of others, and actively breaking down barriers and building bridges. People infected with love are committed to unifying and not dividing.

Faith-filled

"Faith-filled people are captivated by the means of grace and rooted in the spiritual disciplines. As a result, they are risk-taking God chasers. These people are determined to see the promises of God, as outlined in Scripture, become real in people's everyday lives. They pray for and expect miracles, and they seek to be a miracle to others. They serve as healers because they have been healed. They forgive others because they know about the power of forgiveness in their own lives.

Available

"If you have someone who is REAL, faith-filled and teachable, they will make themselves *available* to serve. If they aren't available, either something traumatic is happening in their life or their priorities don't include serving and leading on behalf of the church. If it is a priority issue, then they are missing one or more of the other elements of REAL FAT people. It is our responsibility to make sure that every person understands that following their call and serving God must be a priority. If we are successful in this, more people will become available, and then more can be used by God to positively impact the lives of others on an even broader scale.

Teachable

"We have to keep in mind, of course, that just because people have shiny eyes doesn't mean they know how to lead. Just because they have experience leading outside the church doesn't mean they know how to lead God's people in a godly fashion. Many leadership qualities are the kind we are born with, but others we need to learn. When I'm teachable, I'm not arrogant or too proud to say I don't know. When I'm teachable, I'm open to learning something new. I am eager to grow and to be equipped with the gifts and skills of God that can radically improve my effectiveness for the kingdom of God."

Got it, thought Daryl to himself. REAL FAT. I like that.

"Thanks, that was really helpful," he said aloud. "It looks to me like your approach is really good. Can we just copy what you have here?"

"While you are welcome to use whatever you find helpful, I wouldn't recommend just copying it," Rachel replied. "There is much value in discussing what each block looks like in your context and tailoring it to create the culture you seek to create. Any other questions?"

"I have one!" came a voice from the side of the room. "I'm assuming your Journey to WHOLEness stops are a series of things that create the evidence. Do you have a description that you'd be willing to share?"

"Absolutely! You'll find that on Resource G in your handouts." Seeing another hand up, Rachel responded, "Yes, Janelle, you have a question?"

"Yes. I was wondering what core competencies you are talking about in the evidence block in the 'Lead Others' column. At work, they have a grid of competencies for each level of leadership."

"Well, at the Fellowship, we like to talk about competencies in terms of habits, not steps. They are behaviors we hope consistently happen in the heart, walk, and talk of each person who is in a formal leadership role. We are still developing our competencies but would be happy to share where we are thus far. We want our leaders to do a number of things and exhibit certain qualities.

She directed the room to a slide on the screen behind her, which Elvin had cued up as she spoke. It read:

- Be humble
- Take risks
- Discern next steps
- Build teams
- Understand the role of grace
- Promote the welfare of the people
- Survey the situation
- Communicate the situation
- Cast vision
- Gain commitment
- Provide loving accountability
- Lead people to something greater than themselves

"These aren't teachable in the classroom," Rachel explained, "but they are catchable in the right arena with the right accountability relationship. This is how Jesus's disciples caught it, and this is how we must position our people to catch it. One of the simplest drawings I've seen of how 'each one, teach one' can inform and influence the leadership capacity and missional impact in our churches comes from the Ferguson brothers' book *Exponential: How You and Your Friends Can Start a Missional Church Movement.*

Leadership Plan

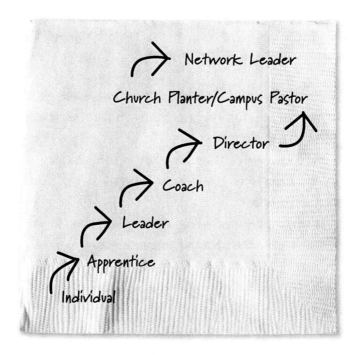

"This creates a much bigger pond. What if we were growing and developing leaders who were courageously calling people who had the vision for being and multiplying REAL church in a variety of contexts? What if each individual understood that being an agent of God's mission in the world and starting a missional movement was the main idea? What if our leadership development system were based on apprenticeships and mentoring people up to the place God created them to serve in the body of Christ in the world? What if every person who participated in the life of our church understood that they could start a missional church movement?"

Leadership Development

Spiritual leaders are called, committed, caring, capable, and courageous callers of other leaders.

Questions our leadership development process needs to answer:
1. How are we ensuring our leaders have the ability to thrive and adapt?
2. What environment are you creating for leaders? Is it large enough to allow people to grow into all God would have them be?
3. How do we know when a leader is ready to make the leap to the next level of leadership?

Lead Self -> Lead Others -> Lead Leaders (See Resource H)

Leadership capacity determines personal and organizational capacity.

We know someone is ready to lead others when they are REAL FAT:

* Relevant	* Faithfilled
* Enthusiastic	* Available
* Authentic	* Teachable
* Loving	

Chapter 20
Having a Heart for the Marginalized

The Edges. Love. Touch.

Eric ended up heading over to the "Ministry to the Marginalized" track by himself. As he walked down the street and around the corner to one of the Fellowship's transitional houses, his prayers were with his ministry partner, Sandy. He had really been looking forward to participating with Sandy in this track. The two of them were extremely passionate about reaching out to the marginalized, and of the various tracks offered in the REAL Church revival, they knew beyond a shadow of a doubt that this workshop had their names all over it.

Both of them had personal reasons for wanting to take this track, and Pastor Joe, in inviting them to the training weekend, had encouraged them to follow their hearts. Eric was a recovering alcoholic who had been sober for twelve years and was now serving as a trustee at Last Chance. Sandy was a single mother; a painful divorce had left her working two jobs simply to survive while trying to raise her son on her own. Church had been her one place of peace; her son, Jimmy, was fighting an addiction to cocaine. Eric and Sandy saw the Church of the Last Chance as a place where the least, the last, and the lost of Hopeville might find some hope. They knew that disenfranchisement looked different from place to place, but they also knew that it felt the same no matter where you lived.

As Eric walked in the front door of the house, he asked one of the workshop facilitators, Barbara, if she would pray for Sandy. Jimmy had suffered a bad relapse on Friday night, and Sandy, upon hearing the news, had rushed back to Hopeville to be by his side. Barbara didn't just say, "I'm praying for you," the standard church line given when prayer really wasn't happening; instead Barbara invited all the workshop participants to intercede in prayer with her on Jimmy's behalf, asking the Holy Ghost to cover and comfort Sandy as well.

After the riveting prayer, and after everyone had hugged Eric and encouraged him, Sharon opened the meeting.

"Hi, I'm Sharon Grey. Barbara Johnson and I we will be facilitating the 'Ministry to the Marginalized' track. Right now, we'll be leading the workshop, 'Having a Heart for the Marginalized.' It's great to have you here!"

"May I ask," interrupted one of the participants, sounding a bit miffed, "why we are out here? Why are we in this house, away from the rest of the people at the church?"

"That's a great question," replied Sharon. "We wanted to give you a sense of how it feels to be separated, lonely, and detached. That's often what marginalized people feel. Plus, this is a place where we do a lot of ministry to marginalized people."

Eric was impressed that so much thought had gone into even that aspect of the workshop.

"Before we get started, though," continued Sharon, "tell us why you signed up for this track."

People began calling out reasons from around the room:

"Alcoholism is prevalent amongst the membership in our church and in our community."

"We have a growing homeless problem in our city."

"Unemployment and underemployment are taking a toll on the people in our region."

"There's just been too much youth crime and violence in our area, and people always say, 'This kinda thing doesn't happen in our neighborhood,' when it does."

"My pastor asked me to come."

"Good, good," replied Barbara. "We're going to get at some of that, but let me begin by saying that we look at marginalization and disenfranchisement differently than perhaps many people do. We consider anyone who is outside of the 'majority culture' of your congregation and community, those who are being judged or feel as though they are being judged for some reason, as being marginalized and disenfranchised. This opens the door to do ministry with a whole lot of people, not just those we typically would call marginalized. Society tends to limit marginalization or disenfranchisement to those who are addicted to something, homeless, poor, immigrants, and so forth. But we broaden the circle to include those suffering from the '–isms' of life—things like racism, classism, sexism, age-ism, sexual orientation-ism . . . I know that's a new word!"

"That's a lot of people and a *lot* of issues," Eric interrupted.

Identify your own places of disenfranchisement

"It sure is," said Sharon, "but it just goes to show you how vast and wide marginalization can be. In order to have a heart for the disenfranchised, you have to be able to identify your own place of disenfranchisement, just like I have to identify mine. When we see marginalization that doesn't look like ours, many people cast judgment. But the fact of the matter is, many of us are just a paycheck away from homelessness, a medical crisis away from financial ruin, and a drink or a snort away from addiction. In fact, each day that we arise clothed and in our right minds, we should tell God thank you, because 'but by the grace of God, there go I.' I can minister to the disenfranchised when I tap into my own disenfranchisement."

"What if you don't have any disenfranchisement?" one person asked.

"Well, I guess you've reached perfection then," Barbara said, as laughter filled the room.

"You've brought us to our first exercise already," Sharon said once the laughs had died down. "I'd like us to take a look at our own places of disenfranchisement. Over the next ten minutes, I'd like you to reflect upon your own congregational and community contexts and write down all the places and spaces where you feel judged, not welcome, or on the margins. Then I'd like you to get with a partner and share those that you feel comfortable sharing."

The group got busy writing. As Barbara and Sharon walked around the room and peered at the participants' papers, they were amazed to see the things that were mentioned and the length of some people's lists. Here is some of what they saw:

- Living with breast cancer
- Being lesbian in a predominantly heterosexual congregation
- Being a man who can't seem to attract a woman in an area where the ratio of women to men is twenty to one
- Having more education that most people in the congregation and community
- Being white in a predominantly black congregation
- Being from the 'small island' in the midst of bigger island countries and feeling 'less than' because of it
- Being unemployed in a congregation that is predominantly employed
- Being divorced and single around so many married people
- Not being able to find a date when so many others seem to have one
- Having a different accent than everyone else

As the two listened to people sharing, the list seemed to extend even further.

"Very good," Barbara said, raising her voice to transition to the next segment of the session. "It appears like you have more marginalization and disenfranchisement in your life than you thought you did, huh?"

Some people said yes as others nodded their heads in agreement.

"Hopefully you now have a better idea of what we mean when we say that unless you've really tapped into your own disenfranchisement, you will have a difficult time authentically connecting to those who feel disenfranchised," replied Sharon. "People—especially those on the margins—will read through you and see whether you are phony or for real in your help of them."

"Reminds me of the movie *The Blind Side*," Eric chimed in. "Mrs. Touhy had to be real if she was going to help Michael Oher."

"Yes, I've seen the movie . . . you're right. That's a great connection," said Barbara. "But in addition to identifying your own disenfranchisement, to have a heart for this ministry, you've got to evaluate how deep and how far you are willing to unconditionally love someone."

Dwell on possibilities not deficiencies

"What do you mean by unconditional love?" asked a man named Bill, from the back of the room.

"We mean the desire to work for the well-being of others regardless of who they are, what they've done, what they look like, how they smell, or whatever," said Barbara. "At the Fellowship, we encounter people from all walks of life, with all kinds of issues—drug and alcohol addictions, homelessness, being undocumented, domestic violence and relationship turmoil . . . you name it. You've got to love people, if you're going to help people. Most of us usually hang around people we think are 'safe.' Our tendencies are to minister to people who allow us to be comfortable. But to do the ministry Jesus calls us to, we have to avail ourselves to minister in love to people who have all sorts of disconnects with mainstream society.

"In doing so, we do not dwell on their deficiencies, we look at their possibilities. And we don't participate in people's pity parties or conduct such parties on our own either. We lead people in love to the plans and purposes that God has for them and for us."

Be willing to become vulnerable

"And to truly love someone, you have to be willing to become vulnerable. Most people don't want to be made open to hurt or pain, particularly emotionally. But we can only help someone if we can tolerate being hurt. Isn't that the message of the cross?"

"I'm not sure I understand," Eric said.

"Well, during a particular season, we were helping an alcoholic get up on his feet, gain basic life skills, and present himself for employment," Sharon offered. "We even found him a job cleaning the streets in the neighborhood for a good wage. We spent a lot of time helping him, but then we discovered that he started drinking on the job, having binges on the weekend, and coming to work drunk. We had to terminate him, and he went off. He was so drunk the day we had to let him go, that he threatened to go home, find a gun, and 'bust a cap' in Pastor D!

"It hurt all of us to see him in that predicament—particularly when it seemed like he was turning the corner—but we couldn't jeopardize the employment program for everyone else. Things like that are what we're talking about. You have to be able to love unconditionally."

"Okay, so, answer this for me," Barbara said to the group, "who do you love?"

"Well, I love my family and my friends . . . my church family," a woman named Nancy said.

"That's good. But would you love anybody who sat next to you in church, even if they were a complete stranger? Do you love your neighbor in the community who you don't know well, but whose life is a recipe for disaster?"

The room was quiet for a while.

Examine who you love

"Well, this leads us into our second exercise—you guys are a great group!" said Sharon. "Please turn to Resource I in your resource packet and have a look at 'The Touch Test' by Pastor Rudy Rasmus from St. John's Downtown in Houston.[21] Please take ten minutes and answer the question, 'Who do you love?' Many of the people listed will disturb you, but the exercise will bless you. What will you do if you find these folks sitting next to you in the pew one Sunday?"

Eric was fascinated by the exercise. The list was phenomenal. This track was already broadening his ideas for ministry at Last Chance. As he was doing the exercise, he could not help but think about Sandy. He was hoping and praying that her son Jimmy would pull through and could find a support base to help him in weak moments. Jimmy had been shunned by Last Chance in the past; the church loved Sandy, but by its actions showed that it really didn't want to be bothered with Jimmy's problems. It was Eric's hope that this mentality could change within the congregation.

"Okay, how'd you find this exercise?" Barbara asked.

"I'm taking this back to church tomorrow and asking several of our leaders to fill it out," said Bill. "Interestingly enough, we don't talk about unconditional love much in our church . . . and I don't know why. We mention love, but we don't really teach it or learn how to really model it. I became aware of that during opening worship when Pastor D was laying out what it meant to be REAL church. Now you've taken it one step deeper. You're helping me view love in an entirely different context, though, specifically what loving the *marginalized* is all about."

"Yes, thank you for sharing that. You've got to know your own disenfranchisement and be willing to love others unconditionally as they battle theirs," Barbara said. "It's at the heart of what we do. Because we deal with marginalization at the Fellowship at all levels. We minister to the divorcee, to the cancer patient, to the individual in danger of deportation. We minister to the gay or lesbian individual, the young boy or girl who does not have a father or mother. We minister to families who have children or close relatives who are incarcerated. All of these folks and many others are judged, and even live in the margins. We seek to pull them out of the margins and assure them that God loves them. But to do so, they have to see that we are 'love with skin on.' You *gotta* love. There are so many outcasts in the world today because the world has stopped loving—or perhaps never started.

"Remember, love is one of our basic foundations for being REAL. And when you authentically love, outrageous things can happen, and all kinds of people can be reached. For example, not long ago, we had a leadership summit at the church. Any and everybody was invited. One woman came whose husband left her; she'd had a son die of AIDS, another son was sent to the war in Iraq, and another was strung out on drugs. She had been fighting depression following a series of treatments for cancer followed by unemployment. She ended up at the Fellowship at someone's invitation, and she's found love despite all her challenges.

"That's what you want," Sharon said. "You want your congregation's heart for the marginalized to be so big that people who come to you *feel* the love, regardless of the twists and turns their lives have taken. Love that leads them to be whole again.

"Your church can become that, if you start teaching love, preaching love, and modeling love to everyone in the congregation and community, particularly those who are feeling least, last, and lost. We are a witness at the Fellowship that this can happen. But it hasn't always been this way. There were some people that our ushers used to escort to the door because we simply didn't want them here. Every three months, a transvestite would visit the Fellowship. We believe this person had a 'thing' for Pastor D. Every time he'd show up, folks would escort him to the door. I wonder what would have happened back then if we had tried to love him?"

The room became very contemplative as Barbara continued.

"There's one last thing we'd like to share with you before we take a break," said Barbara. "And that is that a heart for the disenfranchised begins expanding as people practice the spiritual disciplines."

"What do you mean by spiritual disciplines?" queried Nancy. "And what does that have to do with having a heart for those who are often judged?"

"Well, I'm glad you asked," Barbara replied. "You see, love is an expression of spiritual discipline. We say that because we've found that the vast majority of the people who engage meaningfully with marginalized and disenfranchised populations are people who have had an awakening to God through worship, prayer, fasting, and Bible study. In fact, you are in the house that we named after our transitional housing coordinator, Ms. Velma. Ms. Velma heard God's call to help homeless people while studying and sharing in a Bible study at the Fellowship. The study changed her life and began to bring all the things she'd learned about caring for people, even from a kid and through her career as a hospital nurse, to the realm of helping mothers and young children who had no place to live. It's one of the reasons we brought you here today. Ms. Velma was disenfranchised herself once, a mother with young kids, just trying to survive. Now she's helping others who were in her shoes do the same. All of that emerged out of the Bible studies. In fact, our street pastors who reach out to minister to transient men and women, our homeless coordinators, our counselors for at-risk youth—all of them—sensed a call to this ministry. And that came through worship, prayer, and Bible study."

"That's right," said Sharon. "You can only do this work effectively when you know that God has called you to it. The demands, the commitments, the stresses, and the strains of helping people who have nowhere to turn are heavy—very heavy. And unless you have the heart for it and you've been called to it, there's another ministry you need to pursue."

"How do you know whether you've been called to it?" Eric asked.

"Simply put, God's calls are clear, concise, and personal," said Barbara, "You will know God has called you to this or any ministry when His summons is clear, concise, and personal to you. I had only been attending the Fellowship for a year or two when someone invited me to come down to the Fellowship Hall to serve the meal to our homeless brothers and sisters. I really didn't want to go, but I didn't have the heart to tell my friend no. As I was walking down the stairs I was dreading it. The next week, for some reason, I felt drawn back to serve the meal. Before I knew it, God was revealing to me ideas for how to make their experience better and how to grow the ministry. I started having Bible studies on the bus; I recruited more people to help with the ministry; and I'm now working on my MSW."

As Eric listened to Barbara's testimony, he was convicted that there was no other ministry for him to pursue. God had been calling him to start a support group that ministered to recovering alcoholics and drug addicts, but he'd been ignoring it. Now there was nowhere to run and nowhere to hide. It was time for him to start this ministry at Last Chance. He also knew that the first two members of this ministry would be Sandy and Jimmy.

Having a Heart for the Marginalized

Marginalized = anyone who isn't in the majority culture of our congregation and community and/or feel as though they are being judged or less-than

To authentically connect with those on the margins:
1. identify my own places of disenfranchisement
2. dwell on possibilities, not deficiencies
3. be willing to become vulnerable
4. examine who I love (Resource 1 in resource packet)

We must pull people out of the margins and assure them God loves them...and so do we.

To lead a ministry with the marginalized, I must be called. God's calls are clear, concise and personal.

Chapter 21
Assessing Power in Your Community

Government. Private. Public.

Gary and Pamela made their way down the hallway with other participants to the room marked "Community Development." For a change,
Gary had arrived on time that morning; the topic had him so riveted that
suddenly he became very prompt. He had been looking forward to the
opportunity with great expectation ever since Pastor Joe had invited him to
lead Last Chance's effort to connect with the community. It had been one
meal in that diner he'd never forget.

"The sign is over here, Pamela," Gary said after spotting their destination. Pamela crossed over to where Gary was, and the two entered the classroom where the session on community partnerships was being held. Pamela
entered the room with mixed emotions. On the one hand, she was excited
about the idea of community development, but she was also very apprehensive about being tasked with one more thing. She simply wasn't quite sure
how much she was willing to commit to the community transformation
process. After all, as the resident "Jill-of-all-trades" at Last Chance, she had
taken on leadership in almost every area of the church and was feeling a

little burned out. But because she loved her church dearly, she continued to make those sacrifices.

Pamela and Gary thoroughly enjoyed the first session. It was a gorgeous fall day, and the workshop leaders, Nelson and Laura, led them on a tour of the neighborhood that helped all of the participants experience how to conduct a community inspection. They interacted with small business owners, talked with police officers, played with kids, and encouraged homeless men and women squatting on the stoop of community buildings. The tour truly gave a broad picture of the number of community issues that the Fellowship was called to address.

When the group returned to the classroom, they engaged in a lively discussion of how to conduct a community inspection back home, and Gary picked up a few tips he planned to add to what he was already doing.

"Before we continue," Laura said, "I'd like you all to introduce yourselves, let us know where you are from, and tell us one reason why you wanted to take this track on community development as opposed to the other offerings this weekend. Surely there was something compelling in your community or congregation that moved you to sign up to be here today!"

As people began to share, it became evident to Laura and Nelson that there were many diverse communities in the room. While the Fellowship was in an urban community, in the room with them were people from rural areas, the suburbs, towns, and even exurban areas. The recession and slow economic recovery had impacted each of these regions in some unique ways. Nelson and Laura were prepared for the diverse perspectives, needs, and settings in the room. They knew that while all communities are different, there were core principles that crossed every community regardless of location.

Gary spoke up first. "Well, he said, "I'm here because my pastor has asked me to lead the community engagement process at our church, so I'm hoping to learn how to build meaningful relationships in a community that has undergone great transition. We're in what used to be a rural community that's now become a suburban community. But as we are seeking to transform our church, the reality is, we have no connection with our community. Small businesses are trying to survive as big-box businesses plant their roots. What was once an area noted for its slow pace is now a sprawling suburb with traffic issues. Just two miles down the road from the church, there are new communities being built faster than you can say 'hello,' even while money is tight for people. And our church hasn't begun to engage itself in the change that is taking place."

The next person to speak was a middle-aged woman whom Gary had chatted a little bit with on the neighborhood tour.

"My name is Lisa," she said. "I'm here because I want to know what my church can do to get these drunks and drug users off the corner next to my church. We don't like the fact that they are there, but no one in our congregation seems to want to do anything about it. I *do* want to do something about it—but I need a plan and tangible skills."

"I'm George," said the man seated next to Lisa, "and I'm here because my church and neighborhood do not have any say in who comes here or who does not. The city wants to build a new grocery store right across the street from our church. First of all, it will be a traffic nightmare. Secondly, while this store is popular, its employment practices have been under fire. It appears to be a done deal, but I want to know how we can get in the game, engage community partners, and make sure that as a neighborhood, we get what *we* want out of the deal."

The next attendee spoke up in a loud, clear voice. "I'm Mark from First Church," he said. "I'm here because my pastor wanted me to find out about the establishment of a separate 501c3 entity from the church that might assist us in accomplishing the church's vision and mission."

Finally Pamela introduced herself. "Hi, I'm Pamela from the Church of the Last Chance. To be honest with you, I don't know why I'm here. I've done everything there is to do in church, to the point where I don't want to do any more. But there's some reason why I agreed to sign up for this track . . . I just can't put my finger on it."

Gary tried to hide the surprise he felt at hearing Pamela's almost painfully honest comment. He knew that Pamela was always busy around the church, but he hadn't realized that it was taking such a toll on her.

"Sounds like you are a candidate for a divine vision," Laura responded. "Perhaps the Lord is about to speak to you today."

Gary and Pamela looked at one another after hearing Laura's comment. They both knew that things were about to change in their lives, and in the lives of their congregation, because of this experience. They just didn't know how. But the change was coming.

"I've been at the Fellowship even longer than Pastor D," Laura bragged as she began her presentation. "I've served in many different roles here at the church, from personnel chair to finance chair to trustee chair. I love my church. But now I've settled into something that really pulls together all of my diverse passions and skills—and that is in serving as the president of the board of directors of the Fellowship's 501c3 community development corporation, which is called the Beacon. We will be talking about how to set up a 501c3 in the next teaching block. I promise it will be a blessing to you! I love this work. I live two blocks from the church, so this community and what happens to it are very important to me. The first thing I have to say is that, after doing an inspection, it is so important to identify and engage community partners."

"Absolutely," said Nelson. "I too share a great passion for this neighborhood. I grew up here, went to schools here . . . Now I live seven blocks from here, and I really want to see this community become a place where anyone would want to live."

Gary and Pamela perked up, each for different reasons. Like Nelson, Gary's life had been tied up in the town where the Church of the Last Chance was. Many people had left; but after his long career in the community as a firefighter, he had stayed, and he wanted to see that those who stayed had a great community to enjoy just as much as those who were just moving in. Like Laura, Pamela knew all too well the story of having so many different hats to wear in leadership. But unlike Laura, Pamela hadn't found her true ministry passion yet. Was it about to come?

"Let me cut to the chase," Laura said. "Before you can engage community partners in your congregational and community transformation process, you have *got* to first understand clearly how all communities work. You have to understand the power dynamics that take place within every community structure. They are complex and dynamic; yet, once you understand them, they are very simple and straightforward. Most people don't understand them—I surely didn't until I got involved with this—so don't feel bad if you find out that you don't either. Those who know how to analyze power in a community have an advantage over those who don't. Simply put, communities work through the interaction and interplay of three basic sectors. Does anyone know what they are?"

Mark spoke up before anyone could venture a guess. "What is a sector?"

"Good question. A sector is a distinct part or branch of a nation's economy or society, or of a sphere of activity," Laura answered.

"Okay, well in that case, the government must be one," Lisa answered. Nelson wrote "government" on the flip chart.

"Are publicly traded companies a sector?" Gary asked.

"They are a part of what is called the 'private sector,'" Laura answered. "The private sector includes every major entity that infuses a community with revenue and jobs. For example, corporations, farms, banks, media outlets, agricultural equipment companies, professional sports teams, major hotel chains, automobile manufacturing plants, major restaurant chains, universities and colleges, hospitals, utility companies, transportation agencies, farms, etcetera, etcetera—all of those form the private sector. This sector serves as the economic engine every community needs in order to thrive."

"Okay, got it," said Gary.

"Can anyone tell me the third?" Laura continued.

"Well, if there is a private sector, is there a public one?" a voice called out.

"You got it. There is a public sector. So those are the three sectors: private, governmental, and public. And these three sectors are at work in every community. They may look differently in an urban setting as opposed to a rural setting or a suburban setting. But trust me, they function the same way.

The Private Sector

"So, let's start with the private sector. The more representation the private sector has in a community, the stronger that community can become. There will be more revenue, which means there will be more jobs, which means there will be more housing built and owned, more kids in schools, more parks, and so on. No community can survive without a strong private sector. Research will show that when the private sector is weak, several factors kick in—an increase in crime, poor education, multiple signs of poverty in the community. And, just let one or more major corporations leave a city or town and watch what happens in that area. People will suffer unless there is a replacement in the private sector and it comes soon. We're going through that right now with a major military hospital right up the street leaving our neighborhood. Everyone thinks that the federal government is the major private sector employer, but the fact is that if you take the educational institutions and the medical hospitals out of this town, we would be in severe economic trouble. If you are seeking to organize and understand community, you've got to build relationships with and within this sector."

Heads nodded, and inquisitive expressions formed around the room as Laura continued talking. Just then Nelson spoke up.

"Laura and I are going to be conducting several checks as we interact with you today," he said. "The first is a private sector check. With a person or persons from your church team, I'd like you to do the following assignment. Write "Private Sector" on a piece of paper. I'd like you to list all of the private sector entities that exist in your community. Take five minutes and write down who brings revenue and jobs to your community."

As the teams got to work, Gary and Pamela could not help but think about all the change that had happened in their town, just over the last five to ten years. The new stores, shopping malls, and restaurants began to fill their list. Even the corporate offices of several technology companies were there. Gary was happy that his favorite restaurant, the one where he had met with Pastor Joe, had hung on. But the exercise really began to touch Pamela deeply.

In the town near the Church of the Last Chance, there were the remnants of a once-thriving auto plant. The property laid dormant now. In the last recession, the auto plant had closed. With it, went her father's job of forty-three years. Though he was at retirement age, Pamela's father had not been ready for retirement. He had loved his work and enjoyed working. He was a fixture in the community and very visible at many community meetings. Two years after the plant closing, and his subsequent layoff, however, Pamela's father died. His life had been wrapped up in that plant. The depression of not being there had rapidly sucked the life out of him.

"Everybody finished?" Laura asked. "Let's just shout out some of the private sector companies you've put on your list."

"Macy's, Walmart, Host Farms, Marriott, Holiday Inn, John Deere, our NFL team, Chrysler, Wells Fargo, our state universities, Google, the state detention centers," people called out.

"The detention centers?" somebody asked. "Are they private industry?"

"Yes, they are," Nelson said. "They keep a lot of rural communities employed today. With the droughts in some areas that took place several years ago, many farms couldn't survive. As a supplement, the state began to move their prisons and detention centers to these farm areas, and with the rise in crime in urban and suburban areas, the prison industrial complex has become big business. You can now buy stock in prisons on the Dow Jones 30 industrials."

"What?" somebody shouted out. "That's crazy!"

"He's right, though," Laura said. "You can. And that's why you must understand and get to know the private sector in your community. This sector can make or break a community."

The murmurs around the room confirmed that some attendees knew from experience exactly what she was talking about.

"I was born in Pittsburgh when the steel industry was thriving," Laura continued. "I had uncles and some cousins who spent time working in the mills. It was rough employment, but it was employment. And they were able to help feed their families through the income they received. In the 1970s however, the steel industry in America began a severe decline. The growing global economy made it more profitable at the time for companies to import steel instead of manufacturing it here at home. And as a result, US steel mills began to shut down, and jobs began to disappear.

"I can remember being able to smell the steel mills at least seventy-five miles outside of Pittsburgh. When the steel industry tanked, you could barely smell steel at all as you came up the highway. Many people left Pittsburgh during that time because jobs were hard to find, and many families suffered as a result of it. Yet today, Pittsburgh is thriving once again because the city reinvented itself. Once the home of steel, today the city is now known as one of the health care capitals of our country. People are working again. The point is that you've gotta have a strong private sector if you're going to have a strong community."

The Governmental Sector

"Now let's talk about the governmental sector," Nelson transitioned. "The governmental sector provides law, order, and services to the community. This sector spends a lot of time supporting the private sector through creating and maintaining legislation that enables the private sector to earn as much as it can. Additionally, the governmental sector ensures that basic community services—water, sewers, schools, safety nets for the poor, police, fire and rescue, transportation, and so on—are provided to the community. Without the legislative arm of government in a city or town, there would be sheer chaos.

"Here in Columbia, I work in what is probably the most unique city in the country," he continued. "There are several government agencies that function more as a private sector entity, and then there's the local government, which actually oversees city operations. One of the challenges that our local government has is that it is often given a city budget to manage what are essentially state-level issues. And so its interaction with the private sector is critical to the city's ability to operate efficiently. In the governmental sector, you find your elected officials, including the mayor, city council members, and other government agencies. A weak government is a set up for a weak community because without order you have confusion. The strongest communities have well-organized, efficient governmental sector. The weaker communities display governments that struggle to get anything significant done."

"What if you don't have a mayor?" Pamela asked. "What does government look like then?"

"Good question," Nelson said. "Every municipality has a government. I would venture to say that if you don't have a mayor where you live, then you have a county executive or supervisor of some sort who is an elected official and responsible for leading the governance of your community."

"Yes, in Hopeville we have an executive."

Laura spoke up then. "Okay, time for another check. Take out a piece of paper and title it 'Government Sector.' Write down all the federal, state, and local government entities that are in your town, city, or region."

As Gary and Laura worked together on this, they couldn't help but recall all of the Last Chance members who held jobs in the government sector. As they talked and took notes, they began to share with each other the ideas that could emerge if somehow they were able to encourage church members to start community partnerships. The possibility of using school buildings and other government entities for community programs began to race through Gary's mind. *That would be a great way to broaden David's program with the youth,* he thought.

The Public Sector

"Okay, good," Laura said after she finished humming the jingle to *Jeopardy*, signaling that time was nearly up. "I think we all have a good idea who is in our government sectors, so let's push on to the public sector. The public sector is you and me, the people who live in community. This ranges from doctors, trash collectors, lawyers, and police officers to citizens, undocumented individuals, and people from all walks of life. People in the public sector work in all three sectors. In this sector as well, you find citizen organizations, community associations, churches, synagogues, mosques, boys' and girls' clubs, sororities, fraternities, and other community-oriented groups. You even have mayors. Who are your mayors?"

"What do you mean?" one woman asked. "I thought mayors were in the government sector. We just elected ours to a third term last week."

"Oh, no term limits, huh?" Nelson quipped as he prepared to address the group.

"Let me clarify—Laura is not talking about the *elected* mayors. She's talking about the unelected ones. People like Aunt Susie and Uncle Fred, who may sit in rocking chairs on their porches all day long or hang out in the barbershop or at the beautician's for hours. But I guarantee you this: few major decisions are made in their community without their approval being secured. These are major players in the community. They can kill a project before it even gets off the ground. Or they can ensure a project gets completed even though you may never hear their voices. You have to know who your mayors are. They are an important part of the sector."

Pamela began thinking of all the people she knew in Hopeville; a few seemed to fit exactly the description Nelson had just given.

"Without a public sector," Nelson continued, "you have a ghost town. For example, years ago my brother worked for GM in Detroit, Michigan. Detroit was a thriving metropolis whose heart was the 'Big Three' auto industry: GM, Ford, and Chrysler. With the rise in popularity of international car brands including Toyota and Nissan, the American car industry began to suffer. And with it, so did Detroit. Today there are neighborhoods in Detroit that have all but been abandoned because the public sector has moved elsewhere to survive. You can't have community without people. So obviously this sector is critical to community as well. Take a quick check and write down all of the public sector groups in your community."

After the participants had done so, Nelson began to walk them through the power dynamics connecting the three sectors. "How these three sectors operate in tandem with one another determines the strength of the community where your church is located. You can tell a strong community because there are well-paying jobs, good schools, an efficient government, clean streets and parks, plenty of amenities, strong churches and civic organizations, multiple family units, and very little crime. In strong communities, all three sectors are working in tandem with each other. But if you enter a suffering or struggling community, you can now identify the central reason why: one or more of the sectors in that community is lacking or not in healthy relationship with the others."

"So which sector is usually the most powerful?" Gary asked.

Before Laura or Nelson could speak, shouts from the room could be heard all over the place. "The private!" somebody said. "They got the money; they got the power."

"No, the government does," another person argued. "They make the laws and keep order—an orderless society would produce chaos."

Nobody mentioned the public sector until Laura spoke up again.

The church should be a major catalyst for community transformation in the public sector, private and governmental sectors.

"Herein lies the challenge for you and others like you who feel
compelled to transform or strengthen your congregations and communities. As the church, you've got to begin looking at yourself as the catalyst
for community wholeness in your neighborhoods. After all, you are a major
public sector player, and in God's economy, you are the centerpiece of any
community with all of its sectors combined. And so you need to begin to
act like it. Anyone disagree?"

Sensing no pushback, Laura went even deeper. "If you are in a strong
community, and your church is struggling, that means that you haven't
stepped up and acted as a major public sector player. If that is the case, you
are irrelevant. And God does not establish irrelevant churches. Obviously, if
you are in a marginalized community, one or more sectors is failing. In that
context, what becomes imperative for you and for those in the community
with you, is to do an analysis of how power operates in your community so
as to bring strength to whatever sector is weak.

"In some struggling communities, the problem is obvious. For example,
in Detroit there aren't enough private sector companies. And as a result, the
government and public sectors are hurting. Teachers are being laid off; school
systems are struggling; the unemployment rate is high, and families are in
crisis. Then, in other communities, sometimes the government sector suffers
because of corruption. Corruption will scare private sectors away to other
areas. I'm not picking on East St. Louis, Illinois, but if you were to do a background check on them in past decades you'd find this to be the case.

"There are other reasons affecting this, of course; the '-isms' of life can
do a lot of damage to a community. But for the vast majority of communities where there are significant community needs, whether they be problems
with kids and drinking and driving, or problems with crime and violence,
the issue is not just with the private or governmental sector, the issue is the
public sector. And more specifically, the public sector's lack of community
organizing. And the only way for that to be changed is for some entity in the

public sector to begin organizing people for change. And the best entity to do this is the one that has or should have divine vision—the church."

Lightbulbs began to turn on in Pamela's head. She had always wondered why her community had struggled while others thrived. Her wonder often turned to anger as she went to community meeting after community meeting, addressing issue after issue—something her dad had done as an active member in the community—only to find that the subject of the meeting was already a moot point before she got there. Now she knew why. Politics—transactions and deal making—was going on in the private and governmental sectors all the time. And a disorganized public sector never got wind of what was happening until it was too late.

A burning sensation began to penetrate Pamela's chest, and a sense of call began to sit in her stomach. Could it be that the reason she was here was because God was calling her to become a community organizer in her neighborhood near the Last Chance? An organizer who would help Last Chance and other churches transform their towns, cities, and neighborhoods for the betterment of all?

"What Laura is trying to tell everybody is that this is where the church can make the gospel real in the community," Nelson continued. "Remember Luke 4, verses 18 and 19: Jesus himself declared, *'The Spirit of the Lord is upon me because he has anointed me to preach good news to the poor. He has sent me to proclaim release to the captives and recovery of sight to the blind, to let the oppressed go free, to proclaim the year of the Lord's favor.'* And he did this by organizing twelve people who would end up transforming the entire world. If Jesus organized twelve people to transform the world, then surely you and I can organize people to transform our communities. But community partnerships and community organizing are the key because the private and governmental sectors by and large do what their resources allow them to do. After all, they control revenue, jobs, and governance. You and me, for the most part, only interact with these sectors if we are buying something, looking for a job, or if it is election time. It is usually at election time that your streets get paved and your trash gets picked up on time—if you are even fortunate enough to get that.

"These two sectors are very well organized, and they know each other well. They live in the same neighborhoods together; they socialize together, take vacations together, play golf and go to the community pool together.

They craft deals for one another in their neighborhoods. There's nothing wrong with this, unless your neighborhoods are being locked out of their plans and resources, or unless they have limited themselves to acting self-ishly and not caring about the well-being of all. And so the only way to get the private and government sectors' attention is by organizing people and organizing money and building community partnerships. People equal votes. And resources provide the ability to act in ways that lead to trans-formation. If you are going to be a church that is a catalyst for community transformation, you must organize your community so that it can flex its muscles in the public arena to get what it needs to have in order to thrive. While you are doing this, you will find great opportunities to reach people for Jesus Christ. That is our overall mission, you know."

Folks nodded their heads as they listened.

"I remember Pastor D telling us a story," Laura continued, "of a man at a community rally where we were seeking to get resources from the private and governmental sectors to train and hire unemployed workers. The rally was held at a neighborhood church, and the man, who was a member of a union, came up to Pastor afterward and said, 'Rev, if you all keep doing stuff like this, we will come flocking to your church.' Because this is what being the church is all about—helping people in their time of need and helping people live abundant lives."

Tears began to well up in Pamela's eyes. Like her father had done outside his auto plant work, all her life she had served in capacities to try to help other people's lives. As Pamela sat in the workshop trying to contain her emotions, Gary grabbed her hand and whispered, "I don't know all of what I need to know about God, but I know that when He calls you, you gotta answer. If he's calling you to community organizing and development work, I'd love to partner with you to make a difference at Last Chance and in our town."

Unable to speak, Pamela simply nodded her head in agreement, and the first community partnership through Last Chance was formed. Now she knew why God had had her press her way to the REAL Church Revival even when she was so tired. She felt reenergized and ready to continue the trans-formation that Pastor Joe and others were working for.

Now she was more eager than ever to learn the nuts and bolts of how to organize her beloved community.

Power Analysis

Communities work through the interaction and interplay of three basic sectors: public, private, government

The private sector is the economic engine of a community. It includes every major entity that infuses a community with revenue and jobs.

The governmental sector provides law, order, and services to the community. It includes all branches of government. Elected officials need votes from the public sector and cash from the private sector.

The public sector is made up of the people who live in a given community and community organizations like citizen organizations, community associations, churches, synagogues, mosques, boys' and girls' clubs, sororities, fraternities, etc.

The church should be a major player in the public, private and governmental sector; as the organizer and catalyst for community wholeness in your neighborhoods.

If you are going to be a church that is a catalyst for community transformation, you must organize your community so that it can flex its muscles in the public arena to get what it needs to have in order to thrive.

Chapter 22
Engaging Community Partners

Relationships. Reputations. 501c3s.

"To organize your community effectively, you must build relationships with people in each of the three sectors and learn specifically about how your unique community functions," Laura stressed. "You've been doing or should be doing relational interviews and house meetings from your initial community inspection. Pastor D told me that some of you have been doing this already."

Gary and Pamela answered in the affirmative while others looked on.

"Well, you and those in your congregation must never stop doing these relational interviews," Nelson continued. "Rather, they need to intensify and expand. Particularly now that you, the congregation, and the community have the beginnings of a vision for what God wants your community to look like. Take out your private sector sheet. Here are the specific entities that make up the private sector in your community. You need to conduct relational interviews with their leaders—presidents, vice presidents, board members—and get to know them while allowing them to get to know you. You need to share the information you've learned from these meetings with others in the town hall meetings you continually have with more and more people from your community. Additionally, you need to use these interviews to hear the private sector's vision for your community and then look for partnership opportunities so that common ground can be reached. The same thing needs to happen with the government sector. While God has a vision for your overall community, you need to learn the visions of others to see where they are compatible—or at odds—with what God desires.

"Furthermore, you need to conduct relational interviews with all those you have listed on your government sector list: your congressional representatives, your mayor, your city council persons, and others in government that make decisions that impact you. You want to share with them your ideas, ultimately your vision for community transformation, and explore ways that they can partner with you. You need to continue to conduct these meetings with people in your neighborhood, the 'mayors,' teachers, principals, small business owners, and so on.

"Some of these people are in your churches," he continued, "and others of them want to be in your churches, but they need an invitation, or they simply need to see that you are working, living, and functioning as the embodiment of Jesus Christ. Through these meetings with people in the private, governmental, and public sectors, you want to forge a seat for you and others at the decision table as well as establish a prominent role in shaping decisions that impact your people. It's not enough to sit at the table; you want to be able to impact decisions that pave the way for God's vision of community transformation to become a reality. This is what the church needs to be doing!"

Laura jumped in, "I'm reminded of what former South African archbishop Desmond Tutu said years ago. He had just emerged from his first relational interview with then-president F. W. de Klerk, who was attempting to dismantle the apartheid regime. The media assembled outside to interview Tutu on this historic occasion. One reporter asked the archbishop how it felt to finally have a seat at the table of power. Tutu responded: *I am not interested in picking up crumbs of compassion thrown from the table of someone who considers himself my master. I want the full menu of rights.*" [22]

"That's right, you don't want to just have a seat at the table. You want to be able to set the menu," Nelson agreed. "Most of the time, if you cultivate an environment of positive relational interviews in these sectors, you can get a lot of positive things accomplished for your community, particularly if you are able to see that mutual self-interests are met. However, there will be times when flexing your muscles in the public arena will be necessary to demand what you need. That's why you need to be organized. Frederick Douglass once said, 'Where there is no struggle, there is no progress.' Don't be afraid to flex your muscles when you need to, particularly when you have God on your side and when you have organized people and organized money to support kingdom plans and purposes. Politicians, God bless their souls, are excellent mathematicians: they know how to count people and their votes. And if you have organized votes, they will respect you. Private sector leaders know all about money. When they see that you have organized people and organized money, they will be more than willing to talk because they know that the wellbeing of the people is paramount to them making money. It is best to cultivate as many community partners as possible, however, so that you can create the most opportunities for progress."

"Wasn't Nehemiah in the Bible a master at this?" Gary asked the group, before rushing ahead to answer his own question. "He was on a mission from God, wasn't he? He even built a good relationship with his king and his officials; this paved the way for him to go back and fulfill God's mission of rebuilding his community. And he knew the power of organized people and organized money. It helped him to stave off the opposition that other politicians, like Sanballat and Tobiah, brought against him. It also helped him build community partners."

"You are right, Gary," Nelson said. "As you are moving seriously toward transforming your community, the need to build community partners is an important step along the journey. Nehemiah highlights this as well. Because like us, he finds that the work that God has called us to is too great for us to do on our own. We need help. If you are faced with a task for God that you can't do on your own, ask for help!"

"How many of you remember rent parties?" Laura asked. "The generation in my parent's age bracket really remembers rent parties. I have some family members who thank God for rent parties. These were the parties that people used to throw in their apartments when the rent was due, but the money was short. People would cook some food, throw on the tunes, and have a neighborhood party. Everybody who came would dance a hole in your rug, eat up your food, but leave you some money in the shoebox so that you could pay the landlord before getting kicked out. To improve the lives of people in the community, we need help. Your church is not going to have the capacity, no matter what its size, to handle or to respond to every community challenge. We need partners and we need a network of best practices that can be shared amongst people in the community. For example, if the Fellowship is providing an excellent free immigration clinic for the neighborhood, it doesn't make sense for the church down the street to recreate it and try to do the same thing when that might not be their strength or calling. We need to identify what we do well, what we have the potential to do well, and what we don't do well. As you do this, you can focus much more clearly on the possibilities that you bring to transformation and the resources from other entities you need to find. These entities may include residents of the community, community organizations, associations, affiliations—anybody who you've identified in your inspection as someone who can help you.

Identify potential community partners

"Now I'd like you to take ten minutes to consider what people or groups in your community look like potential community partners. Who do you want to have a rent party with?"

The room became alive with excitement as people began talking around their tables. Nelson and Laura walked around the room and saw groups with their sector sheets out, crossing off some names and starring others.

When time was up, Nelson brought the exercise to a close.

"Now that you have a list of potential partners, I want to caution you. As you continue to survey your community to identify potential partners, you need to be very careful whom you partner with. Just like we should check out somebody thoroughly before we get married, before we partner with another church or community organization, we need to check them out thoroughly. The reason for this is that your community reputation and integrity are always on the line. You've got to be sure that the people you partner with have the same agenda and level of integrity that you do. You don't need to partner with people who can secure job opportunities for folks in the neighborhood, but whose reputation is lousy or counterproductive—because sooner or later, their reputation will come back and burn *you*. "

Laura continued, "Fifteen years ago, the Fellowship was just getting its feet wet with the possibilities of economic development. The two apartment buildings adjacent to the Fellowship—we are in one of them now—had been tied up in tax court after many years of serving as crack houses and squatters' residences. Finally, the buildings were being released from court, and we had a chance to purchase them. Because we were so green in the development world, we didn't understand the possibility of political railroading and underhanded deal-making at high levels. But, boy, did we get some quick on-the-job training!

"To make a long story short, there was another community organization competing against us for the buildings. We found out that this group was funded by Columbia's city government, was politically connected to our city councilwoman, and had a notorious reputation for getting projects, but never completing them. So many of their projects around the city were left undone. One day one of their leaders approached us and said, 'If we partner together, I have inside information that will get us the project.' Having done our homework about this potential community partner and having listened to other community partners who we trusted, we politely declined and pursued the project on our own. Later on, the director of housing for the city at that time told us that we had the best proposal for the properties but we were not awarded the properties because the deal had been rigged. We were devastated, but in the long run, we were blessed because we had not soiled our own reputation in what would have been a horrendous partnership decision."

"Well, what do *we* need to do so that that doesn't happen to any of us?" Gary asked with hopeful expectation.

"I'm glad you asked," replied Laura. "Before you partner with anyone, you need to be clear about the answers to five questions."

She directed the participants' attention to the screen behind her, which read:

1. Do they share your vision for the community?
2. Do they have a solid, positive reputation in the community?
3. Do they operate their organization with integrity?
4. Do they have a proven track record of rendering service to community members and to other community organizations?
5. Are they really committed to securing the community's well-being through the services that they deliver?

"If the answers to all these questions please you, then you should prayerfully consider becoming partners. If at any point the answers to these questions change, you need to have the boldness and the courage to sever ties with that particular group. You never burn bridges, but you don't need to stay tied to groups that have the potential to destroy you.

"Now, going back to Nehemiah's community partnering process, he identified and built relationships with different community partners. With Jews and priests—that's with other churches and other faith traditions if called to do so. With nobles and officials—which means government officials and corporate gurus who have the resources to help you revitalize. With community residents, community organizations, associations . . . anybody who was identified as potential partners in the inspection phase.

"In our own experience at the Fellowship, we have partnered with a Jewish community development corporation and other synagogues who embrace what we're doing with transitional housing, with our developing work with the homeless, and in the storefront improvement project for the small business community surrounding us. We've partnered with government officials who share our passion for community development, and they've funded us to do work around business improvement, crime prevention, and drug abuse prevention, particularly among teenagers. We have built relationships with and partnered with private entities, banks, construction companies, developers, architects, community organizations, and associations to develop a hundred-unit multipurpose housing, community, and commercial development project for revitalizing the neighborhood where the Fellowship is located. We have even built relationships and partnered with our own denomination and with immigrant justice groups to provide free legal services for immigrants in our community. Fannie Mae helps us with our homeless efforts. There are folk out there who are going to help you do the work of community transformation if you investigate the community and build relationships with community partners. Pastors and church leaders must be *compelled* to do this.

"Often times, creating a formal alliance with city-wide, faith-based organizations and other groups can be extremely beneficial to your local neighborhood transformation efforts. We are a vital part of a fifty-member church organization that built 150 houses for poor folk in Columbia in spite of constant pressure from government and private sector forces to quit on the project. Because of this organization's efforts, 150 families making between $20,000 and $60,000 a year at the time—which in Columbia is definitely poor—moved into their own homes, with major equity. We had to go to Capitol Hill, City Hall, and the boardrooms of major corporations to ensure it got done. It was a seven-year battle. But it got done. You see, what God has for you will be for you. If we are faithful to God as we follow His guidance in developing community partnerships, God will make a way. Do you get it?"

"Yeah, we get it!" Gary and Pamela said in unison.

"Okay, good! Well, now I want you to take ten minutes to make a plan for reaching out to potential partners," Laura said. "Using the list of potential community partners you created before, cross out any names that you already know won't answer the five questions correctly. Then for all the remaining names, I want you to make a schedule of when you are going to contact them for a meeting and who you are going to take with you. Remember, Jesus always sent people out two by two. It is wise to follow this model. The purpose of the meeting is to continue building relationships and determine the answers to the five questions."

Folks got busy with the assignment, and a tremendous buzz filled the room. Partners were being identified on paper; at the same time, partners already written down were being scratched out. It took Laura a couple of minutes to shift the energy that had built up in the room.

"This is fabulous," she said. "Your energy is giving us the energy to keep doing what you are doing. Do you have any questions about your homework before we transition to talk about 501c3s?"

"I do," said Pamela. "I'm curious to know what one of these relational interviews looks like. I'm not sure that I know how to build a relationship while at the same time getting answers to some very big questions."

Building relationships by asking the right questions.

"Let's use the basic questions we talked about in the community inspection as the basis for a role play," Laura answered. Pointing to the screen, she read the six questions aloud.

- Where are you from?
- How did you get here?
- How long do you see yourself here?
- What would you like to see this community become?
- What is your perception of our church?
- How can we help you or help the community achieve your vision?

Nelson said, "Let me and Laura give you an idea of what we are talking about. We're going to role play, and while we do that, please take notes on what you see me doing. Make notes about the things I do that will build relationship and about the things I do that are off base." As Laura took a seat, Nelson began the conversation.

"Hi, Laura. How are you?"

"Fine, Nelson, it is a pleasure to meet you."

"Thanks for taking time to meet with me today. Have you been in the community long?"

"No. Actually, I came here from North Carolina," Laura answered. "I was working outside of Greensboro and got a promotion that brought me here to Columbia about two years ago."

"Is North Carolina home?"

"Yes, but not that part of North Carolina. I'm originally from Charlotte."

"Oh, I have family in High Point," said Nelson.

"I have an uncle in High Point."

"Where about? My uncle lives off of Penny Road."

"Wow, mine lives off of Greensboro Road. I'll bet they aren't too far from one another."

"My uncle's name is Mark Jones—what's your uncle's name?" Nelson asked.

"John Jackson."

"Okay, well, I'll call Uncle Mark tonight to see if he knows your uncle. You never know—we might be related!"

"Wouldn't that be funny!" Laura said with a laugh.

"It would. So tell me, as the bank manager who hasn't been here that long, what are your impressions of this neighborhood?"

Laura took a moment to think and then replied, "Well, it has tremendous potential, but I get the sense that it is fragmented."

"Hmmm . . . why do you say that?"

"Well," Laura continued, "we don't get a lot of accounts from local businesses or organizations. In my past work, in other communities, I was much more accustomed to having a larger business client base from the immediate community. While this community is not suffering, it is also not taking advantage of the many opportunities that we as a bank could provide. For example, do you bank here?"

"Well, uhhhhhh . . ." Nelson began looking uncomfortable.

"My point exactly. And you told me when you set up this meeting that you lived here in the neighborhood. What's keeping you from banking with us?"

"Nothing really," said Nelson. "I've just been with my bank for a long time."

"I can understand that, but I'd like you to know we'd love to have you as a customer," Laura pressed.

"Okay, well, thanks for the invitation. Do you work with churches?"

"Absolutely," Laura assured him. "However, churches have a great opportunity that they often squander."

"What do you mean?"

"Well, we are an extremely church-friendly bank. We'd love to offer specials on checking and saving accounts. We'd even be interested in making loans as it is feasible. We have extended the invitation to many churches and haven't heard back from any of them. Why do you think that is?"

"That's a good question," replied Nelson. "I'm going back to my pastor tonight to let him know about your interest. It is obvious that you would like to do business in the community."

"Yes, we would—but not just for selfish reasons. Sure, I would like your business, but I come from a background of strong community ties. I like to see people in a community benefit from various strong community connections."

"That's great to hear. I'd love to find out what your vision is for this community?"

At that point, Nelson brought the role play to an end and addressed the workshop participants. "So, did you get a feel for how the relational meeting flows? What did you see and learn?"

"I saw and heard that she has an interest in being a community partner, but that the community is not interested for some reason," Pamela offered.

"Yeah, a broad community vision hasn't been crafted yet," someone else said.

"The church has been slow to make a connection with this bank," Gary added.

"But the door is open for a greater community partnership," Lisa said. "Do you always spend so much time talking about family and where people are from?"

"Yes," Nelson said. "Because this allows you to connect with others on a personal level. And relationships build their foundations at personal levels."

As they wrapped up their conversation, Laura announced that the group would take a fifteen-minute break. When they returned, she noted, they would talk about why and how to establish 501c3s and their roles in establishing community partnerships.

"Anybody heard of a nonprofit 501c3 community development corporation?" Laura began after the group had returned from their break.

George yelled out, "It sounds like the IRS is involved to me!"

"Aren't they in everything already?" joked Laura, who happened to be a career certified public accountant.

Several in the room laughed, and a few more cracked jokes about the IRS. In the brief interlude, Lisa moved to the snack table in the back of the room and picked up a chocolate chip cookie and bottle of water. When the laughter had died down, she commented, "I think my brother used to work for one, but I'm not sure what he did."

Laura smiled and said, "Okay, let's start from scratch. If you position it properly, the nonprofit 501c3 community development corporation can help your congregation and community become major players in community development in your municipality for years and years to come. Our church first learned about it from a church in another part of the country—and we've never been the same since."

"How is that?" Pamela asked with great interest.

"Pastor D heard about a church establishing a 501c3 to do community ministry while attending an urban church conference in 1996. The workshop presenter was a Baptist pastor of a church on the south side of the city whose congregation worshiped with an average of ninety people a Sunday. It was a small church, yet it was instrumental in starting and administering a highly regarded private school for elementary kids in one of the south side communities. He was amazed that this small church was running a million-dollar operation and became very intrigued.

"The pastor of that church explained in his presentation, 'We must tithe, and we must offer because God does wonderful and powerful things through this command; however, to accomplish the deep, far-reaching visions that God gives us as a church to do, we must develop alternative strategies that allow us to access greater funding resources that the church, because of the separation of church and state, simply cannot attract.' By the time the pastor finished running down the list of places where he raised money, Pastor D realized that after four years of pushing the gospel plow in this community in Columbia, it was time for us to put together our own separate nonprofit entity to be better positioned to pursue the dreams God gave us for our city.

"And I was one of two people he invited to help make it happen," Laura said.

"I tried to talk him out of it at first. Have y'all read the story of the friend at midnight in the Bible?" she asked. "You know, the one where the man is persistent in knocking on his neighbor's door at midnight until the man got up and helped him with a need. Well, Pastor D came at me so much, I felt like he was knocking at my door constantly! I would say to him, 'But we are already a 501c3 as a church,' and truth be told, we were. But Pastor D would come back and say, 'But we need a separate entity, related to the church, but separate from the church.' If we do that, we can do far more. And finally I saw what he saw, and I'm so glad I did."

The benefits of creating a 501c3

"Well, what are the benefits of having a separate 501c3?" Gary asked. He was getting the sense that a 501c3 could function like an arm of the congregation without being the congregation.

Nelson responded, "There are four distinct benefits you don't want to miss.

Seeing Lisa enjoy her cookie like she was a kid in a candy store made Gary want to join in the fun. Gary ran to the table quickly to snatch a sugar cookie and a bottle of water for himself. In an instant, he was back in his seat and ready to take notes.

Nelson continued, "The first benefit of having a separate 501c3 entity is that it allows churches to gain access to greater resources. Private donors can give all they want to a congregation, but government and other private industries are severely limited in what they can give a faith community because of the laws around separation of church and state in the United States."

"I think industries and banks at one point could only give between $2,000 and $2,500 annually to a church, right?" Gary blurted out.

Nelson kept rolling, "Gary, you might be right. That isn't much money, is it? Particularly when you have multimillion dollar dreams! But if a church gets wise and establishes this legal entity separate from its existence as a church, and in partnership with its community, it can creatively pursue resources to help its community become WHOLE."

"But how do you do that?" Pamela asked eagerly.

"We will tell you in a minute," Laura said, "but before that let me give you the second benefit. A separate 501c3 allows churches to become more actively involved in the community development world, knowledgeable about how community development works, and engaged with private and governmental forces seeking to develop their neighborhoods. Two things are upon us, even as we are sharing with you today. One is that the congregation and the Beacon are planning to build a hundred-unit housing and community services facility that will move individuals and families from homelessness to permanent residency. Without a separate nonprofit 501c3, it would be impossible for us to partner with various financiers because most financiers do not want to cut deals with churches. Another is that there are serious plans to build an urban Walmart across the street from the Fellowship. Because we have the separate 501c3 in place and have been doing development projects in this part of the community, the government and Walmart approached us early to see how we might engage the community in figuring out how such a project might work here. Without the entity, the public sector is not at the table nor is it helping to set the menu.

"So, what I hear you saying is that the separate 501c3 becomes a vehicle for you to do business with the private and governmental sectors, yes?" Gary inquired.

"That's right," said Laura. "And if we are going to be churches who transform our communities, we better know how to advocate for our community with the private and governmental sectors. The third benefit is that the separate 501c3 enables the church to focus on the work of the church and allows the community development entity to focus on community development matters. The two are able to support a common vision without co-mingling finances or governance in detrimental ways. This helps to protect the church from potential lawsuits related to community development efforts. The last thing a church wants is to be sued by its neighbors as it seeks to work with them to strengthen the community. Jesus did not die and rise from the dead for his ministry in the world to be compromised by lawsuits."

"The final benefit of forming a 501c3 is that it allows churches to form stronger community partnerships. That's what we've been emphasizing in this session," Nelson said. "What you may not know is that the private and government sectors need strong public sector organizations to carry out a lot of their work in the community. While the private sector generates money in communities and the government sector distributes money for communities, each of these sectors needs organizations in the community that can carry out services to meet community needs. For example, if HIV is a major problem in your community, both the private and governmental sectors may have money they can give the community to address the multiple issues surrounding HIV. But in and of themselves, they do not have the capacity to establish the organizations that serve people on the ground and benefit the people who are in need. When a church can help a community establish a separate 501c3 that responds directly to community needs, then that church and the separate nonprofit entity can become a powerful voice and a powerful presence for hope and healing for all people.

"The money has to land somewhere, right?" Nelson continued. "Why can't it land on you so that you can help those who are sorely in need—in need of affordable housing, quality education, health care, job skills, job training . . . ?" His voice tapered off as he let the participants imagine all that they could begin to do in their communities.

"I'm loving this," Pamela said as she too succumbed to the cookie urge. Then, in Kate-like fashion, she asked yet another question.

How to construct a separate 501c3

"So, what's required to construct a separate 501c3? How do you do it?"

"Simple," Laura said. "All you really need is a good CPA and a good lawyer. You may have a good CPA and lawyer in your congregation. Many congregations do. But even if you don't, as you are doing your community inspections and relational meetings, and building your community partnerships, you will discover that there are legal and accounting firms that will construct such an entity for you, pro bono—free of charge.

"Then," she continued, "you need to construct a board of directors. A nonprofit board steers the direction, raises funds, hires and evaluates the executive director, and champions the cause within the community. You might not have the funds right away to hire staff, but don't worry—keep working. The resources will come. Your board is critical to not only the implementation of the vision, but also the mission and long-term strategic plan necessary for fulfilling your vision."

"With that said, let me stress this vital point," Nelson jumped in. "It's critical that your board members are committed to a common vision of what the community should look like and a shared understanding of the needs in the community that should be addressed. The size of the board should be determined by the capacity of work you intend to undertake. If the board is too small—say, less than seven—it can limit the inroads necessary for raising funds and creating enough community awareness. A board that's too large—more than eighteen—can stall decision making and forward movement."

"Okay, so, the third and final vital requirement is the construction of your bylaws," Laura shared. Looking at her watch, she noticed that time was almost up.

"Your bylaws simply state what you are going to do and how you are going to do it. The bylaws help you remain aligned to the shared purpose and vision for the separate 501c3. Once you construct your board of directors, the board, in prayer, needs to ask God for specific instructions that will become your bylaws. Then it needs to ask God for guidance on pursuing its initial project and subsequent efforts. In the Fellowship's community, we initially sought to transform two abandoned apartment buildings—where there was a lot of drug abuse, prostitution, and gross disenfranchisement—and make them affordable housing. Your projects will be informed by your inspection and discernment process. As you submit all of this to prayer, God will instruct you on the steps to take and the moves to make. Bylaws should reflect your vision: if they're too specific, they'll be outdated easily, and if they're too general, they won't be helpful."

"We've covered a lot this afternoon, I know," said Nelson. "Does anyone have any burning questions?"

"Yes," Pamela said, "would you guys be willing to mentor us once we get something like this off the ground?"

"Certainly," replied Laura. "We want all of you to know that we are in this ministry thing together. Doesn't the Word of God say, 'When one member suffers, we all suffer, but when one member rejoices, we all rejoice?'"

Heads nodded all around the room, as participants looked on happily, their eyes shiny with anticipation. Laura said, "We are here for you."

With that, applause and an impromptu standing ovation broke out. Laura and Nelson smiled at one another with gratitude; they looked to the audience and then to the ceiling as if to say, "God, thank you!" Then, by the prompting of the Holy Ghost, Laura asked Pamela to close the session in prayer. During their time together, God had made it clear that Pamela's ministry was community ministry—community organizing to be exact.

Timid, but surrendered, Pamela prayed so powerfully that for a moment, heaven came down and kissed earth. After many of those gathered had wiped tears from their eyes, everyone embraced and then prepared to assemble together in their church groups to process all they had learned that day.

Identify community partners who:
1. Share your vision for the community
2. Have a solid, positive reputation in the community
3. Operate their organization with integrity
4. Have a proven track record of rendering service to community members and to other community organizations
5. Are committed to securing the community's well-being through the services that they deliver

Build relationships by asking:
* Where are you from?
* How did you get here?
* How long do you see yourself here?
* What would you like to see this community become?
* What is your perception of our church?
* How can we help you or help the community achieve your vision?

Create a 501c3 in order to...
...gain access to greater resources
...become more actively involved in community development
...maintain focus
...form stronger community partnerships

Creating a 501c3 requires:
* A good CPA and a good lawyer
* A board of directors
* By-laws

Chapter 23
Aligning Activity with Purpose

Mind. Heart. Spirit.

The groups filed back into the Fellowship Hall from their various tracks, both excited and exhausted. Joe watched as his leaders came toward the table. He saw shiny, tired eyes, but he also sensed that his leaders had gotten what he'd hoped for. He greeted them with prayerful anticipation. The energy he got back from them confirmed that the Holy Spirit was about to move in a profoundly new way.

Pamela was the first to arrive to the table. "Pastor Joe, I'm ready to get our community organized around what God is doing through our church," she said. "My eyes have been opened to what you've been trying to get us to see during the last several months. I can't wait to get home to start working."

"We've got some really fresh ideas," Gary continued, "about how we can connect our government sector to the work we want to do with youth. It was made so plain in our track—now we just need to make it happen!"

"The worship track has been an unbelievable experience for David and me," Kate chimed in. "On the one hand, it is clear that we are on the right track. But on the other hand, we can see that we're going to have to make some major changes. And we're going to have to be in prayer about when and how to make them."

"I second that emotion," David said in agreement. For his part, Mr. Wilson just seemed confused. He looked at both of them and wondered what in the world they were talking about.

The excited chatter in the room was interrupted by Pastor D who was preparing to lead the last session of the training.

"Good afternoon, everybody! Have you had a great day?" Spontaneous applause and cheers erupted.

"Well, from the sound of things, it appears that the sacrifice you made to get here this weekend has been worth it. That's great. Praise God for that! If you are not seated with your teammates, I need you to rearrange yourselves so that ministry teams are intact."

After a few people changed seats, Pastor D continued.

"I know you guys are tired and ready to get out of here to see the city and get a little break. But we need to work with one more concept before the end of the day so that you leave here with a unified sense of purpose and a clear ninety-day direction. I have found in my own experiences at conferences and training events that if I leave with good ideas, but no plan of implementation, the ideas quickly get lost in the daily stresses and strains that greet me when I return.

"So, we want to be intentional to help you leave with a ninety-day plan that your team can begin implementing right away."

Pastor Joe looked at his team and asked, "You guys ready?" All except Mr. Wilson nodded their heads in agreement.

"If your church is anything like our church is, every now and then we need a little realignment work. If you are driving an older vehicle, you have experienced the need for a front-wheel alignment. We need those every now and again in the course of regular driving conditions, but we need realignment more frequently when the driving conditions are brutal. If you've ever run into potholes, had to make a sudden swerving maneuver to avoid an accident, or slammed on your brakes, you might know what I'm talking about. Sometimes if the vehicle has neglected basic maintenance or is severely misaligned, a big bump can cause huge issues—you might end up needing a new axel or other types of major repairs. So, think about this for a moment: how have the driving conditions been in your congregation? Is it time for realignment or major repair?

"From the laughter, I'd say that it is past time for an alignment job!

You may be asking what we need to be aligned to? Ephesians 4 gives us one image of alignment in verses 15 and 16:

> [15] *'But speaking the truth in love, we must grow up in every way into him who is the head, into Christ, [16]from whom the whole body, joined and knit together by every ligament with which it is equipped, as each part is working properly, promotes the body's growth in building itself up in love.'*

John 15 provides another biblical image of alignment. Jesus is the vine; we are the branches. We must abide in him or be cut off.

"So, keeping all of that in mind, let me walk you through a process that we are using here at the Fellowship to help us consistently realign ourselves and our ministries to the purpose for which we were created. Most of you probably have mission, vision, purpose, or some other guiding statement or slogan that seeks to communicate who you are and where you are going. Hopefully the statement includes the notion that you are aligned with Christ and includes elements of the Great Commandment and the

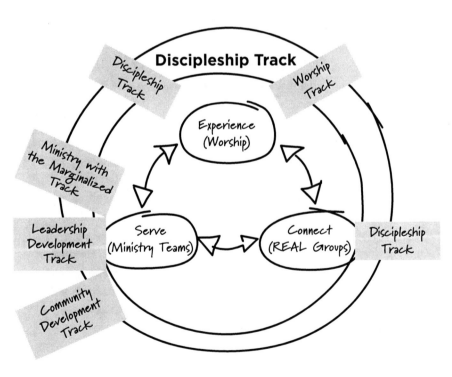

Great Commission that Jesus left for us to fulfill. You'll see them both on the screens behind me," Pastor D said, gesturing behind him.

"Essentially the commandment is about loving God, neighbor, and self; and the commission is about making disciples of Jesus Christ who transform the world.

"All of the different tracks you've just been through have addressed various aspects of the Great Commission and Great Commandment. Now I want us to take a look at how those tracks are connected to each other and our core mission as a church.

"Let's see a show of hands for those of you who attended the disciple-ship track? I'm glad to see we have at least one disciple maker per table. As you learned, the disciple-making process involves—but is not limited to—worship, small groups, and serving. Like the graphic on the screen suggests, the process flows in a variety of ways. The worship track intersects with discipleship at the 'experience worship' part of the cycle," said Pastor D, pointing toward the top of the image in front of them.

"In worship, we make faith decisions; we deepen our experience with God; we learn His Word collectively; and we are empowered to serve him in creative and fresh ways in the world. The leadership development, community development, and 'Ministry to the Marginalized' tracks each inform the 'serve' aspect of discipleship. We understand 'serve' to have both congregational and community aspects. And, like Jesus, we always need to reach the least, the last, and the lost.

"So, now that you see how all of this is lining up, I want to invite you to begin connecting what you've learned with what you are going to be doing in the next ninety days. The first task is easy: take five minutes to find a time in the next week or so to share with one another the ideas and goals you have from your various ministry tracks. Each of you should come to the meeting prepared to report on ideas that you'd like to implement in the next ninety days, six months, nine months, and eighteen months based on what you learned today. Give yourself enough time to really share. You will find a sample agenda in your resource packets on Resource J."

Immediately, the hunt for dates began.

After five minutes had elapsed, Pastor D interrupted.

"Can I have your attention back up here, please? We're going to move on to your next assignment. If you look again at the diagram behind me, you'll see that disciple making from a foundation of loving accountability can be the aligning force for your ministries in the congregation and community. If everything we do as a church is focused on leading more people to become connected learners and followers of Jesus Christ, then we should see more people in worship, more people in small groups, and more people leading and serving. And out of that, we should see healing and transformation happening in our communities. So, let me ask a few pointed questions." Pastor D focused the group's attention on the screen behind him. It read:

As a congregation, if you were really serious about achieving Christ's mission in the world,

- What would you stop doing?
- What would you continue doing (with modifications or as is)?
- What would you start doing?

"Those who attended the discipleship track already spent some time with these very questions. So, your team's starting point will be having your discipleship track people share with you their lists in each category. After you hear what they've said, you're going to add to or edit what they presented. Keep in mind, if something you are doing is not leading more people to and through the discipleship journey or if it isn't transforming lives in the community, *you should stop doing it!* You have twenty minutes to do this, so use your time wisely. If you have any questions, please raise your hand and one of the Fellowship's leaders will stop by your table. On your mark, get set, go!"

Monica and Crystal were so glad to have the opportunity to check their thinking with the larger group. As they walked through their list of things to stop doing, start doing, and keep doing, they received confirmation about many of their thoughts. There were also happy to add new ideas from the group to the mix.

Monica shared with the group her discomfort with the fact that so many people in the serve area were focused on serving on committees rather than on serving the community. Quickly, the group decided that they needed to stop putting so many people on committees. They also needed to streamline the decision-making process at Last Chance. They added, "Simplify committee and decision-making structure" to the 'start doing' list. Soon, time was up, and Pastor D was talking again.

"I know you probably didn't get through all the discussions and debates you needed to," he said. "But that's okay. What you just did was a mini-realignment session. We recommend that you do a full realignment session once a year. This is a time set aside for you to evaluate your ministry—looking at every activity you are doing and asking those three basic questions. If you really want to be disciplined, you will force yourself to stop doing at least as much as you start doing.

"Alright, well, now it's time for your next step: narrow your focus. You're going to look through your 'stop doing' and 'start doing' lists and identify a few things.

"First, figure out one simple thing you can do right now that will result in an increase in worship attendance within the next ninety days. This might include starting a new worship service that is relevant to those who aren't yet a part of your congregation, even though they drive by your church every Sunday. Or it might be to stop including things in worship that aren't part of the Core Four—worship track attendees will know what I mean by that. Or it might be something else entirely.

"Second, I want you to identify the one simple thing you can do right now that would result in an increase in small group or study participation. This might include anything from starting a small group for potential small group leaders to having an exciting small group sign-up party to doing an easy-to-publicize worship series tied to a small group book.

"The third and last thing is to name one simple thing you can do right now that would result in an increase in number of people serving the community.

"We're going to take these one at a time. Please text your answers to me so that we can capture everyone's ideas. Notice, I said 'text,' which means it needs to be brief. I'll give you five minutes to determine the one simple thing you can do right now that would result in an increase in worship attendance within the next ninety days."

As the exercise continued, people's exhaustion seemed to be replaced with the energy of possibility. Soon a flurry of ideas filled the screen:

> call anyone who has missed more than 3-4 Sun b4 missed attendance is a habit

make invites 4 next sermon series & ask each person @ worship 2 distribute 5 & bring 1 visitor

emphasize membrshp expec. incl. weekly worship attendance

monthly recognition 2 the person bringing most guests ea. month

make worship more REAL

make worship more welcoming 4 guests

"This is wonderful," Pastor D enthused. "If you saw something on the screen that you think would work better than what you had written, you have my permission to steal that idea—but only if it will work in your context!"

He repeated the same approach for generating ideas to increase small group participation and the number of people serving the community. As each batch of ideas appeared on the screen, participants began to sense more and more that transformation was within their reach.

"Finally, I want you to take ten minutes to do four things."

"First, identify an owner for each of your ninety-day ideas. Who will be responsible for implementing it? There might be many people required to make it happen, but in implementation, we need to identify an owner.

"Second, clarify each of your ninety-day ideas so that everyone understands it. That means that everyone understands what 'done' looks like. It could mean that you need to quickly sketch out the who, what, when, and why of the idea.

"Third, fill out the worksheet in your resource packet on Resource K so that our prayer team might pray for your team over the course of the next ninety days. We want you to feel undergirded by prayer. And that leads us to one more thing we want you to do in the next ninety days.

"The fourth thing is to establish an intercessory prayer team that will pray specifically for the transformation of your congregation and community, for your ninety-day goals, and for any other items brought to the team's attention by those leading the transformation.

"We've spent a good bit of time wrestling with the nitty-gritty of keeping our activity aligned with our mission," Pastor D continued. "This is important. Equally important is to keep our hearts aligned with our spiritual leader so that we more deeply and intuitively understand the spiritual reasons and purposes behind the decisions we make along the way. As we prepare to close, I'd like to ask each lead pastor to share your heart with your team. Let your folks know what you are begging for in your congregation and community."

The mood in the room shifted as the hubbub of many voices sharing strategies gave way to hushed contemplation, and the band started playing, "I Give Myself Away." As teams finished listening to their pastors' hearts and provided affirmation, lyrics went up on the screen, and a few people began singing along to the music.

I give myself away,
I give myself away,
So You can use me . . .

Here I am
Here I stand
Lord, my life is in your hand
Lord, I'm longing to see
Your desire revealed to me . . .

After all of the teams had completed their conversations, Pastor D moved to wrap up the event.

"I want to extend three invitations for you to come forward for prayer this afternoon as we prepare to close. The first is for those who are ready and prepared to go back home committed to being change agents for congregational and community transformation. If that speaks to you, won't you come?"

As the music continued in the background, many people rose and came forward. It started slowly, but then people started rushing to the makeshift altar for prayer.

Pastor D continued the invitation, "Secondly, I want us to pray for those who are not quite sure yet. It's alright to be not quite sure. This is heavy work, and you've got to be clear that God is summoning you to it."

Several more people made their way to the altar. Pastor D sought to provide a hug of encouragement to as many of those as he could reach.

"And thirdly, if you are sensing that, after this weekend, God is calling you to a specific aspect of ministry, would you raise your hand?"

By that time, there were only a handful of people still in their seats at the tables, and many hands were raised as the Holy Spirit began to minister to people in prayer. People began praying out loud and praising God for what God had done that weekend. In the midst of the pandemonium that was breaking out at the altar, Pastor D took oil and began anointing people whose hands were raised. For those gathered it felt like a fresh Pentecost moment.

When the euphoria in the room quieted down, Pastor D began to pray:

"Lord, we thank you in the name of Jesus. For you have visited us here this weekend, and you are particularly speaking to us right now. I pray in the name of Jesus that the very things that you are speaking into our spirits would come to pass. May we be reminded of your words through Paul, that He who has begun a good work in us would bring it to completion in the day of Jesus Christ. I pray, God, that You would bring revival, revitalization, transformation, and a Holy Ghost invasion to every church and community represented in this room. And, Lord, I pray that you would use each one of us to expand your kingdom here on earth, as we await your glorious kingdom in heaven. Please hear our collective prayers. In the name of Jesus we pray, AMEN!"

As people hugged each other, cried, embraced, laughed, and shared, Pastor D gave his trademark benediction: "This is the best day of your life. It is the only day you have to live. Yesterday is gone; tomorrow may not come. So live today to the fullest, in the grace of our Lord and Savior Jesus

Christ. Go in peace, and may the peace of Christ go with you!"

The joy and anticipation in the room were nearly palpable, and those gathered there continued to embrace each other tearfully.

"God bless you, everybody," said Pastor D. "Don't forget to sign up to review your ninety-day plan with one of our REAL church coaches! See you in worship tomorrow!"

It was another thirty minutes before the fellowship hall was empty. God had done something powerful. From that point on, many churches and communities would never be the same again.

Realignment is necessary under normal driving conditions and critical in more treacherous ones.

If we were really serious about achieving Christ's mission in the world,
* What would we stop doing?
* What would we continue doing?
* What would we start doing?

Need to make this an annual habit.

Building a ninety-day plan
* generate ideas that can be implemented now in each core area of discipleship
* identify an owner for each idea
* clarify ideas so that everyone understands what 'done' looks like. Sketch out the who, what, when, and why of the idea.
* ensure that our intercessory prayer team is undergirding and bathing our efforts in prayer.

Chapter 24
Putting Steps in Place for Progress

Purpose. Simple Steps. Owners.

As Aida approached Pastor Joe and his team, she could tell they were ready to make change happen.

"Good Afternoon," she said. "It was great worshipping with you today!"

The team was relaxed and smiling. Each of them was looking forward to their final meeting before heading home.

"My role here is to make sure you have some solid steps in place so that when you leave, you can hit the ground running and actually make progress within ninety days or sooner. I will be available to you for the next ninety days via email and short phone calls to answer questions, be a sounding board, or just to celebrate your progress. Why don't you share your ninety-day plan with me now, and then I can answer any other questions you might have."

Pastor Joe asked Monica to read their items since she had taken notes during their group time the day before.

"One: meeting on September 18 at 7:00 p.m. at Pastor Joe's house to review all ideas from the training event and prioritize them. He's buying the pizza."

"Great," responded Aida. "You have a time, location, purpose, and food," she affirmed as the team laughed.

"Two," continued Monica, "increase worship attendance within ninety days by asking members to distribute five invitations highlighting an exciting sermon series. Kate is the owner for this."

Monica paused to see if Aida had a comment about this ninety-day goal. "Go ahead and read through the list," Aida said, "and then we'll come back and review."

"Three: increase small group participation within ninety days by identifying eight spiritual leaders who will go through a six-week study and then each start their own group doing the six-week study. Pastor Joe is the owner.

"Four: increase the number of people *serving* the community by working with community partners and mayors to identify tangible ways we can serve and by reducing the number of people tied up in committee meetings. Gary is the owner on this one.

"Five: ask our intercessory prayer team to continue praying specifically for the transformation of our congregation and community, our ninety-day plan, and any other items brought to its attention by those leading transformation. Joan—our new prayer team lead—is the owner."

"Wonderful!" beamed Aida. "You have owners for each—and they aren't all the same person. Now let's step through each one. Does any one of these feel unrealistic in terms of the time frame? Are there any that you think you need more than ninety days to accomplish?"

Kate spoke up hesitantly, "The serve strategy seems like it will take more time to do. I know that we have already been in relationship with our community, but I have a hard time understanding how we could reorganize our committee and decision-making structure in just ninety days, let alone have new serve ministries founded *and* people shifting from their committees to those groups."

Monica, David, and Crystal agreed. "I think you're right about that," said David.

"Well, I wasn't thinking about a full-blown reorganization," Gary began to explain, "but simply seeing if we could reduce the committee size by two or three people who feel called to the particular community ministries we will be starting. We're getting close in our conversations with the principal of Battlefield Elementary to uncovering what a partnership there might look like. We also have a meeting set up in a couple of weeks with the local Meals on Wheels and Alcoholics Anonymous chapters."

"Oh, well. that sounds very reasonable," Kate said. "Sorry that I didn't understand what you had in mind."

"And thanks for providing a perfect illustration of the difference between an idea and an implementation plan!" Aida said. "Gary started to walk us through an implementation plan. I would ask that he—and whoever else is connected to the serve part of disciple making—continue laying out the steps. These steps should include the people involved and a time line so that we might all be better able to evaluate and support the plan. After we take a look at the other ideas, we'll divide up into teams to formulate a plan for each item that has clear steps.

"Now, are there any thoughts or questions about either the strategy to grow worship or small-group attendance?"

Hearing none, Aida offered her own. "I'm wondering if the strategy to increase worship attendance assumes that visitors will come back if they just step across our threshold. What percentage of your visitors return a second time?"

"We actually don't know," Joe admitted. "It seems like about one in twenty visitors ends up sticking—but I don't know for sure."

"Okay, well, thanks for being honest! That's important. I would encourage those who will be working on the plan for this area to work step by step on how you are engaging people along the pre-guest to active participant journey. If you don't have simple steps in place to walk with someone intentionally along this path, even a great idea—like invitations—will not yield the result you are looking for. Did you work that out in the discipleship track?"

"We started to outline one, but if you hadn't brought it up, I wouldn't have seen it as related to this ninety-day goal," Crystal said.

"Increasing worship attendance is more than getting a new person to come to church once," Aida said. "Some churches have an active revolving door: for every new person coming to the church, there is at least one person leaving or reducing their participation in the church. Additionally, people are attending churches more erratically. Put all of this together, and you'll discover that in order not to see a decline in your average worship attendance number, you have to be bringing in many more guests *and* not letting them fall through any cracks in your assimilation process."

"That makes a lot of sense," Monica said, nodding her head.

"Okay, good," said Aida. "So, the only question I have about the small group idea is whether or not you have ever tried to start small groups before."

Crystal jumped to answer. "We have been talking about it over the past few months and have read about different approaches . . . but we haven't done anything yet. Having a ninety-day goal will help us act."

"Great!" said Aida, and then, shifting gears, she continued, "Now, please divide yourselves into the appropriate goal teams and map out the steps. As you do so, I want you to imagine placing stepping-stones in a raging river. Much like the Israelites did in the third chapter of Joshua. Take note, if you place the steps too close together, it will take people longer to cross the river. Place the steps too far apart, and you may lose people in the river or create too much anxiety for people to even try to cross.

"Let's take about twenty minutes to write down steps that need to be taken to implement your ninety-day idea. Each step should be sequenced and include the what, why, how, who, and when."

"That sounds like my journalism professor talking," Monica said. "I get how to use those questions to write a story, but I'm not sure how to use them to create a plan."

"Well, let's take a look at what those questions yield in the context of an action plan," Aida encouraged.

"'What' refers to the action itself. 'Why' is just that—why the action is needed *and* the desired outcome of the action. So, this could include the change you want to see in the people impacted by the action. 'How' refers to any details surrounding the action; and, of course, 'who' is the person or people responsible for taking the action. The 'when' is your due date.

"For each action you need to take to implement your ninety-day plan, you need to identify the why, how, who, and when. By outlining your plan in this way, you will clarify the needed steps. This detail will also help you easily engage people in the implementation process."

After Aida had wrapped up her explanation, the Last Chance team got to work converting their ideas into implementation plans. Joe forced himself to sit back and watch the team get to work. He had to actively refrain from interfering in the planning process so that his newly empowered leaders could spread and test their wings. It was a beautiful thing to see.

Chapter 25
Casting a Compelling Vision

Wait. Clarify. Expect. Move.

A dense fog began to lift over the countryside as Pastor D drove down and around the steep and winding roads leading to Hopeville and the Church of the Last Chance. As the headlights of his black SUV cut through the mist, and the sun made its presence known in the morning glory, the pastor of the Fellowship of the Used-Tos gave God thanks for all that had been accomplished in this once dying, but now growing, church.

As his SUV climbed the last hill before he reached the town limits, Pastor D worshipped God with his favorite gospel group, the Mississippi Mass Choir. He reflected on the many things God had done at Last Chance in fifteen months: fifty professions of faith, the foundations of a prayer ministry established, the beginning of partnerships between the church and local government, the exploration of public/private partnerships to help children and needy families, and much more. Joe and his team were making significant strides. Pastor D was filled with gratitude as he cruised down the hill to his favorite restaurant in Hopeville to have a final mentoring session with Joe and then meet with Last Chance's lead team.

"Pastor D, how are you this morning?" Joe asked, as he embraced his mentor in the parking lot of the diner. "It is so great to see you again!"

"I am well, my brother. Just giving God thanks for all He is doing through you at the Church of the Last Chance. A lot has happened over this year, hasn't it?"

"You can say that again and again and again!" Joe said. His eyes suggested that his mind was racing in five different directions at the same time. "I remember when I was on the verge of giving up. I'm so glad I listened to my family, you, and everybody else who encouraged me, and stuck with it. God is beginning to show the fruits of our labor for Him. But, come on, let's go in and get something to eat."

The two men sat down in one of the big booths. Joe had his typical country breakfast, with grits and hash browns. Pastor D explored the menu carefully and decided to try some French toast and strawberries, a meal that Nia had been attempting to get him to eat for years.

"I'm looking forward to our time together—and with your team," Pastor D said. "But I'm curious to know from you, what do you see?"

With a slightly puzzled look on his face, Joe replied, "What do you mean? I see you, I see a big order of buttered grits coming down the aisle, I see the beginnings of a beautiful day outside . . ."

"No, no, no," Pastor D cut him off. "I'm not talking about that. I'm talking about what do you see as God's preferred future for Last Chance?"

"Oh, you mean, what is the vision? Oh, okay. Well, to be truthful, I haven't had much time to think about it," Joe replied as the waiter set their plates down. "I've focused all my energies on bringing REAL alignment—from worship to community development to leader development to spiritual disciplines to small groups—and making learners and followers of Jesus Christ who bring WHOLEness to the world. I haven't had much time, or made the time, to really ask God about a vision."

"Understood," Pastor D said, as he sipped on some cold apple juice. "But now it's time. You've been here long enough. You've spent a good fifteen months in this transformation process. You've made good progress developing leaders. You've begun making connections in your community. You're getting to know this town and your congregation's place here. You've embraced the people, and the people are embracing you. But now it's time—"

"Time for what?" Joe interrupted. "You're not giving me another assignment, are you?"

"No, Joe, I'm simply saying to you, it's time for you to begin the process of casting a compelling vision for your congregation and community. You guys have been doing great in this transformation process, but to what end? Where does God want to take your people? What does the detailed future picture look like?"

Joe paused and thought as he ate his fried apples. Pastor D continued, "In order to keep momentum going in your transformation and growth process, you've *gotta* have vision, and you've got to cast vision as God reveals it to you and your people.

"Vision is God's preferred future for a situation and a people," Pastor D explained. "Vision is what has to be, must be, should be, *gotta* be—in a situation that has gone sour. I have read a lot of definitions concerning vision from a number of different people—Caldwell, Wills, Stanley, Collins, you name it. But the best one I've seen comes from Thom Rainer's book, *Breakout Churches*. He says, 'Vision discovers you, you do not discover vision.' He goes on to say that vision happens when the leader's passion intersects with the congregation's passion, which both intersect with the community's need.

Pastor D started scribbling a rough drawing on a napkin as he continued, "As I have been working with Rainer's model, I have made some slight adjustments. I think God yields vision at the intersection of the leaders' purpose, the congregation's passion, and the community's voice. At that point—or in that tiny space where those three things intersect—God speaks vision. This is a very important point. At least for me it was. Because for the longest time, I believed that as a spiritual leader, I had to find the vision and cast the vision—that I was responsible for vision all by myself. That is simply not the case.

"You know you are ready to communicate God's vision when you can clearly paint it for others. Once you have that clarity, which emerges out of interaction with the community and congregation, it is up to you cast what God has shown and then invite everyone to participate in God's vision of transformation. Participation happens as each person finds his or her unique place and position in the process of making that vision a reality."

Joe's face took on a thoughtful expression as Pastor D spoke. "It was interesting to me that we didn't talk about vision earlier in our conversations," Joe reflected. "You mentioned it, but said you didn't want to deal with it yet."

"Right, because neither you nor your people nor your community were ready for it. Shucks, there wasn't a whole lot you could focus on besides just trying to survive—let alone begin thinking about thriving. You had to stop the bleeding before you could get the patient to heal, let alone think about what a healthy lifestyle would look like. Much of what you have done along the way will inform your vision. But you cannot communicate the vision until you have clarified the three circles," Pastor D said, pointing to the diagram on the napkin.

"Okay, Pastor . . . so can you walk through each circle with me to make sure I understand what you mean?"

"I'm planning on going deeper with the three circles at the lead team meeting so that you and your people are of one accord," Pastor D said. "So I'd like to briefly review the leader's purpose and then spend the remainder of breakfast talking about how to cast vision once you have one. Sound good?"

"Okay, sure," replied Joe amiably.

Pastor D cleared his throat and began, "Vision starts with you—it doesn't end with you—but as the vision caster, you have to be clear about your passion and your purpose.

"Have you ever paused to examine what you are most passionate about in life and in ministry?"

"No, not really," answered Joe.

"Well, you need to," said Pastor D emphatically. "Sometimes the things that bother us the most or disturb us the most are things that give us clear clues about our passion. For example, I am passionate about reconciling oppression of all forms. From family oppression to '-ism' oppression, any time any form of oppression shows up, I find myself fully engaged in trying to reconcile it. But what abut you, Joe? What is your purpose?"

"I'm not sure," he replied, feeling a little deflated.

"That's not surprising. So often we as spiritual leaders do not take the time to periodically evaluate what we are really passionate about. It is easy for us to get caught in the daily rut and routine of 'doing ministry' with no clear focus on what God has purposed us specifically to do. One of my mentors, Richard Bright, used to always tell me that there is the work of the church, and there is church work. Church work is oftentimes not the work of the church. You and I must spend the necessary time with God to be clear about our purpose. Jesus spent time in the wilderness praying and fasting with God before he would later declare his purpose in Luke chapter 4. Do you remember his purpose statement?"

"Not right off hand," Joe confessed.

"Well, Jesus declared that the spirit of the Lord was upon him, and then he ran through a simple litany of what it was that he was purposed to do: preach good news to the poor, proclaim recovery of sight to the blind, set captives free, and proclaim the year of the Lord's favor. That purpose came after roughly thirty years of living. In that thirty years, a number of things had to have happened for Jesus to be so passionate about his purpose. Surely, he reflected on the fact that he was born in a stable. Surely, growing up in the poor town of Nazareth shaped his views on how to reduce suffering. Surely, seeing many broken people and wanting to make them whole again was a daily reality in his life. All these things helped mold and clarify his purpose," Pastor D explained.

Joe listened carefully, deep in thought as he considered what the next stage at Last Chance might look like once he discovered his purpose.

"Joe, you need to take some time with God to review your life up to this point and identify some of your patterns of passion that reveal your purpose. What are the situations you've thrown yourself into completely? What are the issues underlying those times when you have gotten so upset you couldn't think of anything else? What themes seem to drive your energies? What wakes you up in the middle of the night or early in the morning? What do you dream of accomplishing?"

"You're right. I need to take some time to answer these questions. They are important ones," agreed Joe. "I'm going to reflect on them during my upcoming spiritual retreat."

"That's a good idea, Joe. But keep in mind that clarifying all three circles takes some time. Don't rush vision. God will begin speaking vision as you identify your purpose and your congregation's passion.

"You're getting deep here," Joe replied, taking a deep breath and hesitating before making his next comment. "I feel like, in my excitement of late, I've been trying to rush vision and rush God to provide a vision. And that has led to frustration and anger. You are telling me I need to wait for it . . . I guess I haven't wanted to wait."

"But you have to," Pastor D said. "Trust me, you have to. That's why I didn't talk with you about vision for the Church of the Last Chance until the end of our mentoring period. I wish somebody had told me what I'm telling you. I had to learn the hard way, and I believe it impeded some of our progress along the way."

"Alright, alright, I'll wait!!" Joe exclaimed with a laugh.

"Good!" Pastor D said. "Trust me, the time will come after all this preparation work for you to communicate God's vision to the people, the people who will participate with you in congregational and community transformation."

At that moment, the waiter appeared with the check. Pastor D paid the tab and added a generous tip for the hardworking student.

So, as I said earlier," he continued, "we'll deal with the other two circles with the lead team. I just want to review some basics with you about what it takes to cast vision. Since we've talked about Nehemiah before, let's allow him to speak to us again here."

"Okay, I'm ready," Joe said as he finished his coffee. The waiter came by with a big smile on his face. "Thank you, sir!" he said to Pastor D. "I hope to serve you again soon."

"I hope so, too, Mark!" Pastor D replied to the waiter. It was a habit of Pastor D's to always get to know the waiters and waitresses in restaurants on a first-name basis. He used this as a chance to get to know people, do quick one-on-one relational meetings, and invite folks to Jesus or the Fellowship if the opportunity presented itself.

"Mark, will I see you at Last Chance on Sunday?" Joe asked. He had picked this up as he observed Pastor D's every movement and remembered something Pastor D had said earlier: "You must model the behavior you want to see."

"I don't know . . . maybe," said Mark, still smiling.

As Mark walked away, Joe and Pastor D resumed their conversation.

"Remember, Joe, that Nehemiah did a thorough inspection—just like I've asked you to do. It was after he surveyed the situation and conducted a thorough inspection that he was prepared to cast vision at the appropriate time and in the appropriate place.

"Keep in mind that Nehemiah believed in provision. He believed that God would make the provision for the vision to come to pass. The great preacher from Chicago, Jeremiah A. Wright Jr., says that whenever God gives a vision, God also makes provision. It's important that you believe that as you continue to lead the revival in Hopeville—because things will happen along the way to discourage you. Plans will be delayed; circumstances will change; folks who are with you for one season will be different in the next season. Sometimes in the midst of it all, the money gets funny, and we don't know how we're going to get it done. But God has a way. If I read Nehemiah correctly, he went to power to get resources, and God gave him everything he needed through that connection. Don't be afraid to go to the king, the president, the mayor, the congressman, whoever God directs you to in order to get the resources God needs to make the vision a reality. Just be sure you remain true to your divine purpose in life, and don't get bought off. Nehemiah got what he needed and stayed true to his purpose. He received materials to build up what was broken and resources to even build up his own situation. He was even offered people from the king's army to help!"

"Thanks for that reminder, Pastor D. As you were speaking, I realized there are a few conversations I have been afraid to have," Joe admitted. "Remembering that God is making provision for God's vision at Last Chance is really helpful."

"Don't be afraid, Joe. Remember, God is with you. When it was time for Nehemiah to communicate vision, he did so by painting a clear picture of what the situation was. He presented before his people, their human condition. He said, 'You see the trouble we are in: Jerusalem lies in ruins, and its gates have been burned with fire.' Every vision ought to paint a clear picture of what is.

"Then, after painting a clear picture of what is, we must declare the action needed while tapping into the community's deepest desire. Nehemiah said, 'Let's rebuild the wall of Jerusalem and rid ourselves of this disgrace.'

"Finally, we have to put all of this in God's context. While casting vision, Joe, you need to always point to the fact that this is of God and not of us. You can only say that it is of God when the evidence speaks for itself and when there is a divine summons to do something about it. Nehemiah illustrated this by telling people that the gracious hand of God was upon him and by sharing his conversation with the king—the king who allowed him to come out of exile and who made provision for the resources needed for the rebuilding. We only get our authority from God. We need to back up all of our claims with divine testimony. And if we don't have any, we need to wait until it comes."

"Got it, Pastor D," replied Joe. "That seems simple enough: paint a clear picture of what is, tie the needed action to the congregation and the community's desire, and keep it all focused on what God is up to."

"One last thing I want to prepare you for before we meet with your lead team is that once you cast a divine vision, you need to know that opposition is just around the corner. Whenever you dare to lead a vision for God, you must always expect and prepare for opposition. Divine movement and opposition go hand in hand. We almost always know that a vision is from God when shortly after it is cast, there is opposition. The reason for this is that not everyone will be excited about divine vision. As soon as Nehemiah cast vision to his community, not everyone was excited by it. In fact, Sanballat, Tobiah, and Geshem mocked and ridiculed Nehemiah and the people's efforts. They did so because if the vision became reality, their political position within the community would be threatened and that would negatively impact their economic reality. As soon as a significant number of people in Nehemiah's community started to make the vision a reality, opposition of all sorts rose up.

"Opposition in the face of divine vision is always a sign that you are headed in the right direction. It may come from people who are near or far. It may come from people in lowly places or from lofty places, from people you expect or from people you don't expect—or both! When it comes, much of it will be unfair. But Joe, let me tell you—you just hold out and hold on, victory will come."

"Well, Pastor D," said Joe, with a grin, "I feel like I've already gotten what I need to move forward. I can't wait to see what you are going to do with my lead team!"

After prayer and study of Mark 6:30–44, Pastor D started laying out the three circles for the lead team's understanding.

"Any questions about the 'Leaders' Purpose' circle?" Pastor D asked.

"Can I ask a question?" Kate said as she raised her hand.

"You lose the bet, Joe. I told you we wouldn't get through this diagram without Kate asking a question!" Pastor D teased. The room erupted in laughter—even Kate cracked up.

"What if we as leaders have different purposes than the pastor?" Kate said as the laughter died down.

"Well, it is alright for leaders to have different purposes—as long as those purposes are aligned with the divine vision for the congregation that is cast by the pastor. If any purpose is not in line, then that leader does not need to be leading."

"Gotcha," Kate said. "Oh, by the way, glad I could make you laugh today!"

"Yes, thanks for that," Pastor D chuckled. "Now let's talk about the congregation's passion circle. One could argue that while Jesus preached to thousands and healed multitudes of their diseases, he really only had a congregation of 120 followers. Those were the people present after his ascension. And those were the people who positioned themselves in prayer waiting for the promise of the Holy Spirit that would empower them to transform the world. What were those people passionate about?"

That's a good question, Gary thought to himself. He had never really considered their perspective in that way.

"Well, I'd argue that their passion was for people to receive the same blessing they had received because of their relationship with Jesus," he offered. "Some of them were healed from infirmities; others had demons cast out of them. Other people were shown that they could fulfill something greater than they ever imagined. So they were passionate about Jesus and what having a relationship with Jesus Christ meant to their lives—that sounds like what our passion ought to be too."

"It ought to be at the core of your passion, but what you have to ask God and your fellow members is, 'What is Last Chance's unique expression of that?' As spiritual leaders, you need to talk with, meet with, relate with, and share with the people in your congregation and community so that you can listen for a common passion that God is speaking through the people. Is the congregation's passion circle clear? Well, then good!"

Pastor D surveyed the room to make sure the group was still following him.

"The last piece," he continued, "involves you identifying your community's voice—heard and unheard. If your community is like my community, then there isn't just one voice, there are multiple voices. Not all the voices get heard or are loud enough to be heard. The fact of the matter is, so many voices go unheard, which means so many needs go unmet. It is up to you to find, listen for, and discover voices of disenfranchisement and voices of hope in your community. If you hear the voices, you'll hear the needs and the dreams. It is then up to you and your leaders to create a movement by which the voices of hope might lift the voices of disenfranchisement. When you do that, a process of restoration can begin. Listen to the voices in Jesus's communities and what they were begging and hoping for. Lazarus's sisters were pleading for their brother to have life. The woman at the well was yearning to live with no more shame. Blind Bartimaeus demanded that his sight be restored. The hemorrhaging woman pressed through crowds and clung to the Christ who could make her clean. Those were the voices from Jesus's community that he responded to. I know you all have been doing community inspections and are beginning to explore community partnerships. What are the voices in Hopeville saying?"

The lead team responded, filling the air with what was on their hearts and minds—and those of the community.

"I hear a cry for unity in the community."

"A safe place for kids to play."

"Good jobs for everyone."

"Health insurance."

"A place where they can belong."

"It is at the place where your purpose, and the passion of the Church of the Last Chance, and the community's voice intersect that God will get busy—in and through you—and start something new," Pastor D explained. "Yes, Kate, you have a question?"

"How do these three circles tie into the be-see-do lists we've been working on?"

"I'm so glad you asked," Pastor D smiled. "Pastor Joe told me that you've been diligently reviewing them at each lead team meeting. Let me explain how they tie into this vision model."

"First, 'be who you are' happens at the intersection of Leaders' Purpose and Congregation's Passion. 'See what you have' is at the intersection of Community's Voice and Congregation's Passion; and 'do what matters to God' is at the intersection of Leaders' Purpose and Community's Voice.

"When these connect, they help you get closer to divine vision. I'd like to spend the rest of our time working and praying through your be-see-do lists in the context of discerning God's vision for Last Chance."

The lead team of Last Chance began to describe what they sensed God was telling them in each circle and in each area of overlap. Soon the wall was covered with Post-its and sheets of paper, and the room was filled with possibility and excitement.

Pastor Joe began to get the sense that vision was about to emerge. He checked his notes before he left for the night:

* Vision is more than a bumper sticker. It is the detailed picture of God's preferred future for our community and congregation.

* You will find divine vision at the intersection of Leaders' Purpose, Congregation's Passion, and Community's Voice.

* "Be who you are," "See What You Have," and "Do what matters to God" focuses us on the vision field.

* Do not cast vision until I can paint a detailed, clear picture for others.

* Expect opposition when you cast divine vision.

Epilogue

Twelve years later, the Church of the Last Chance did not exist. In its place, a dynamic, visionary fellowship had taken Hopeville and the surrounding area by storm. You see, because the congregation reached out to the community, the community took over the congregation. One of the first things the community decided to do was to conduct a funeral for the name "Church of the Last Chance," because it no longer fit.

Many in the community who had reached their last chance had found nothing but divine possibilities when the people of the church had reached out to them in the name of Jesus. What was once a region flooded with stories of impossibility was now filled with testimonies of abundant life.

A congregation that had flirted with extinction was now a rich fellowship that met in seven places. Hope had returned to Hopeville, and the community wanted to be sure that the name of the congregation reflected their belief that hope would never leave.

As Joe looked around at the crowd gathered for the dedication of the Community of Living Hope's latest site, he was overcome with emotion. This community center was the fulfillment of a vision God had given him and his people twelve years before. The community center was designed to meet the community's needs and support its dreams. There was a gymnasium, a coffee shop, a thrift store, a free medical clinic, and a subsidized pharmacy. It included a bank that gave micro-loans for entrepreneurs and new small business owners, and even space for job training, employment services, and day care for children.

The sight of it all blew Joe's mind. It was surreal.

At the same time, he found himself wiping tears from his eyes because, truth be told, the journey had not been an easy one. At various points along the way, people got frustrated and left. Not only did the departure of Mr. Wilson cause much drama but, over time, some dear relationships were severed. He was still grieving over the loss of David who had gone from being a volunteer in the worship ministry to leading it as a staff person. He had experienced much weariness and many sleepless nights, as he had to choose God's vision over the will of people and the comfort of friendship again and again. While the journey had been painful at times, Joe stood there rejoicing. Because God had provided again and again.

Just then, Pamela interrupted his thoughts and introduced him to a young woman, Ann, who was getting ready to start her first pastorate at a struggling church.

"Pastor Joe, I've been so impressed with the work you've done here. Would you be willing to mentor me?" With Pastor D's voice in his head, Joe said without hesitation, "Absolutely!"

As Pamela took down Ann's information, Joe tried to pull himself together for the ceremony.

There had been so many times when Joe didn't think it would happen, but as he stood there with tears streaming down his face, all he could think was this: *Nothing is impossible with God.*

End Notes

1 Exodus 3:7-10
2 Jeremiah 1:4-10
3 Nehemiah 1:5–11
4 http://doroteos2.wordpress.com/2009/05/10/great-and-not-so-great-expectations-in-worship/ Four basic responses were given to the question "Do you expect to have an experience of the living God, the risen Christ, or the power of the Holy Spirit when you worship?"

> No (72%)
>
> Have never thought about it/don't understand what we mean (53%)
> Would like to (13%)
>
> Yes (11%)
>
> (Once again, there were some multiple answers: "no, but I would like to; yes I do, but I would like to more often; I've never thought about it before, but no I don't…")

Additionally, out of 227 pastors/preachers in the survey, only eight (!) claimed that they "expect people to experience God/Christ/Spirit" in worship. Worship in UM churches is "about" God, and often "for" God, but seldom "with" God. Forty-four answered that they "hoped" people would experience the divine, but a hope and an expectation are two very different things.

5 District of Columbia Register, Ward 4 Economic Development Plan, 19 February 1999, (15-4), p. 1835
6 http://www.arenewalenterprise.com/
7 Mark 6:37
8 Philippians 4:13
9 See Chapter 5 for details about Daily Personal Worship
10 Resource A: Worship Culture Assessment
11 Acts 1:8
12 Luke 5:8b
13 Luke 5:10b
14 Resource C: Resource List for Studying the Bible

[15] *Communicating for a Change: Seven Keys to Irresistible Communication.* Andy Stanley and Lane Jones Multnomah Books, 2006

[16] See endnote "4"

[17] a poem by Judy Brown taken from *Teaching With Fire: Poetry that Sustains the Courage to Teach.* Sam M. Intrator, Megan Scribner, Parker J. Palmer, Tom Vander Ark. Jossey-Bass, 2003.

[18] *Transforming Mission: Paradigm Shifts in Theology of Mission* (American Society of Missiology Series). David Jacobus Bosch. Orbis Books, 1991.

[20] www.dictionary.com

[21] *Touch: The Power of Touch in Transforming Lives.* by Rudy Rasmus with Christian Washington and Pat Springle. Baxter Press and Spirit Rising Music, 2006. page 73-74.

[22] http://www.tutufoundation-usa.org/exhibitions.htm

Resource A
REAL Worship Culture Assessment
(Chapter 9)

Here's the checklist Pastor D gave Kate as homework on the call. Here are some questions that you can use to further develop a Relevant, Enthusiastic, Authentic and Loving worship experience.

Relevant (impacts real life)

1. Does the sermon address the human condition in a way that connects with our targeted mission field?
2. Does the sermon encourage people to identify ways of hope that can address the stresses and strains of their daily realities?
3. Does the style of music engage our targeted mission field in praise and worship?
4. Does the music touch the soul and bring healing to hurting situations?
5. Do we start and stop worship on time?
6. Are first time guests clear about where to go and what to do?
7. Does multimedia seamlessly support all elements of worship?

Enthusiastic (possessed by God)

1. Do people come to worship expecting to encounter God?
2. Is there enough space built into the structure of worship for the Holy Spirit to move?
3. Do worship servant leaders—from greeters to ushers to worship leaders to musicians—model contagious and authentic enthusiasm?
4. Is worship creative, surprising and ordered?
5. Do people leave profoundly different in God, than they were when they came through the door?

Authentic (welcomed, comfortable & safe)

1. Is the sermon delivered in a way that is down-to-earth?
2. Do people share their stories transparently?
3. Have people been warmly welcomed and greeted by the ushers and other congregants?
4. Did people get a hug? If so, how many?
5. Is there an atmosphere of "come-as-you-are" and warmth?
6. Does the authenticity of the congregation influence people to come back, and to bring others with them when they return?

Loving (breaking down barriers and building bridges for the wellbeing of all)

1. Have people been influenced and compelled to love others?
2. Does love for others position worshippers to unconditionally work for and desire the well-being of others?
3. Was love the foundation of the sermon that was preached?
4. Was love flowing through the prayers that were shared?
5. Was love seen, heard and felt throughout the worship experience?
6. Have people left with options and opportunities for extending love to others in constructive and transformative ways?
7. Have people been embraced and greeted in love?

Resource B
Parts of the Bible
(Chapter 13)

Torah or Books of Instruction written in narrative form	First 5 books in the Old Testament: • Genesis • Exodus	• Leviticus • Numbers • Deuteronomy
Books of History about the people of Ancient Israel	• Joshua • Judges • Ruth • 1 Samuel • 2 Samuel • 1 Kings	• 2 Kings • 1 Chronicles • 2 Chronicles • Ezra • Nehemiah • Esther
Wisdom Literature: books that offer wise council for our life's journey	• Job • Psalms • Proverbs	• Ecclesiastes • Song of Solomon
Major Prophets: prophetic literature that foretells the truths of God	• Isaiah • Jeremiah • Lamentations	• Ezekiel • Daniel
Minor Prophets:	• Hosea • Joel • Amos • Obadiah • Jonah • Micah	• Nahum • Habakkuk • Zephaniah • Haggai • Zechariah • Malachi
Gospels=Good News: contain the words and life of Christ on earth	• Matthew • Mark	• Luke • John
Introduced to the holy spirit, the creation and movement of the church as directed by the Holy Spirit into the world	• Acts	

| Paul's Letters to the Churches in Macedonia. These read like any letter or email sent to you and me. | • Romans
• 1 Corinthians
• 2 Corinthians
• Galatians
• Ephesians
• Philippians
• Colossians
• 1 Thessalonians
• 2 Thessalonians
• 1 Timothy
• 2 Timothy | • Titus
• Philemon
• Hebrews
• James
• 1 Peter
• 2 Peter
• 1 John
• 2 John
• 3 John
• Jude |
| Apocalyptic Literature: foretelling the end of time. Also a book of worship. | • Revelation | |

For a more detailed outline of the Bible, go to: http://bibleoutline.org/

Resource C
Resource List for Studying the Bible
(Chapter 13)

The Invitation: A Simple Guide to the Bible (The Message) by Eugene Peterson

New Interpreter's Study Bible (NRSV with aprocrypha) Abingdon Press

The New Daily Bible Study Series Westminister Press/John Knox

A Hop, Skip and a Jump Through the Bible by J. Ellsworth Kalas Abingdon Press

Nelson's Complete Book of Bible Maps and Charts, revised and updated Thomas Nelson Publisher

The New How to Study Your Bible by Kay Arthur, David Arthur and Pete DeLacy Harvest House Publisher

NIV/The Message Parallel Study Bible Zondervan Publishing

http://www.biblestudytools.com/: commentaries, encyclopedias, dictionaries, parallel Bible, interlinear Bible

http://biblos.com/: atlas, Bible, concordance, dictionary, encyclopedia, reference Bible, commentary, interlinear Bible, interwoven Bible, thesaurus, devotions, visuals, multilingual, lexicon, GNT concordance, Strong's concordance, apocrypha

http://bibleresources.bible.com: access the Bible, understand and study the Bible, quick scripture links, information about the Bible

http://www.biblemap.org/ and http://www.bible-history.com/maps/: shows and describes the physical location of scripture passages

Resource D
Death by Meeting
(Chapter 17)

Meeting Type	Time Required	Purpose/Format	Tips
Daily Check-In	5-10 minutes	Share daily schedules and activities	Don't sit down Keep it administrative Don't cancel even when some people can't be there
Weekly Tactical	45-90 minutes	Review weekly activities and metrics and resolve tactical obstacles and issue	Don't set agenda until after initial reporting Postpone strategic discussions
Monthly Strategic (or adhoc strategic)	2-4 hours	Discuss, analyze, brainstorm and decide upon critical issues affecting long-term success	Limit to one or two topics Prepare and do research Engage in good conflict
Quarterly Off-Site Review	1-2 days	Review strategy, competitive landscape, industry trends, key personnel, team development	Get out of office Focus on work; limit social activities Don't over-structure or over-burden the schedule

From Death by Meeting. Patrick Lencioni.

Resource E
Connecting the Journey
(Chapter 18)

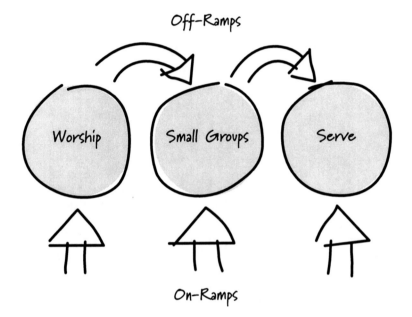

Resource F
Summary of 7 Practices
(Chapter 18)

Practice		Purpose[1]	Explanation	In Baseball…[2]
#1	Clarify the Win	Fuels Momentum	*Define what is important at every level of the organization.* To clarify the win ask, "what's the most important thing?"	The win is getting to home plate.
#2	Think Steps, Not Programs	Protects Alignment	*Before you start anything, make sure it takes you where you need to go.* A step must be easy, obvious, and strategic. Strategic means "it's part of a strategy for moving your people from one place to another." First determine where you want people to be. Then figure out how you're going to get them there. That's doing ministry with the end in mind.	When up to bat, the first step is getting on first base. For a pitcher, the first step is a strike out. The second step is an out. It doesn't matter how hard you hit the ball if it doesn't take you where you need to go.
#3	Narrow the Focus	Promotes Excellence	*Do fewer things in order to make a greater impact* (simplicity and efficiency). Your potential to make an impact with your life is directly related to your willingness to narrow your focus. Choose what potentially works best over what is presently working. The program with the potential to bear the greatest fruit should be your priority.	Pitchers don't need to hit well, they need to pitch well.
#4	Teach Less for More	Guarantees Relevance	*Say only what you need to say to the people who need to hear it.* Narrow the focus say to do one thing and do it well. Teach less for more applies that practice to the information you communicate to your people. Teach with the end (people changed) in mind. Focus on just one truth or principle and you enhance the potential of every listener to really get it.[3]	To improve their game, baseball players focus on the fundamentals: throwing, catching and hitting the ball and running like mad.
#5	Listen to Outsiders	Directs Growth	*Focus on who you're trying to reach, not who you're trying to keep.* What can you learn about the people you are trying to reach? If you don't listen to outsiders you'll be driven by the complaints and demands of the insiders. To effectively listen to outsiders, you must learn their language.[4]	Baseball lost some market share (fans) when insiders created a strike.

Practice		Purpose[1]	Explanation	In Baseball...[2]
#6	Replace Yourself	Assures Longevity	*Learn to hand-off what you do.* Create a process of mentoring and teaching another to do what you do and to do it well. If you fail to develop a strategy to replace yourself you will: a) force talented individuals to remain in the wings; b) cause potential leaders to exit the organization; c) stifle needed insight from valuable team members; d) hinder your ability to recruit volunteers; e) limit the growth of your programs and ministries.	Farm teams provide recruitment and training for potential major league talent. Scouts are trained to spot talent, acquire it, and place it in the right position to be developed.
#7	Work on It	Encourages Discovery	*Take time to evaluate your work—and to celebrate your wins.* If you want a behavior repeated then you need to reward it. Few things are more rewarding for a volunteer than hearing his or her name shared as part of someone's life-changing story.	Spring training illustrates that even the best in the game need a time of focused training and practice.

The above chart comes from *7 Practices of Effective Ministry* by Andy Stanley, Reggie Joiner, and Lane Jones. © 2004 by North Point Ministries, Inc. ISBN: 1-59052-373-3.

[1] page 185
[2] The book is written in two parts. The first part is a story of a pastor who's leadership team tricks him into attending a baseball game. The owner spends the game pointing out the 7 Effective Practices of winning organizations.
[3] page 132
[4] page 152

Resource G
Journey to WHOLEness
(Chapter 18)

Journey to WHOLEness

We have several opportunities to help support people on their journey to WHOLEness. A critical key to growing as a disciple is to find ways to involve your head, heart and hand in the journey. We believe it is essential for every participant to take the next steps by connecting with a fellowship activity and disciple-making small group experiences that will enable you to build your relationship with Jesus Christ and with others.

Like the metro, people get on and off the journey at different places. Here are the stops we've identified as essential for the journey.

Christian Basics Stop: Engage in FOLLOW ME with Pastor D.

If you are curious about Christianity or are new to a relationship with Jesus or have been away from the church for a while or are not sure how to articulate the basics of your beliefs to others, this class is for you! Join Pastor Daniels for four sessions that will help you discover your place in God's story. Questions—large & small are welcome

History, Gifts & Expectations Stop: First Step.

An open, engaging opportunity for participants who are ready to take the 'first step' toward becoming more connected to the life of Emory and Christ-centered wholeness. Participants leave with a sense of their spiritual gifts and which ministries might be best for them based on those gifts.

Worship Stop: Sundays at 8, 10 and noon.

As we seek to help people from all walks of life experience the love of God. We believe worship services are our strongest avenues for God to initiate transformation. We recognize that He is the one who does the transforming, but we want to encourage people to participate in a worship venue that features biblical expressions of corporate worship and teaching of the Scripture. We desire to offer the best possible to God and to the people He brings to us.

Small Group Stop: Participate in a REAL Group.

REAL groups gather in homes, offering fellowship and accountability that moves beyond meeting and mingling to a time of getting to know and love Jesus and one another more. Groups generally last for 6 weeks at a time and contain no more than 8 people.

Deep Water Wednesday Stop (from 7:30-9:00).

An hour and a half devoted to worship, scripture study, prayer and connecting with others in Emory's unique Deep Water Wednesdays. A perfect place for those who haven't yet found a small group or who want to understand the application of biblical truths to their lives better.

Intensive Study Stop: Join in a DISCIPLE Group Study.

New Testament Study: Who is Jesus and what is his significance for our lives? Participants are invited to join this conversation, to study afresh this story of Jesus, and to learn more about their calling to discipleship and to community.

1. Jesus Calls Us Into God's Redemption Story
2. Jesus Calls Us to a Transformed Life
3. Jesus Calls Us to Minister to a Hostile World
4. Jesus Calls Us to Complex Communities of Faith
5. Jesus Calls Us to Serve One Another
6. Jesus Calls Us to a New Relationship With Tradition
7. Jesus Calls Us to Live in Light of His Coming Again
8. Jesus Calls Us to Experience the Gifts of His Dying and Rising

OR

Old Testament Study: What does it mean to be God's chosen people? And how does the story of Israel's covenant with God inform our own identity as heirs of that covenant? Through this study, participants will be invited to listen afresh to the witness of the Old Testament to hear God's call and purpose for their own lives and responds to that call.

1. The Making of the Hebrew Bible
2. The Creation Story of Israel
3. Out of Bondage
4. Promises and Problem in the Land
5. Israel Has a King
6. Division and the Rise of Prophecy
7. Exile and Response
8. Restoration and Renewal

Action Stop: Test Drive a Ministry.

Check out some serving ministries. There are many opportunities that require no prior knowledge, experience or training. This is a perfect opportunity to test drive many different ministry areas and discover which is for you. Learn more at: www.emoryfellowship.org. Of course once you've found your perfect fit, we encourage you to commit to serving and maybe eventually leading a ministry.

God's Call Stop: Living On Purpose.

This highly interactive four-week class helps participants explore their call and discover God's purpose for your life.

Obviously once you've experienced each stop the journey isn't over. In fact it has just begun. Continued practice of spiritual disciplines (worship, prayer, fasting, tithing, small groups, study, etc.) and growth as a spiritual leader are encouraged and expected.

Resource H
Leadership Pipeline Worksheet

	LEAD SELF ➜	LEAD OTHERS ➜	LEAD LEADERS ➜	LEAD NETWORKS
PURPOSE of this stage in leadership development process				
ARENA of operation				
EXPERIENCES to prepare leader for next stage				
EVIDENCE that leader is ready to move to next stage				
ACCOUNTABILITY RELATIONSHIP				

Resource I
The Touch Test
(Chapter 20)

Instructions: Circle the ones you wouldn't feel comfortable touching and sitting next to on Sunday morning.

A heavily tattooed man

Person with piercing through their eyelids

Person who shouts uncontrollably

Elderly single male/female

Barefoot man with a strong body odor

Teenaged male with gold teeth, baggy pants and cap turned sideways

Couple living together, not married

Interracial couple

A Muslim

Divorced female/male

Beyoncé

New Age seeker

Extremely overweight male/female

Couple with crying, screaming baby

Lesbian couple

Convicted sex offender

White male, not dressed in fashion

White female, not dressed in fashion

Female, more than seventy years old

Someone with noticeable hygiene needs

A person who sings loud and poorly

Someone especially quiet and meek

A Caucasian, educated, wealthy female/male

People who are married

A woman wearing pants

An articulate, well-dressed male/female

A person who talks to themselves (loudly)

Recovering drug addict

A Caucasian low-income male/female

Aging white male with financial resources

Woman with dirty bags of belongings

Obviously homeless person

Man wearing baseball cap or hat

Child of middle income parent

Teenager of middle income parent

Disabled person

Gay male

Person who walks around during service

Single male/female under thirty

Unemployed male/female

Person on welfare

Person who snores during service

African-American middle class person

Illiterate adult male/female

African-American male on welfare

African-American female on welfare

Hispanic male or female

Person who answers rhetorical questions during sermon

Asian male or female

A transsexual

Arab male or female

A convicted murderer

Mildly disabled person (needing walkers, crutches)

Person with alcohol on breath

A Buddhist

Emotionally disabled person (unpredictable behavior)

Retarded youth or child

Retarded adult

Smoker

Political conservative

Agnostic/Atheist

Religious fanatic

Person with dirt under fingernails and unkempt, dirty hair

Male wearing one or more earrings

Female wearing tight, short skirt

Ex-Prisoner

Recovering sex addict

Person involved in a sex scandal

Resource J
Sample Agenda for a Post-Training Follow-up Meeting
(Chapter 23)

Joys, Concerns & Opening Prayer (15 minutes)

Each group shares the idea they will be implementing to drive change in their area for the next 90 days, 6 months, 12 months and 18 months

Worship (10 minutes)

Discipleship (10 minutes)

Leadership Development (10 minutes)

Community Development (10 minutes)

Ministry with the Marginalized (10 minutes)

Discussing areas of overlap and opportunities for simplification (30 minutes)

Closing Prayer (10 minutes)

Resource K
90-Day Prayer
Worksheet
(Chapter 23)

Take some time now to outline your prayer requests for the next 90-days. Your intercessory prayer team and our intercessory prayer team will then have a place to start

For Community:

For Congregational Leaders:

For Pastor:

For Spiritual Development:

Other:

If you loved the *Power of REAL*, you may be interested in the book that started it all: *Begging for REAL Church*

What are you begging for?
Where are you begging for it?
Is it transforming your begging to blessing?

Begging for REAL Church makes personal the progression of begging to blessing to boldly reclaiming the role the body of Christ must play in the world. The church gets it right when it gets REAL. Relevant, Enthusiastic, Authentic and Loving relationships that draw people to live and love as Christ did, even when life gets messy and difficult.

Deep change only happens when we acknowledge and embrace what we are begging for, then let God use it to bless us so that we might bless others. Read and practice *Begging for REAL Church* with your lead team, small group and/or friends. Reclaim what it means to be REAL with beggars in your part of the world and watch God transform beggars to blessers.

Visit www.BeggingFor REALChurch.org to:
- Learn more
- Download Resources—including a small group guide
- Read reviews
- Order books (volume discounts)
- Schedule a book signing or REAL event